W9-BLW-941

FAITH

APR 2019

DREAMSIDE

JODY HOUSER | MJ KIM | MARGUERITE SAUVAGE | FRANCIS PORTELA
JORDIE BELLAIRE | ANDREW DALHOUSE | DAVE SHARPE

Chicago Public Library
Bucktown-Wicker Park Branch
DISCARD
Chicago, Illinois 60601

CONTENTS

Collection Cover Art: Marguerite Sauvage

Chicago Public Library
Canaryville Branch
642 - 46 W 43 St
Chicago, Illinois 60609

Associate Editor: David Menchel
Editors: Lysa Hawkins (DREAMSIDE) and
Charlotte Greenbaum (SPECIAL)

VALIANT®

Dan Mintz
Chairman

Fred Pierce
Publisher

Walter Black
VP Operations

Matthew Klein
VP Sales & Marketing

Robert Meyers
Senior Editorial Director

Mel Caylo
Director of Marketing

Travis Escarfullery
Director of Design & Production

Peter Stern
Director of International Publishing & Merchandising

Karl Bollers
Senior Editor

Lysa Hawkins
Heather Antos
Editors

David Menchel
Associate Editor

Drew Baumgartner
Assistant Editor

Jeff Walker
Production & Design Manager

Julia Walchuk
Sales & Live Events Manager

Emily Hecht
Sales & Social Media Manager

Connor Hill
Sales Operations Coordinator

Danielle Ward
Sales Manager

Gregg Katzman
Marketing Coordinator

Ivan Cohen
Collection Editor

Steve Blackwell
Collection Designer

Russ Brown
President, Consumer Products,
Promotions & Ad Sales

Oliver Taylor
International Licensing Coordinator

Zane Warman
Domestic Licensing Coordinator

Faith®: Dreamside. Published by Valiant Entertainment LLC. Office of Publication:
350 Seventh Avenue, New York, NY 10001. Compilation copyright © 2019 Valiant
Entertainment LLC. All rights reserved. Contains materials originally published in
single magazine form as Faith: Dreamside #1-4, and Faith's Winter Wonderland
Special #1. Copyright © 2017 and 2018 Valiant Entertainment LLC. All rights
reserved. All characters, their distinctive likeness and related indicia featured
in this publication are trademarks of Valiant Entertainment LLC. The stories,
characters, and incidents featured in this publication are entirely fictional.
Valiant Entertainment does not read or accept unsolicited submissions of ideas,
stories, or artwork. Printed in the U.S.A. First Printing. ISBN: 9781682152973.

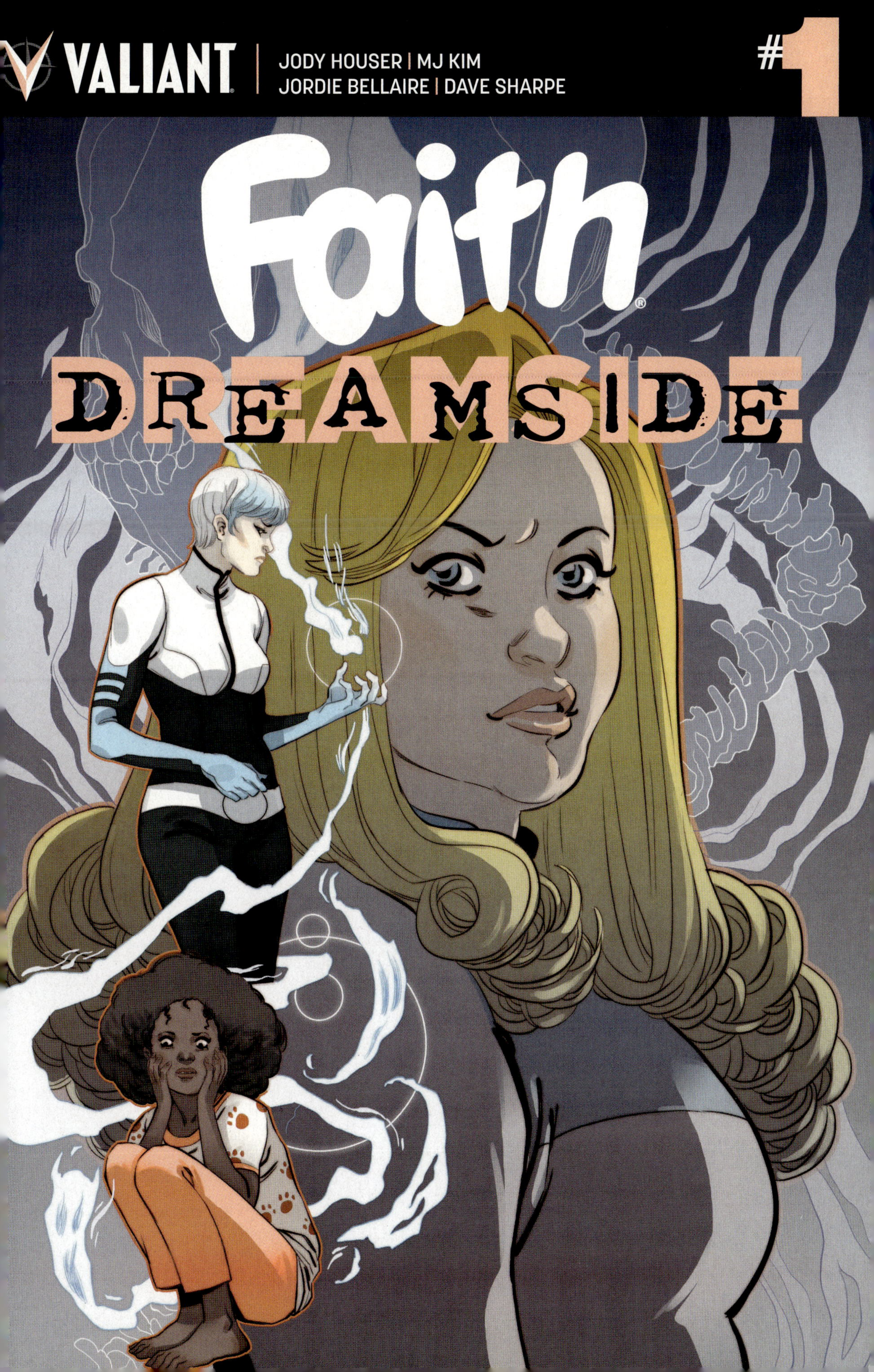
VALIANT
JODY HOUSER | MJ KIM
JORDIE BELLAIRE | DAVE SHARPE
#1
Faith
DREAMSIDE

Faith®
DREAMSIDE

Faith Herbert was just your average super-fan of all things sci-fi and fantasy when she discovered she had superpowers of her very own: the incredible power of flight! She moved to Los Angeles to try her hand at the hero gig as the high-flying Zephyr, where she amassed a fan following along with a rogues gallery of villainous evildoers. She was living her dream, until a group of her most heinous foes framed her for murder, and turned the public against her. Recently returning from Hawaii, Faith finds herself hiding in plain sight under the guise of her alter-ego, Summer Smith, waiting for the day when she can take to the skies once again...

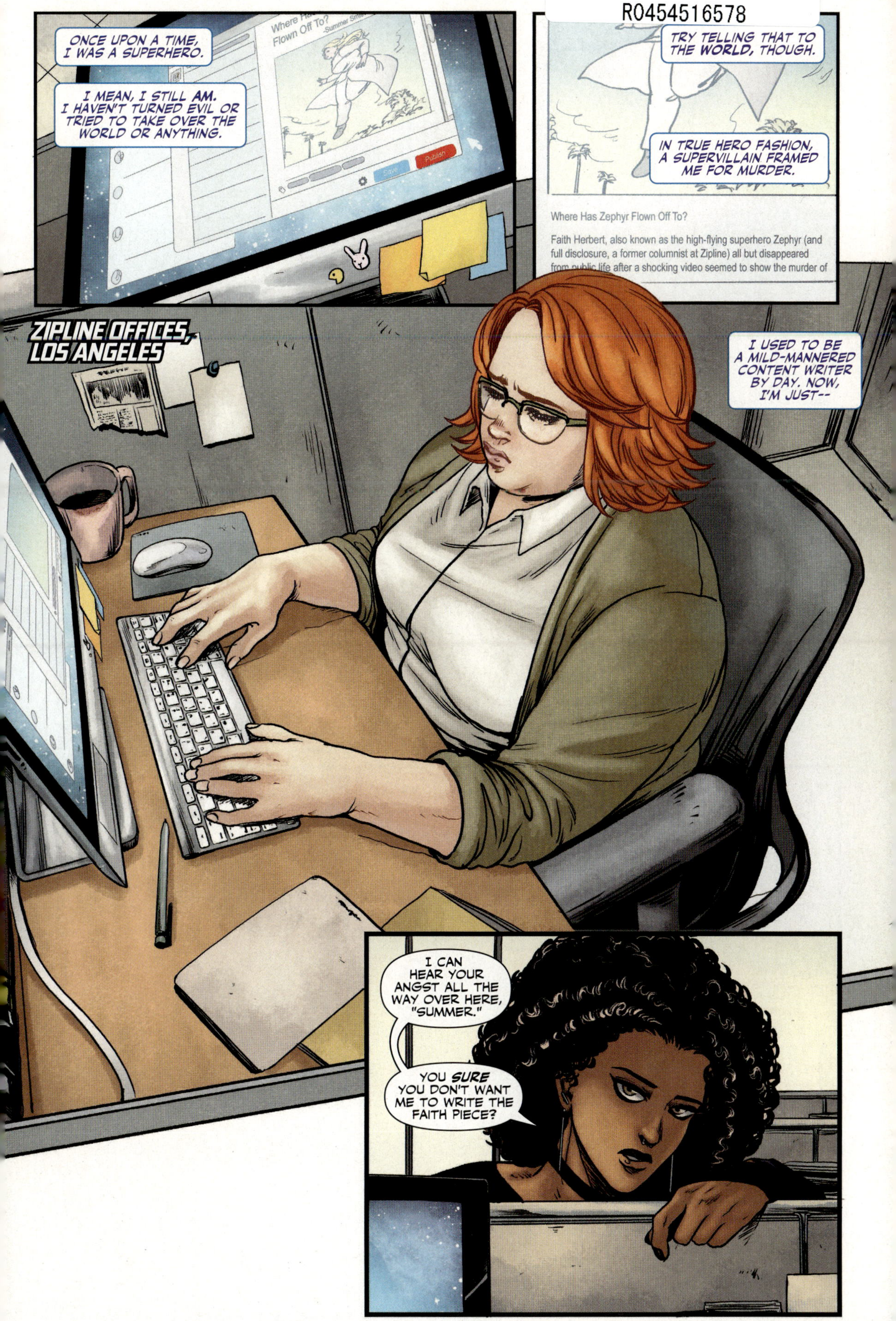
ONCE UPON A TIME, I WAS A SUPERHERO.
I MEAN, I STILL AM. I HAVEN'T TURNED EVIL OR TRIED TO TAKE OVER THE WORLD OR ANYTHING.
TRY TELLING THAT TO THE WORLD, THOUGH.
IN TRUE HERO FASHION, A SUPERVILLAIN FRAMED ME FOR MURDER.
Where Has Zephyr Flown Off To?
Faith Herbert, also known as the high-flying superhero Zephyr (and full disclosure, a former columnist at Zipline) all but disappeared from public life after a shocking video seemed to show the murder of
ZIPLINE OFFICES, LOS ANGELES
I USED TO BE A MILD-MANNERED CONTENT WRITER BY DAY. NOW, I'M JUST--
I CAN HEAR YOUR ANGST ALL THE WAY OVER HERE, "SUMMER."
YOU SURE YOU DON'T WANT ME TO WRITE THE FAITH PIECE?

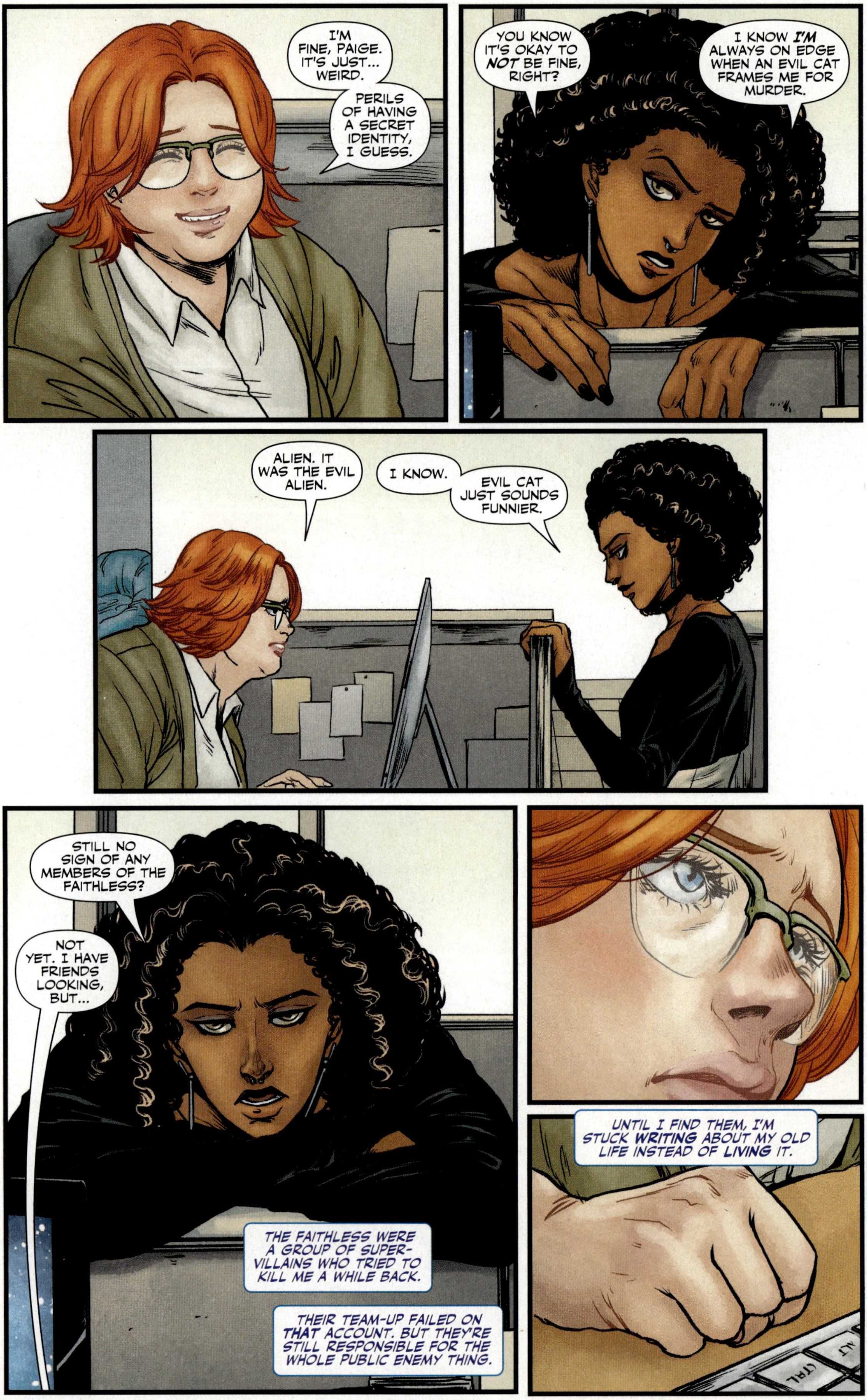
I'M FINE, PAIGE. IT'S JUST... WEIRD.
PERILS OF HAVING A SECRET IDENTITY, I GUESS.
YOU KNOW IT'S OKAY TO NOT BE FINE, RIGHT?
I KNOW I'M ALWAYS ON EDGE WHEN AN EVIL CAT FRAMES ME FOR MURDER.
ALIEN. IT WAS THE EVIL ALIEN.
I KNOW.
EVIL CAT JUST SOUNDS FUNNIER.
STILL NO SIGN OF ANY MEMBERS OF THE FAITHLESS?
NOT YET. I HAVE FRIENDS LOOKING, BUT...
THE FAITHLESS WERE A GROUP OF SUPER-VILLAINS WHO TRIED TO KILL ME A WHILE BACK.
THEIR TEAM-UP FAILED ON THAT ACCOUNT. BUT THEY'RE STILL RESPONSIBLE FOR THE WHOLE PUBLIC ENEMY THING.
UNTIL I FIND THEM, I'M STUCK WRITING ABOUT MY OLD LIFE INSTEAD OF LIVING IT.

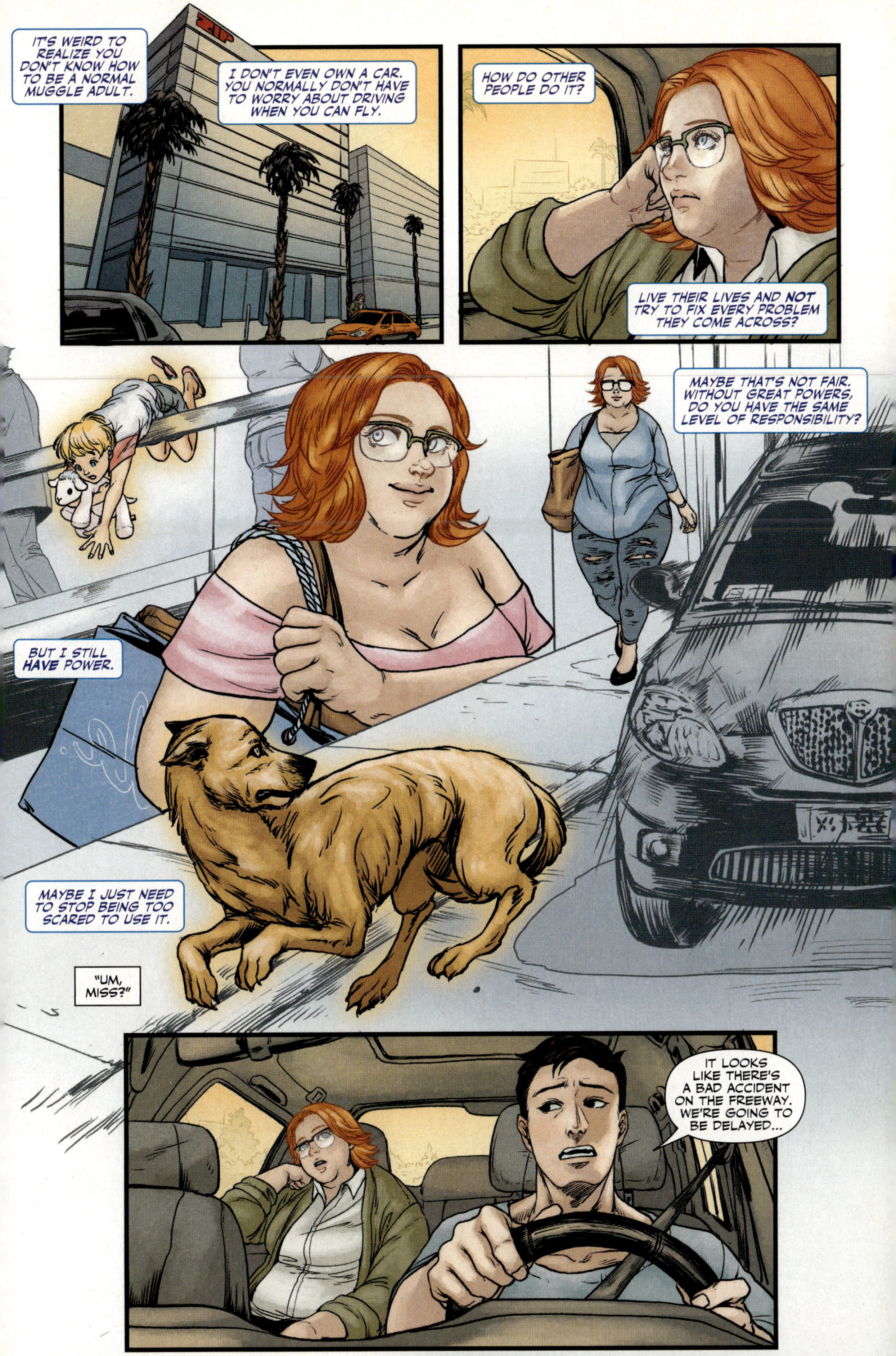
IT'S WEIRD TO REALIZE YOU DON'T KNOW HOW TO BE A NORMAL MUGGLE ADULT.
ZIP
I DON'T EVEN OWN A CAR. YOU NORMALLY DON'T HAVE TO WORRY ABOUT DRIVING WHEN YOU CAN FLY.
HOW DO OTHER PEOPLE DO IT?
LIVE THEIR LIVES AND NOT TRY TO FIX EVERY PROBLEM THEY COME ACROSS?
MAYBE THAT'S NOT FAIR. WITHOUT GREAT POWERS, DO YOU HAVE THE SAME LEVEL OF RESPONSIBILITY?
BUT I STILL HAVE POWER.
MAYBE I JUST NEED TO STOP BEING TOO SCARED TO USE IT.
"UM, MISS?"
IT LOOKS LIKE THERE'S A BAD ACCIDENT ON THE FREEWAY. WE'RE GOING TO BE DELAYED...

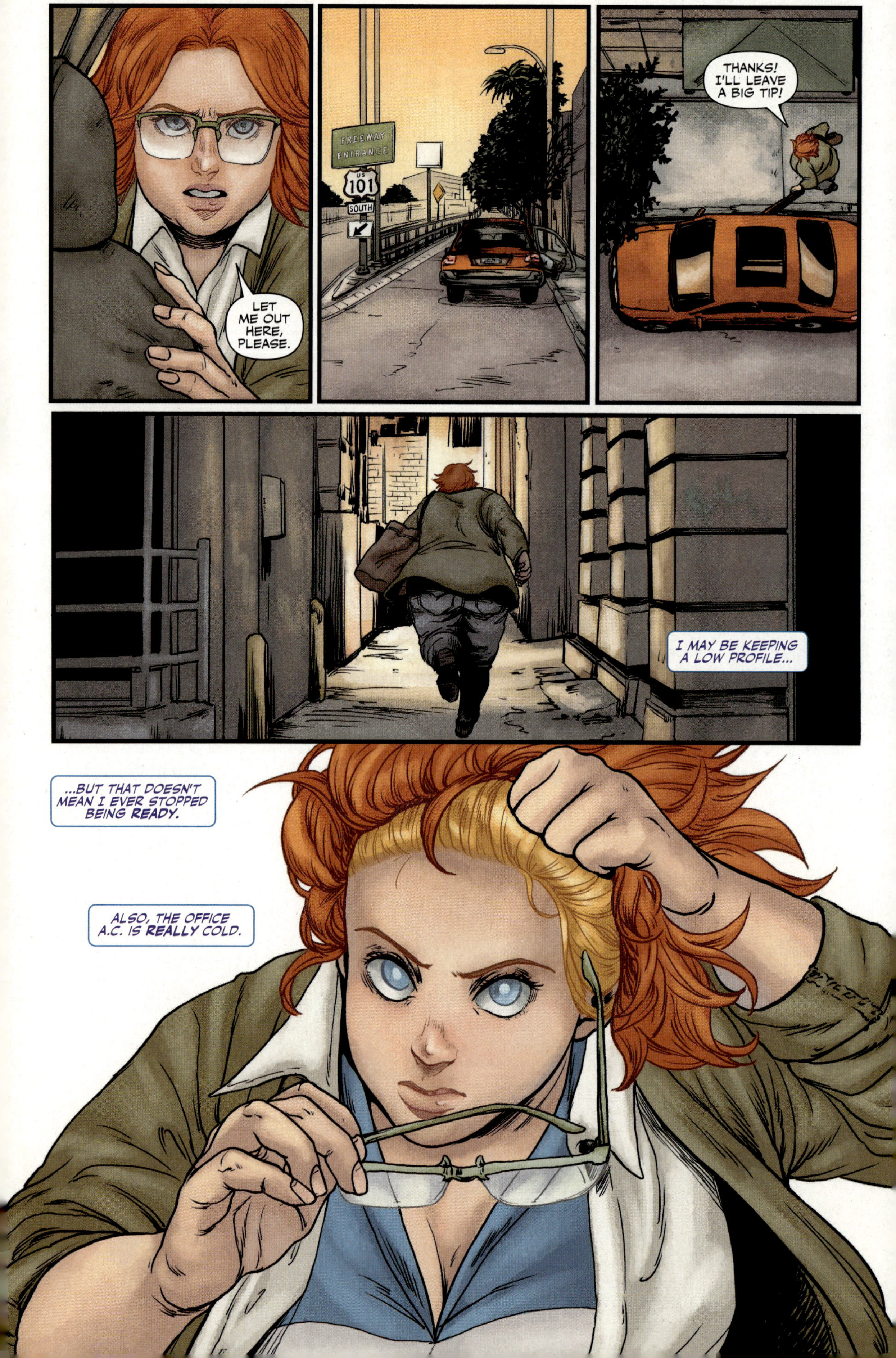
LET ME OUT HERE, PLEASE.
FREEWAY ENTRANCE
US 101
SOUTH
THANKS! I'LL LEAVE A BIG TIP!
I MAY BE KEEPING A LOW PROFILE...
...BUT THAT DOESN'T MEAN I EVER STOPPED BEING READY.
ALSO, THE OFFICE A.C. IS REALLY COLD.

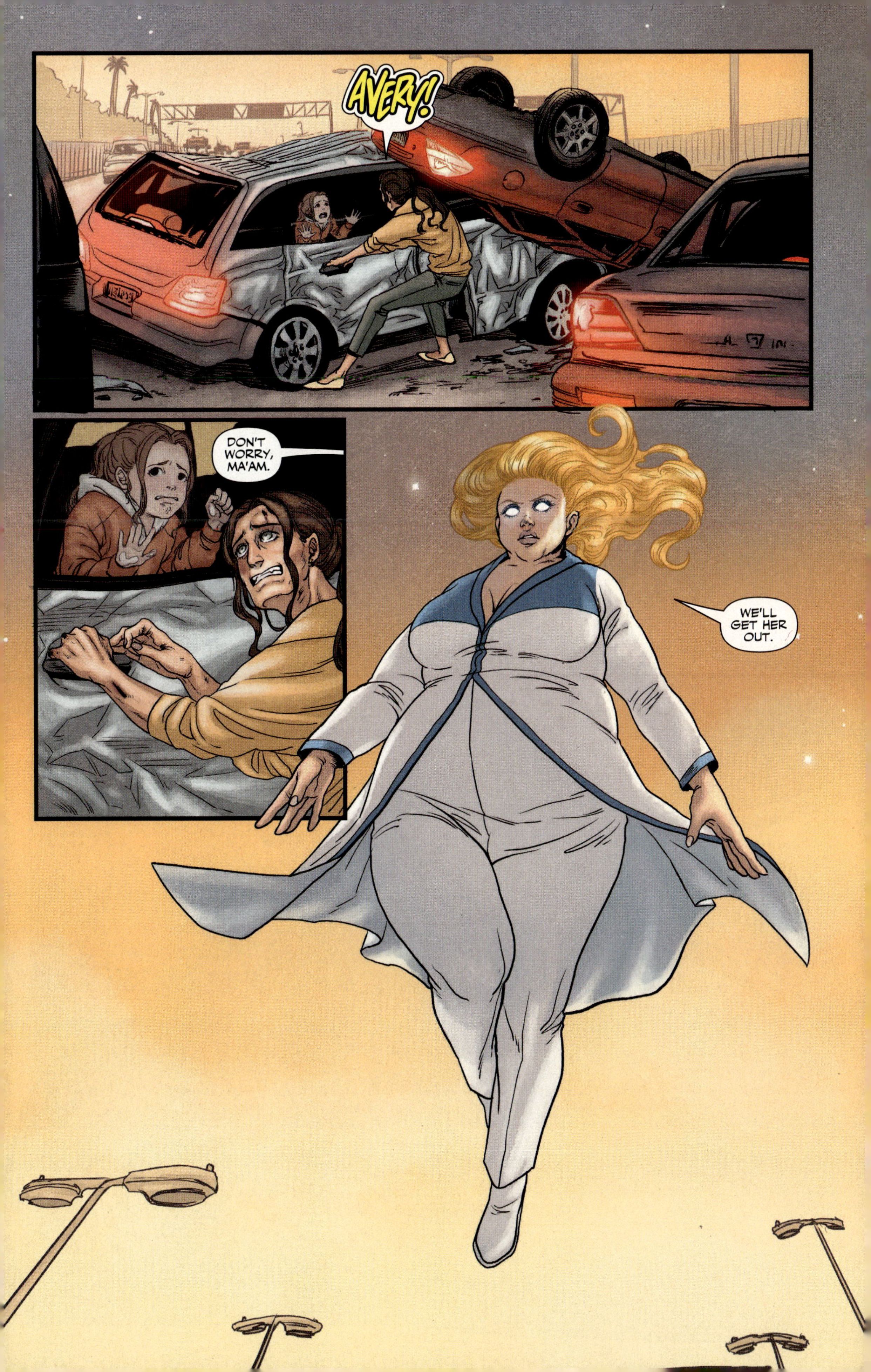
AVERY!
DON'T WORRY, MA'AM.
WE'LL GET HER OUT.

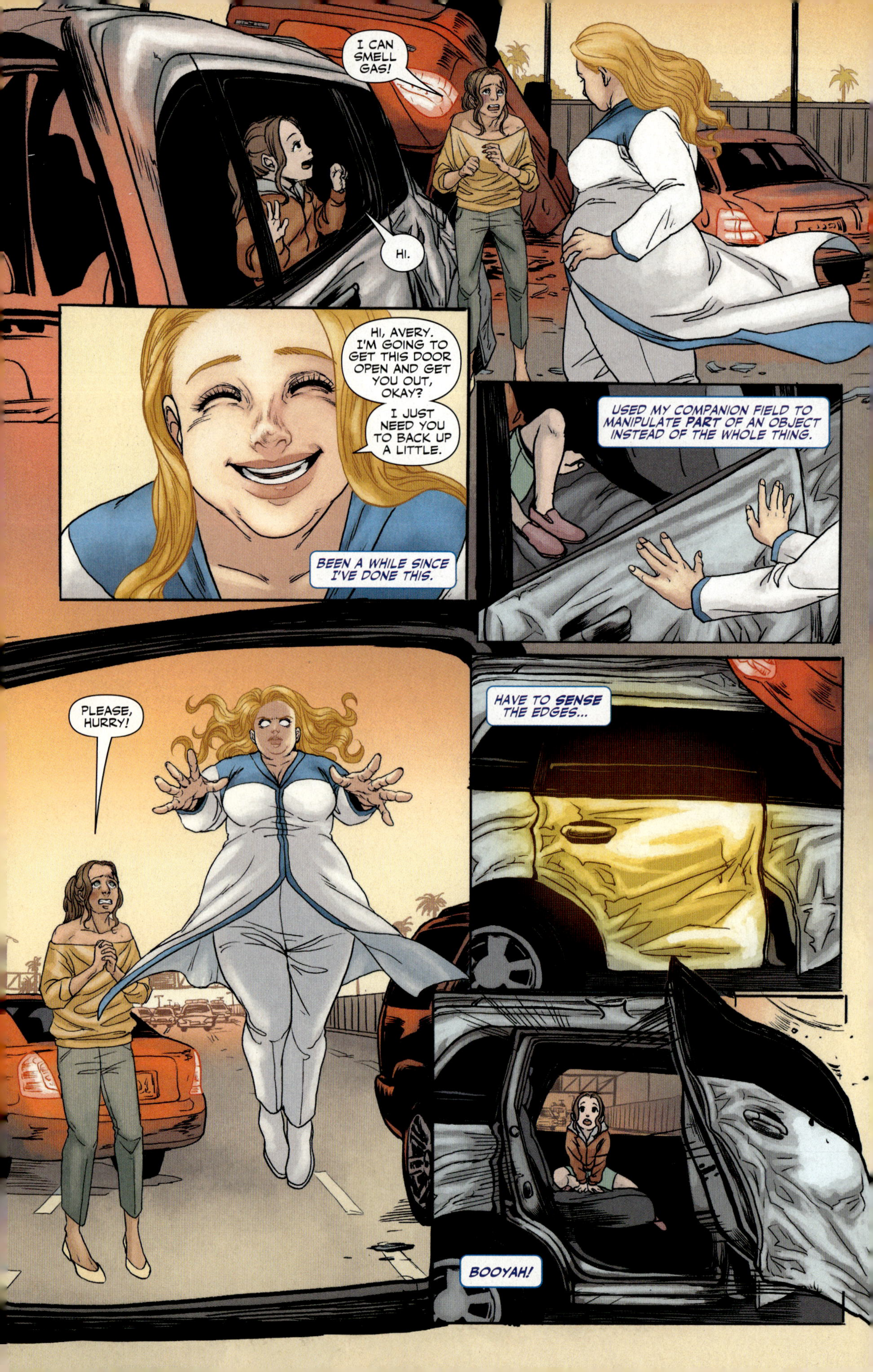
I CAN SMELL GAS!
HI.
HI, AVERY. I'M GOING TO GET THIS DOOR OPEN AND GET YOU OUT, OKAY?
I JUST NEED YOU TO BACK UP A LITTLE.
BEEN A WHILE SINCE I'VE DONE THIS.
USED MY COMPANION FIELD TO MANIPULATE PART OF AN OBJECT INSTEAD OF THE WHOLE THING.
PLEASE, HURRY!
HAVE TO SENSE THE EDGES...
BOOYAH!

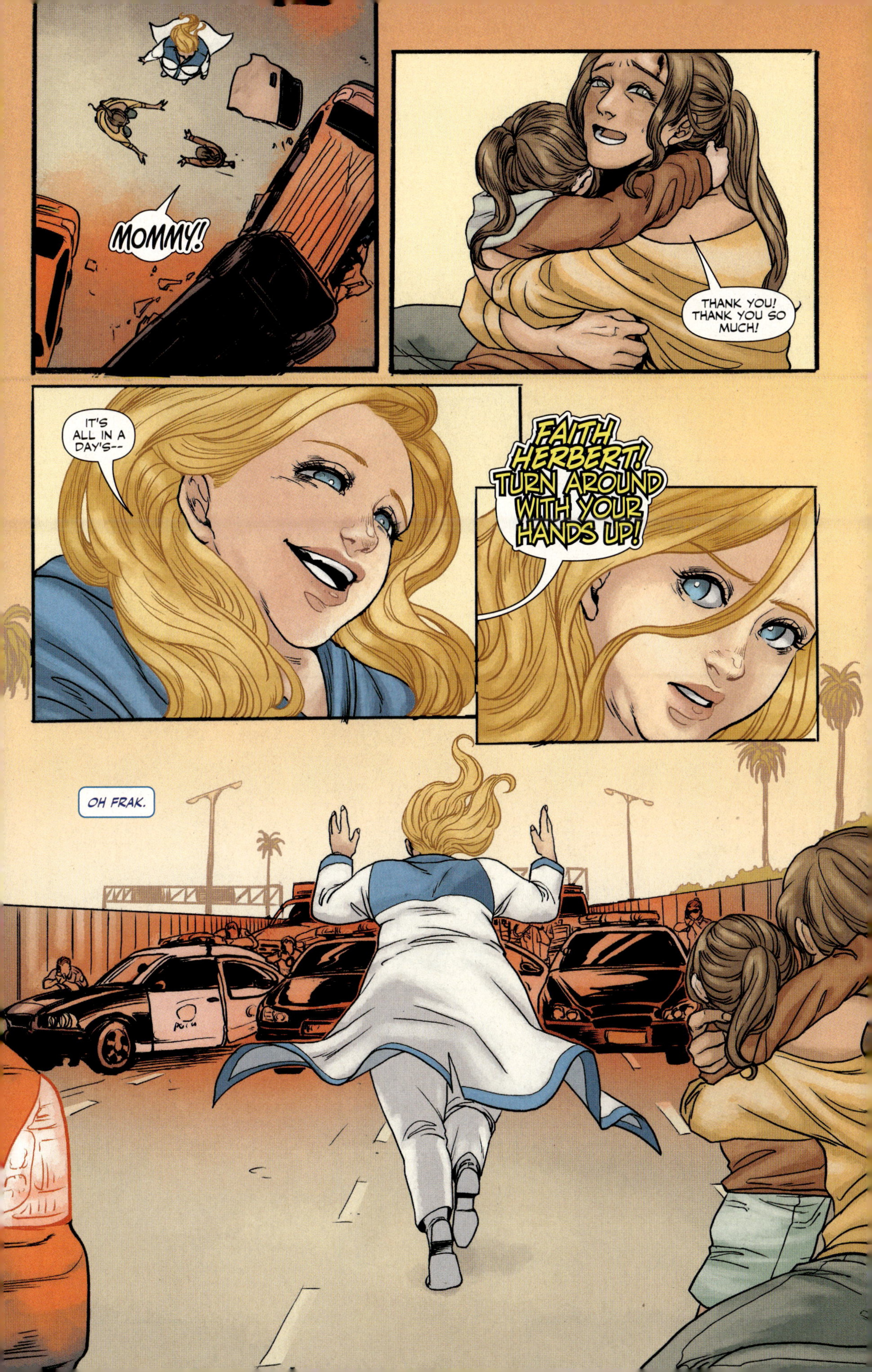
MOMMY!
THANK YOU! THANK YOU SO MUCH!
IT'S ALL IN A DAY'S--
FAITH HERBERT! TURN AROUND WITH YOUR HANDS UP!
OH FRAK.

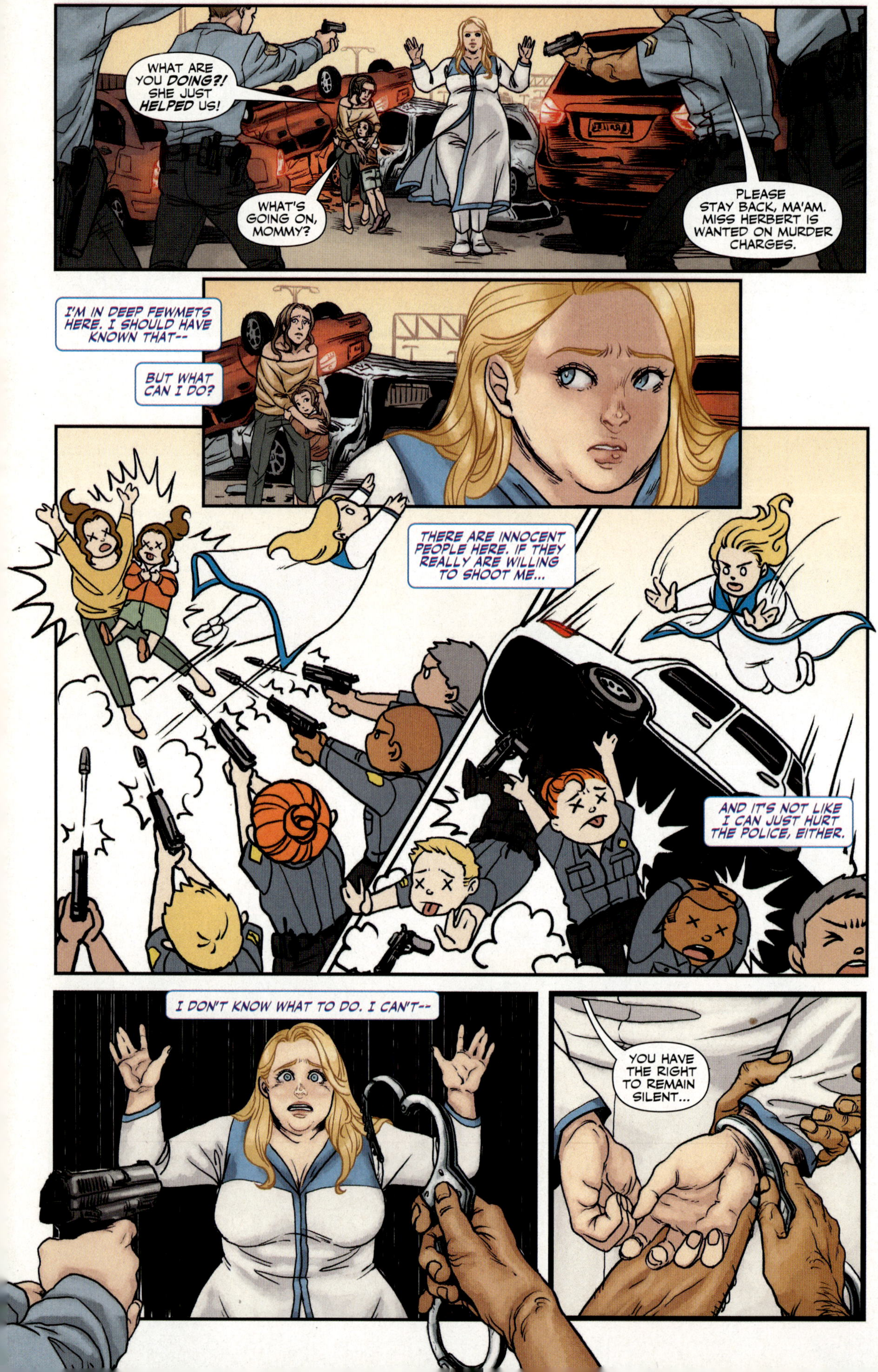
WHAT ARE YOU DOING?! SHE JUST HELPED US!
WHAT'S GOING ON, MOMMY?
PLEASE STAY BACK, MA'AM. MISS HERBERT IS WANTED ON MURDER CHARGES.
I'M IN DEEP FEWMETS HERE. I SHOULD HAVE KNOWN THAT--
BUT WHAT CAN I DO?
THERE ARE INNOCENT PEOPLE HERE. IF THEY REALLY ARE WILLING TO SHOOT ME...
AND IT'S NOT LIKE I CAN JUST HURT THE POLICE, EITHER.
I DON'T KNOW WHAT TO DO. I CAN'T--
YOU HAVE THE RIGHT TO REMAIN SILENT...

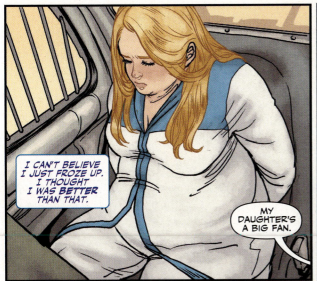

I CAN'T BELIEVE I JUST FROZE UP. I THOUGHT I WAS *BETTER* THAN THAT.

MY DAUGHTER'S A BIG FAN.

SHOULD SAY, SHE *WAS* A BIG FAN.

REALLY?

I CAN'T SAY I WAS *HAPPY* ABOUT IT, BUT AT LEAST IT SEEMED LIKE YOU WERE TRYING TO DO GOOD.

BUT, WHEN SHE SAW THAT VIDEO, THE WAY YOU SHOT THAT MAN...

YOU BROKE HER DAMN HEART.

THAT WASN'T--

"IT WAS AN ALIEN USING HOLOGRAMS" JUST DOESN'T SOUND CONVINCING, DOES IT?

I HOPE THEY THROW THE BOOK AT YOU. JUST TO SHOW HER THAT--

UH, CAMPOS...

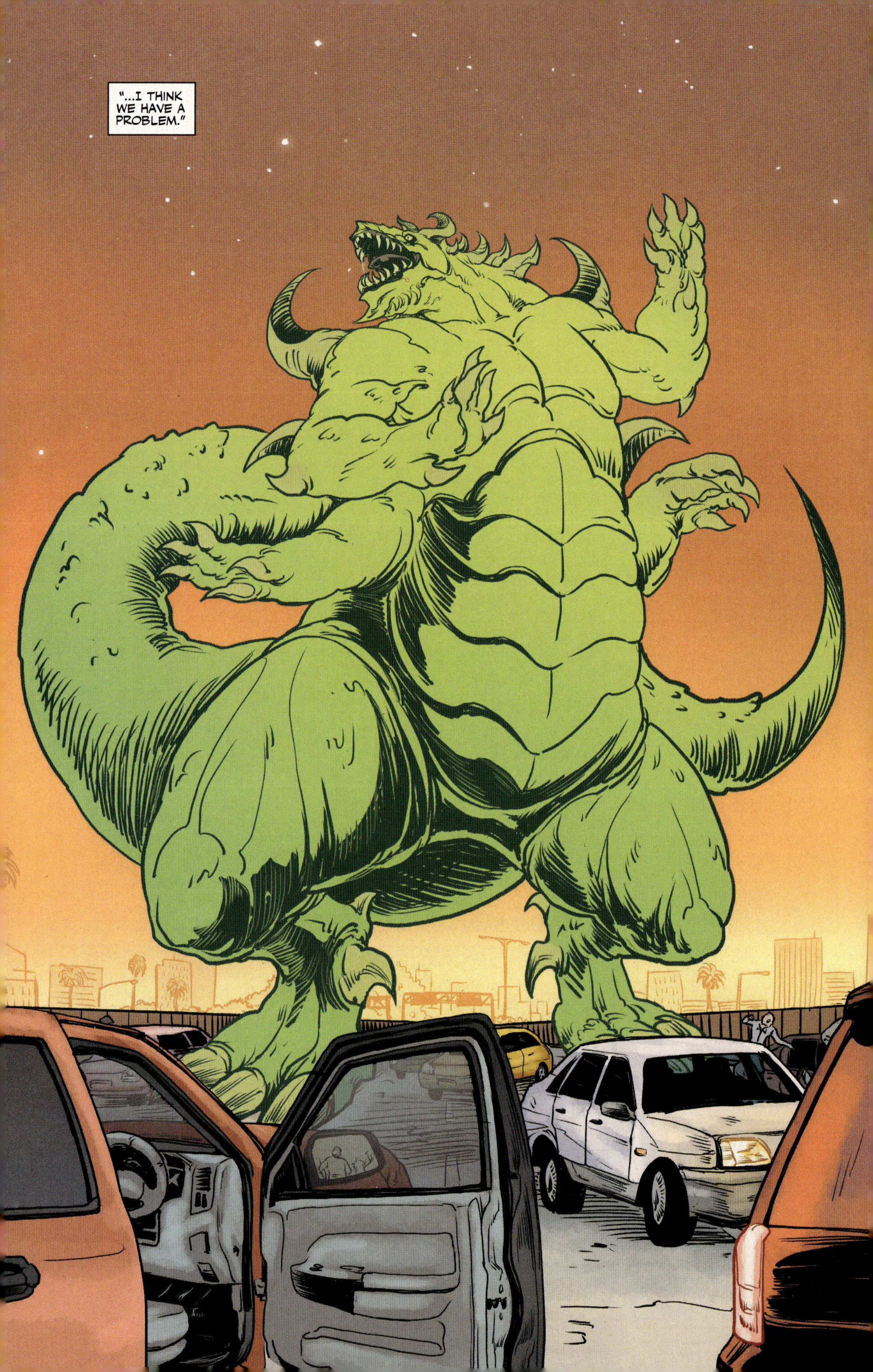
"...I THINK WE HAVE A PROBLEM."

IS THAT A **KAIJU?!**

QUIET!

WHAT DO WE...WHAT ARE WE SUPPOSED TO *DO?*

ARREST IT FOR JAYWALKING?!

I CAN HELP! IF YOU LET ME--

I SAID *QUIET!*

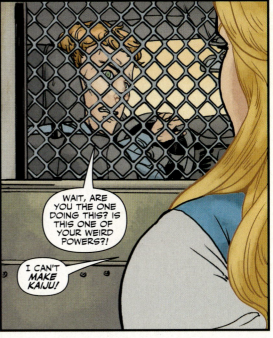

WAIT, ARE YOU THE ONE DOING THIS? IS THIS ONE OF YOUR WEIRD POWERS?!

I CAN'T *MAKE* KAIJU!

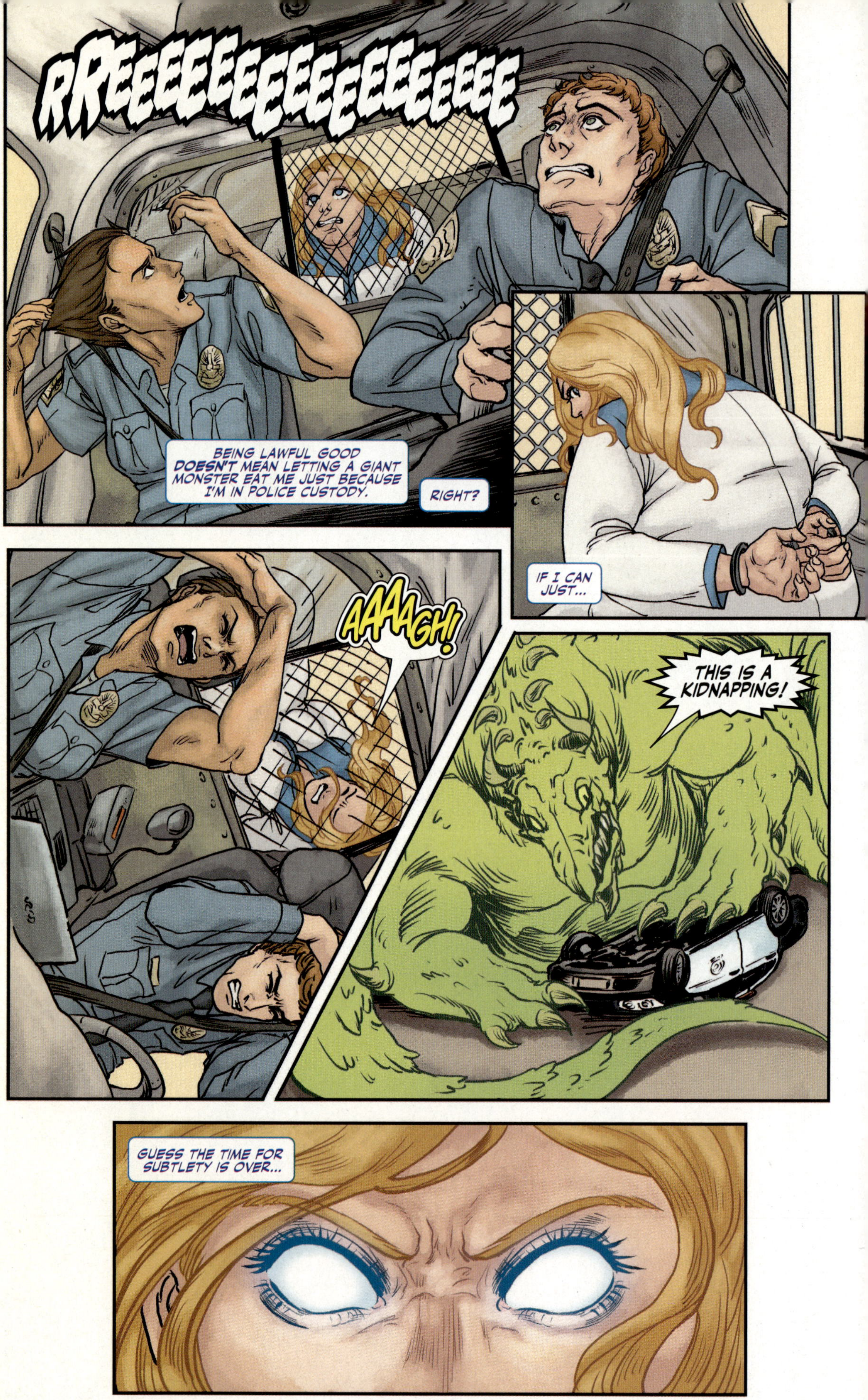
RREEEEEEEEEEEEEEEEE
BEING LAWFUL GOOD DOESN'T MEAN LETTING A GIANT MONSTER EAT ME JUST BECAUSE I'M IN POLICE CUSTODY.
RIGHT?
IF I CAN JUST...
AAAAGH!
THIS IS A KIDNAPPING!
GUESS THE TIME FOR SUBTLETY IS OVER...

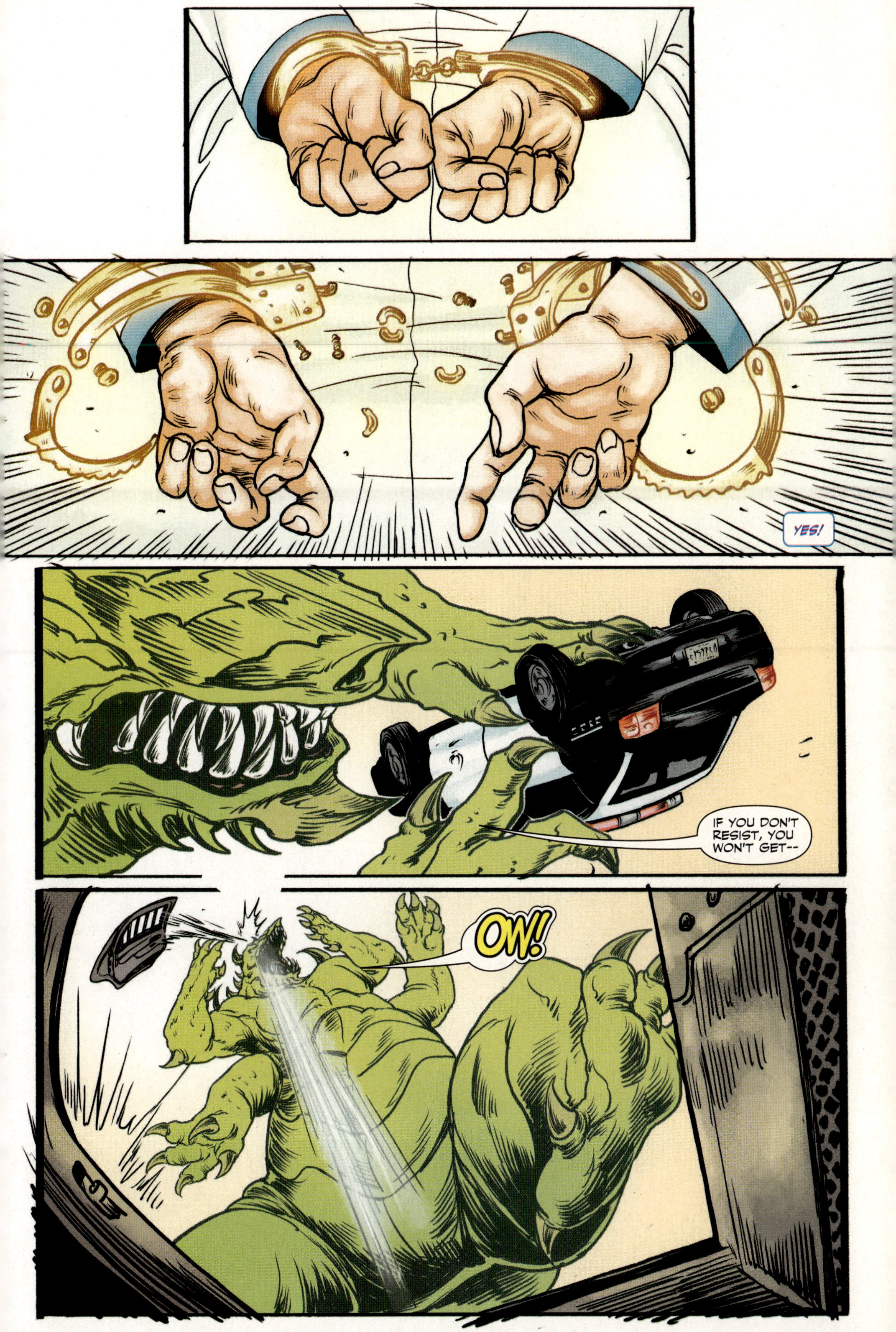
YES!
IF YOU DON'T RESIST, YOU WON'T GET--
OW!

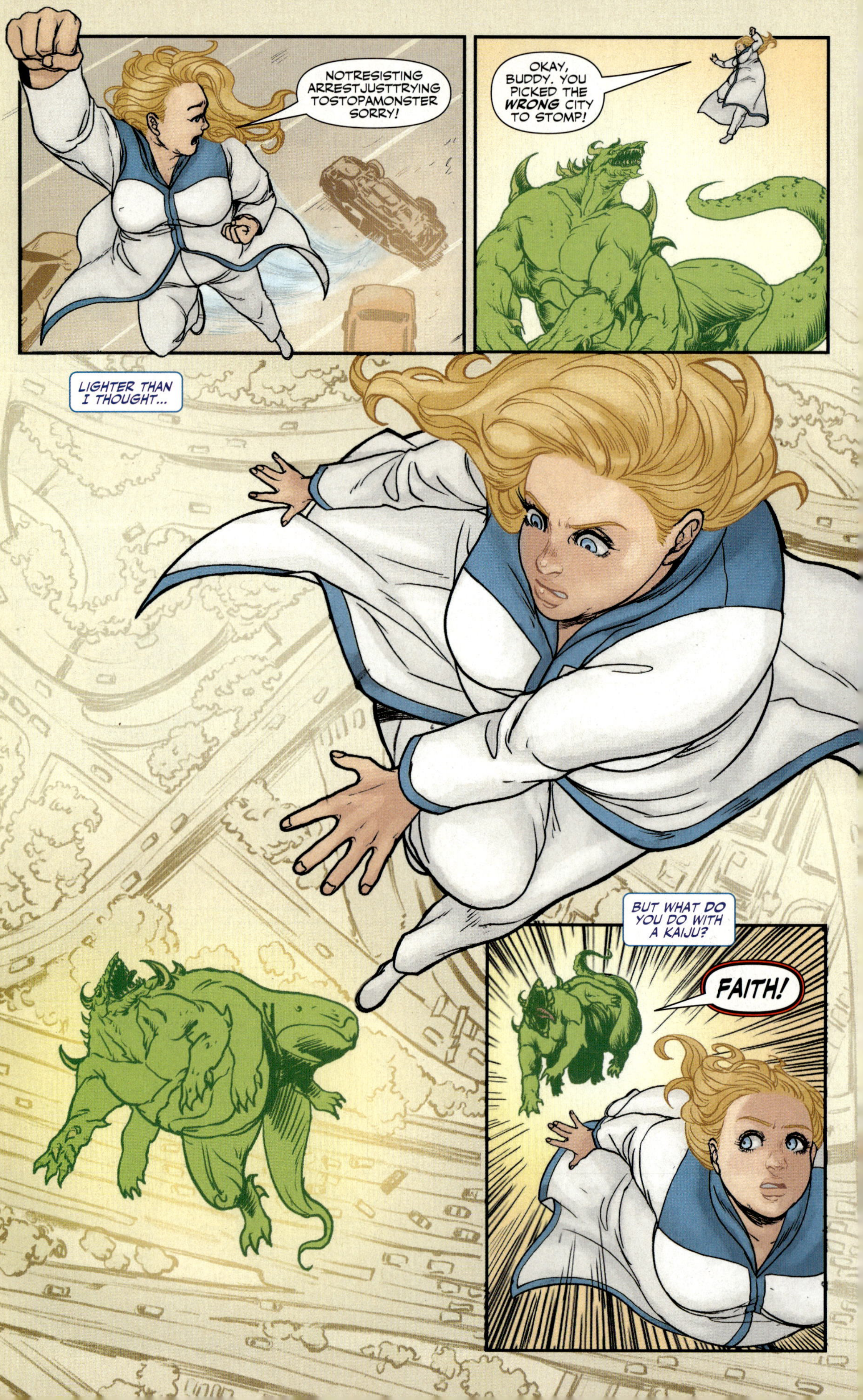
NOTRESISTING ARRESTJUSTTRYING TOSTOPAMONSTER SORRY!
OKAY, BUDDY. YOU PICKED THE WRONG CITY TO STOMP!
LIGHTER THAN I THOUGHT...
BUT WHAT DO YOU DO WITH A KAIJU?
FAITH!

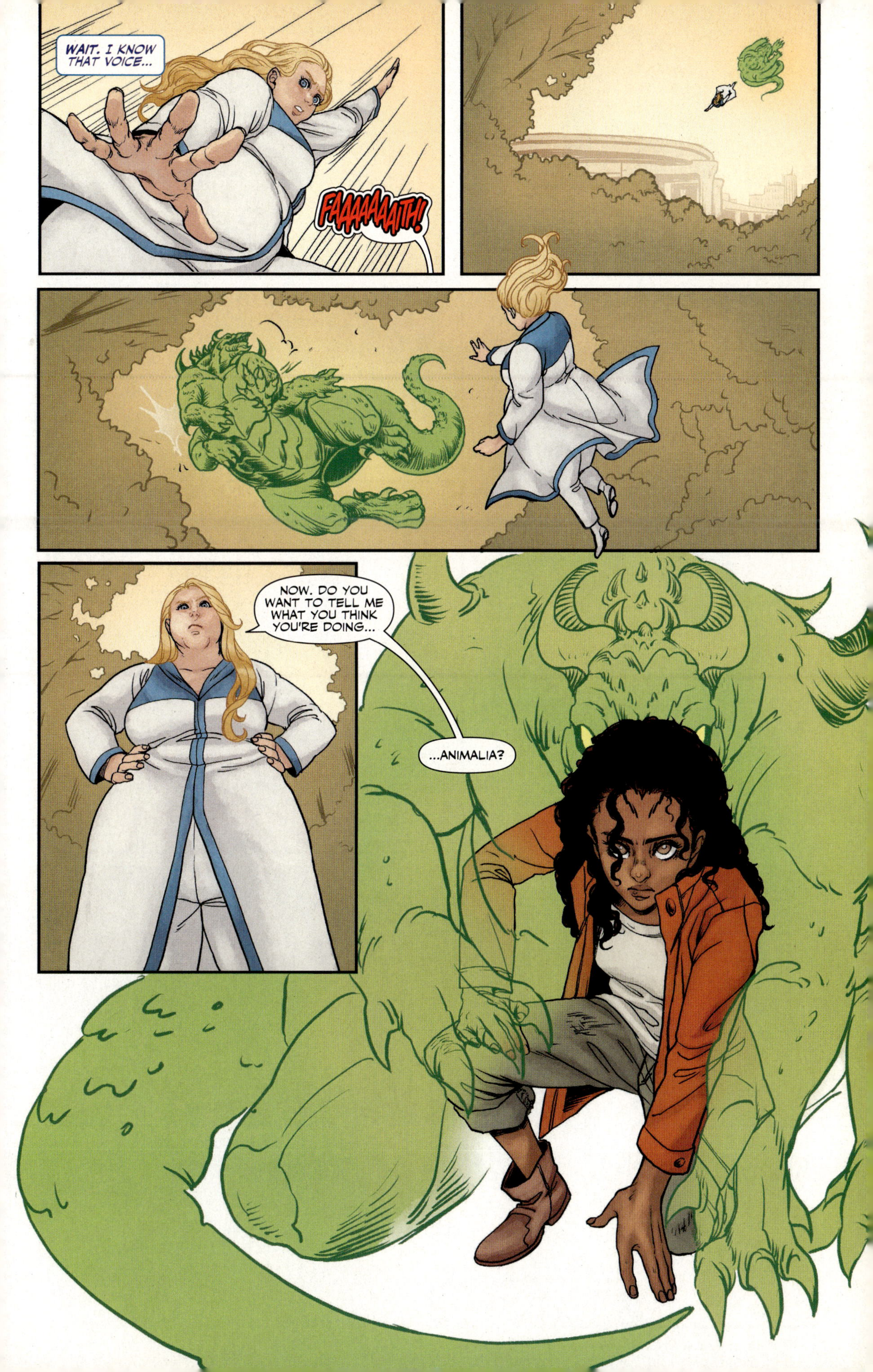
WAIT. I KNOW THAT VOICE...
FAAAAAAAITH!
NOW. DO YOU WANT TO TELL ME WHAT YOU THINK YOU'RE DOING...
...ANIMALIA?

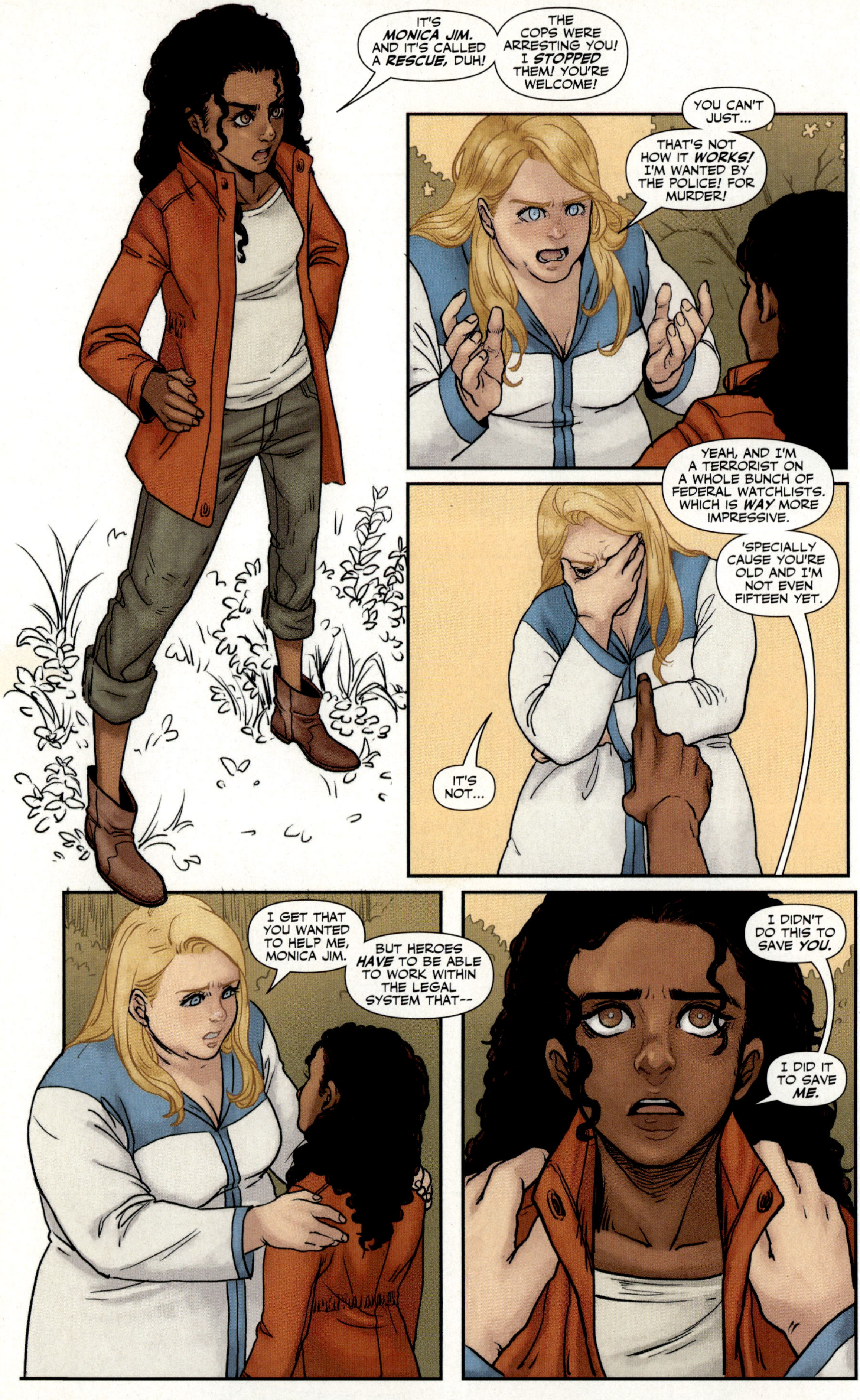
IT'S MONICA JIM. AND IT'S CALLED A RESCUE, DUH!
THE COPS WERE ARRESTING YOU! I STOPPED THEM! YOU'RE WELCOME!
YOU CAN'T JUST...
THAT'S NOT HOW IT WORKS! I'M WANTED BY THE POLICE! FOR MURDER!
YEAH, AND I'M A TERRORIST ON A WHOLE BUNCH OF FEDERAL WATCHLISTS. WHICH IS WAY MORE IMPRESSIVE.
'SPECIALLY CAUSE YOU'RE OLD AND I'M NOT EVEN FIFTEEN YET.
IT'S NOT...
I GET THAT YOU WANTED TO HELP ME, MONICA JIM.
BUT HEROES HAVE TO BE ABLE TO WORK WITHIN THE LEGAL SYSTEM THAT--
I DIDN'T DO THIS TO SAVE YOU.
I DID IT TO SAVE ME.

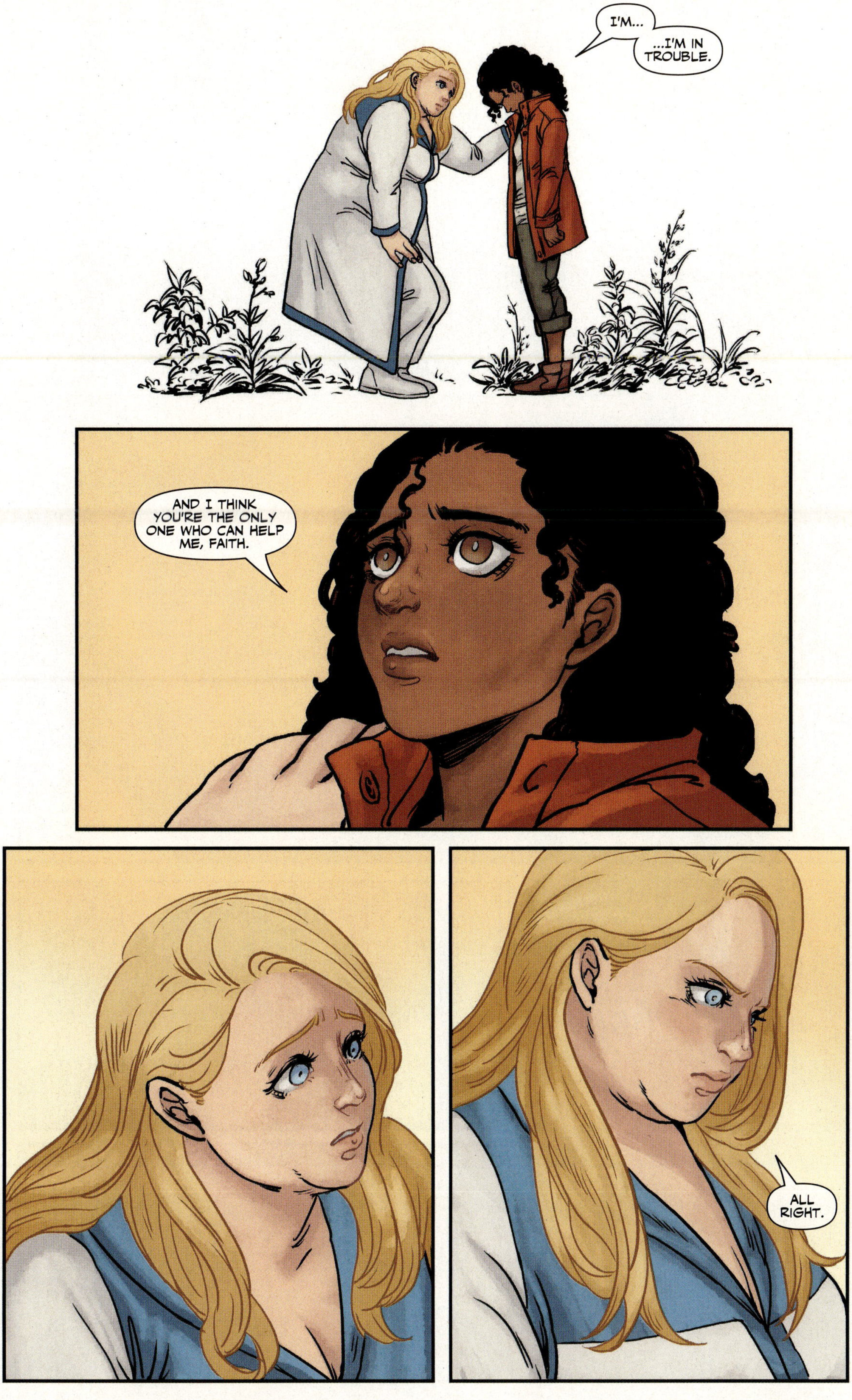
I'M...
...I'M IN TROUBLE.
AND I THINK YOU'RE THE ONLY ONE WHO CAN HELP ME, FAITH.
ALL RIGHT.

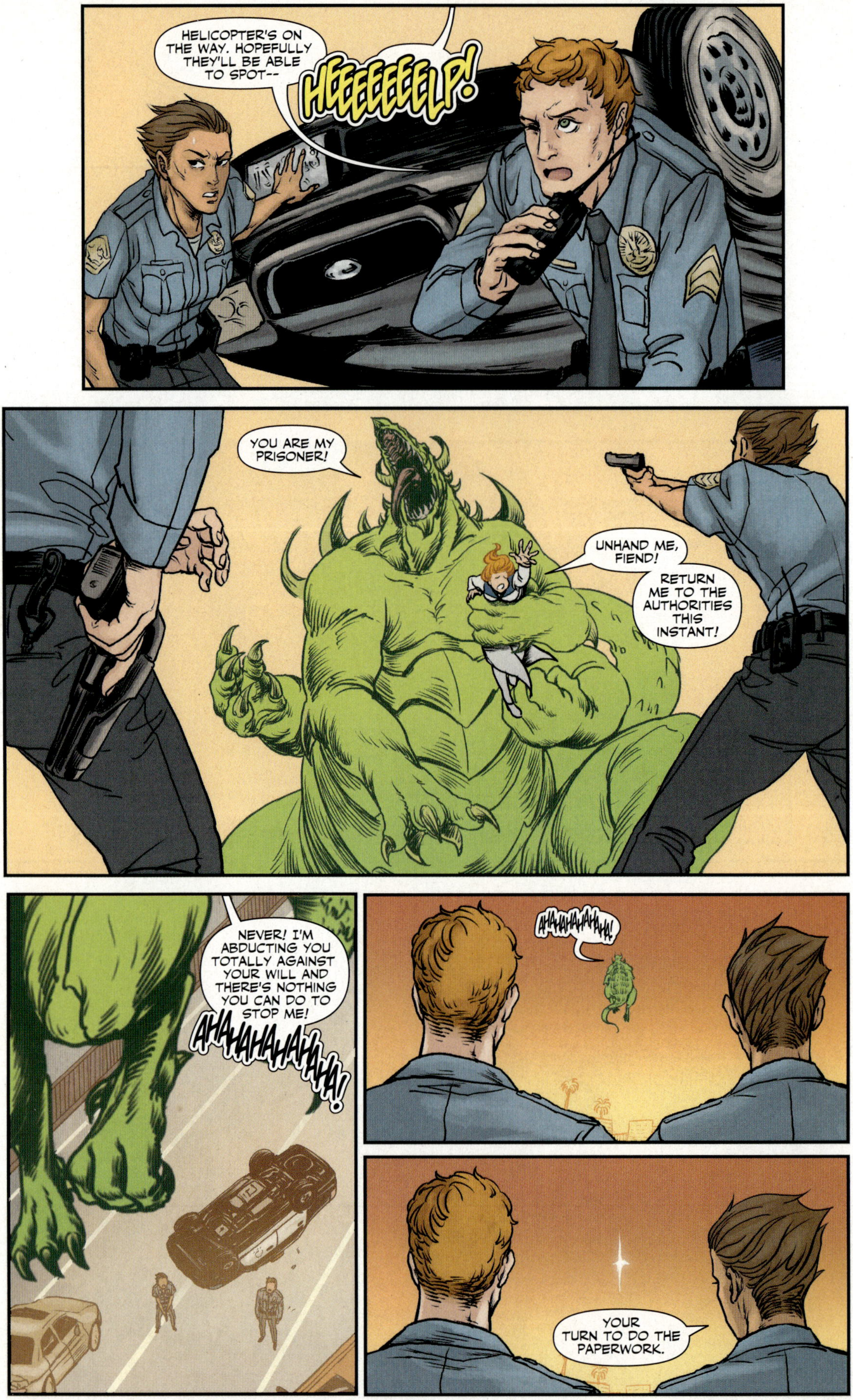
HELICOPTER'S ON THE WAY. HOPEFULLY THEY'LL BE ABLE TO SPOT--
HEEEEEEELP!
YOU ARE MY PRISONER!
UNHAND ME, FIEND!
RETURN ME TO THE AUTHORITIES THIS INSTANT!
NEVER! I'M ABDUCTING YOU TOTALLY AGAINST YOUR WILL AND THERE'S NOTHING YOU CAN DO TO STOP ME!
AHAHAHAHAHAHAHA!
AHAHAHAHAHAHA!
YOUR TURN TO DO THE PAPERWORK.

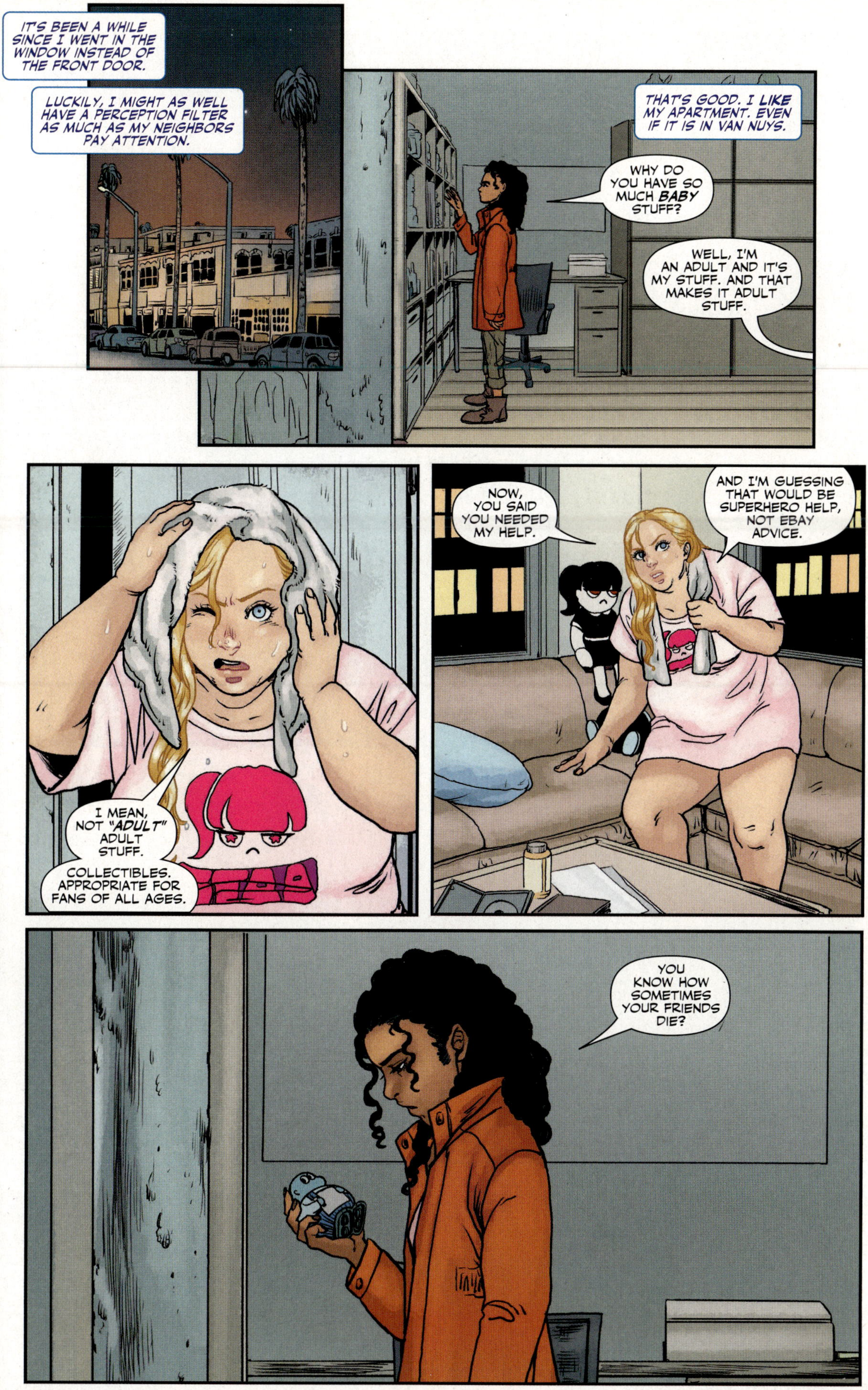
IT'S BEEN A WHILE SINCE I WENT IN THE WINDOW INSTEAD OF THE FRONT DOOR.
LUCKILY, I MIGHT AS WELL HAVE A PERCEPTION FILTER AS MUCH AS MY NEIGHBORS PAY ATTENTION.
THAT'S GOOD. I LIKE MY APARTMENT. EVEN IF IT IS IN VAN NUYS.
WHY DO YOU HAVE SO MUCH BABY STUFF?
WELL, I'M AN ADULT AND IT'S MY STUFF. AND THAT MAKES IT ADULT STUFF.
I MEAN, NOT "ADULT" ADULT STUFF.
COLLECTIBLES. APPROPRIATE FOR FANS OF ALL AGES.
NOW, YOU SAID YOU NEEDED MY HELP.
AND I'M GUESSING THAT WOULD BE SUPERHERO HELP, NOT EBAY ADVICE.
YOU KNOW HOW SOMETIMES YOUR FRIENDS DIE?

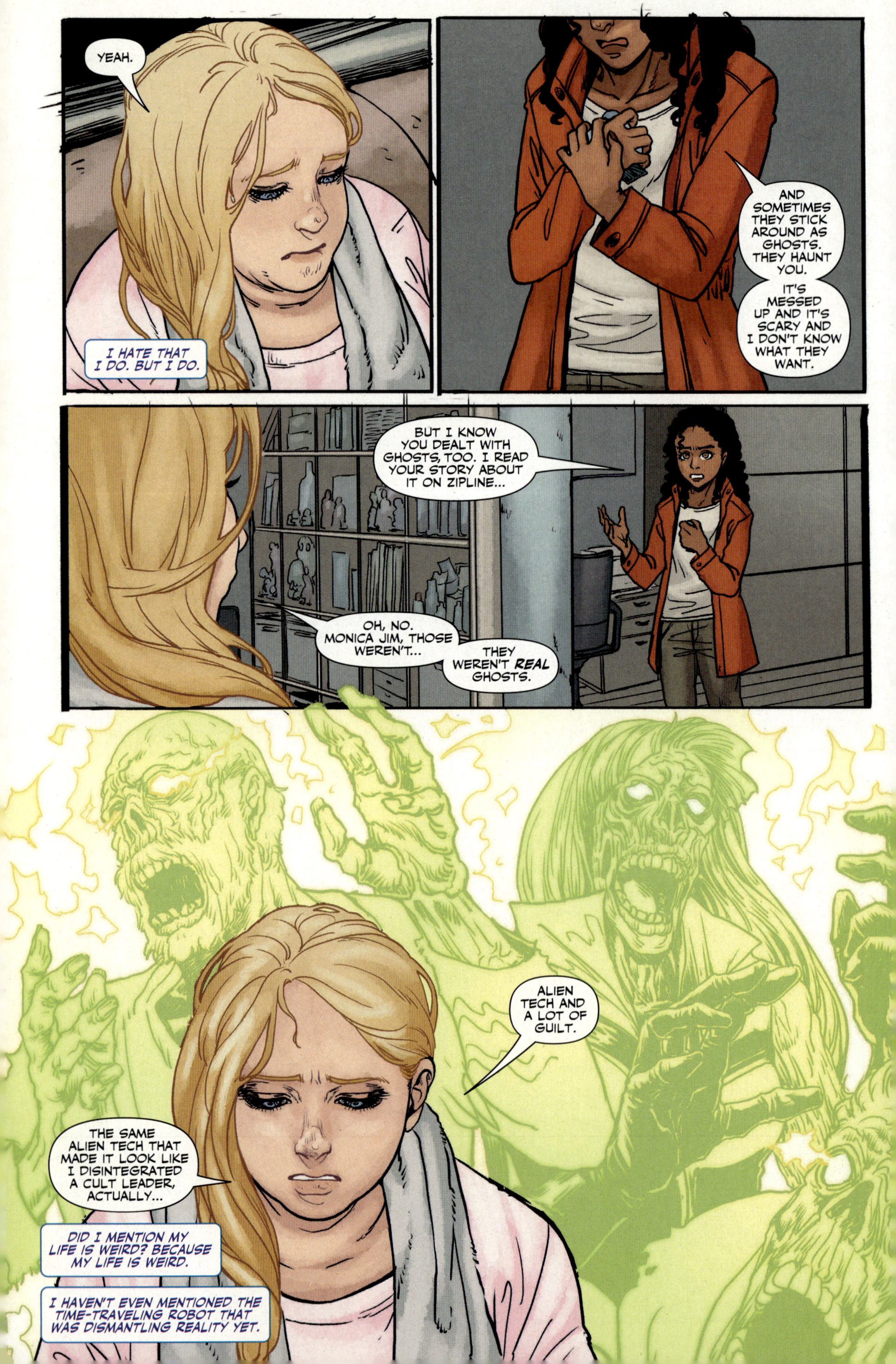

YEAH.
I HATE THAT I DO. BUT I DO.
AND SOMETIMES THEY STICK AROUND AS GHOSTS. THEY HAUNT YOU.
IT'S MESSED UP AND IT'S SCARY AND I DON'T KNOW WHAT THEY WANT.
BUT I KNOW YOU DEALT WITH GHOSTS, TOO. I READ YOUR STORY ABOUT IT ON ZIPLINE...
OH, NO. MONICA JIM, THOSE WEREN'T...
THEY WEREN'T REAL GHOSTS.
ALIEN TECH AND A LOT OF GUILT.
THE SAME ALIEN TECH THAT MADE IT LOOK LIKE I DISINTEGRATED A CULT LEADER, ACTUALLY...
DID I MENTION MY LIFE IS WEIRD? BECAUSE MY LIFE IS WEIRD.
I HAVEN'T EVEN MENTIONED THE TIME-TRAVELING ROBOT THAT WAS DISMANTLING REALITY YET.

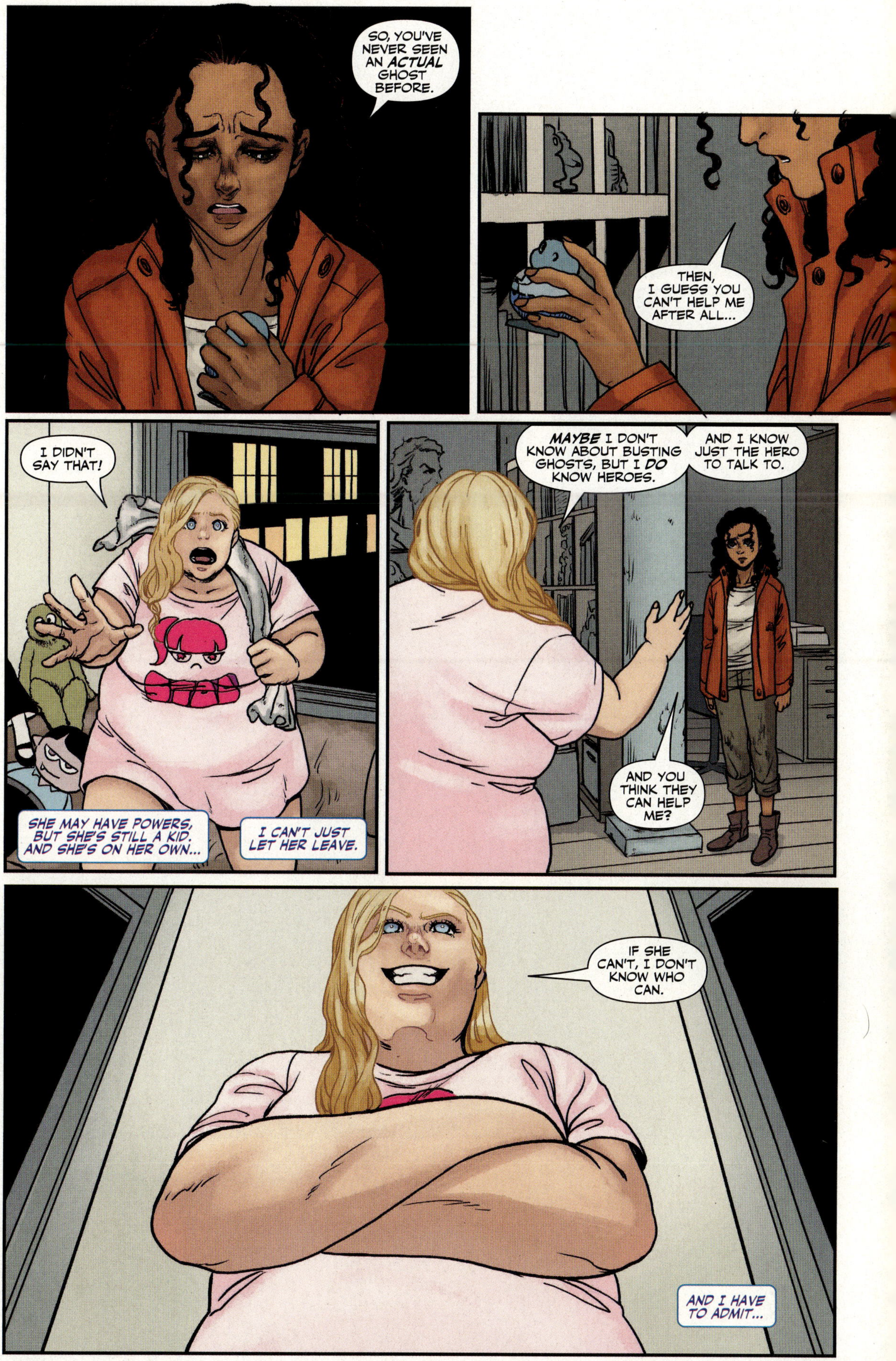

SO, YOU'VE NEVER SEEN AN ACTUAL GHOST BEFORE.
THEN, I GUESS YOU CAN'T HELP ME AFTER ALL...
I DIDN'T SAY THAT!
SHE MAY HAVE POWERS, BUT SHE'S STILL A KID. AND SHE'S ON HER OWN...
I CAN'T JUST LET HER LEAVE.
MAYBE I DON'T KNOW ABOUT BUSTING GHOSTS, BUT I DO KNOW HEROES.
AND I KNOW JUST THE HERO TO TALK TO.
AND YOU THINK THEY CAN HELP ME?
IF SHE CAN'T, I DON'T KNOW WHO CAN.
AND I HAVE TO ADMIT...

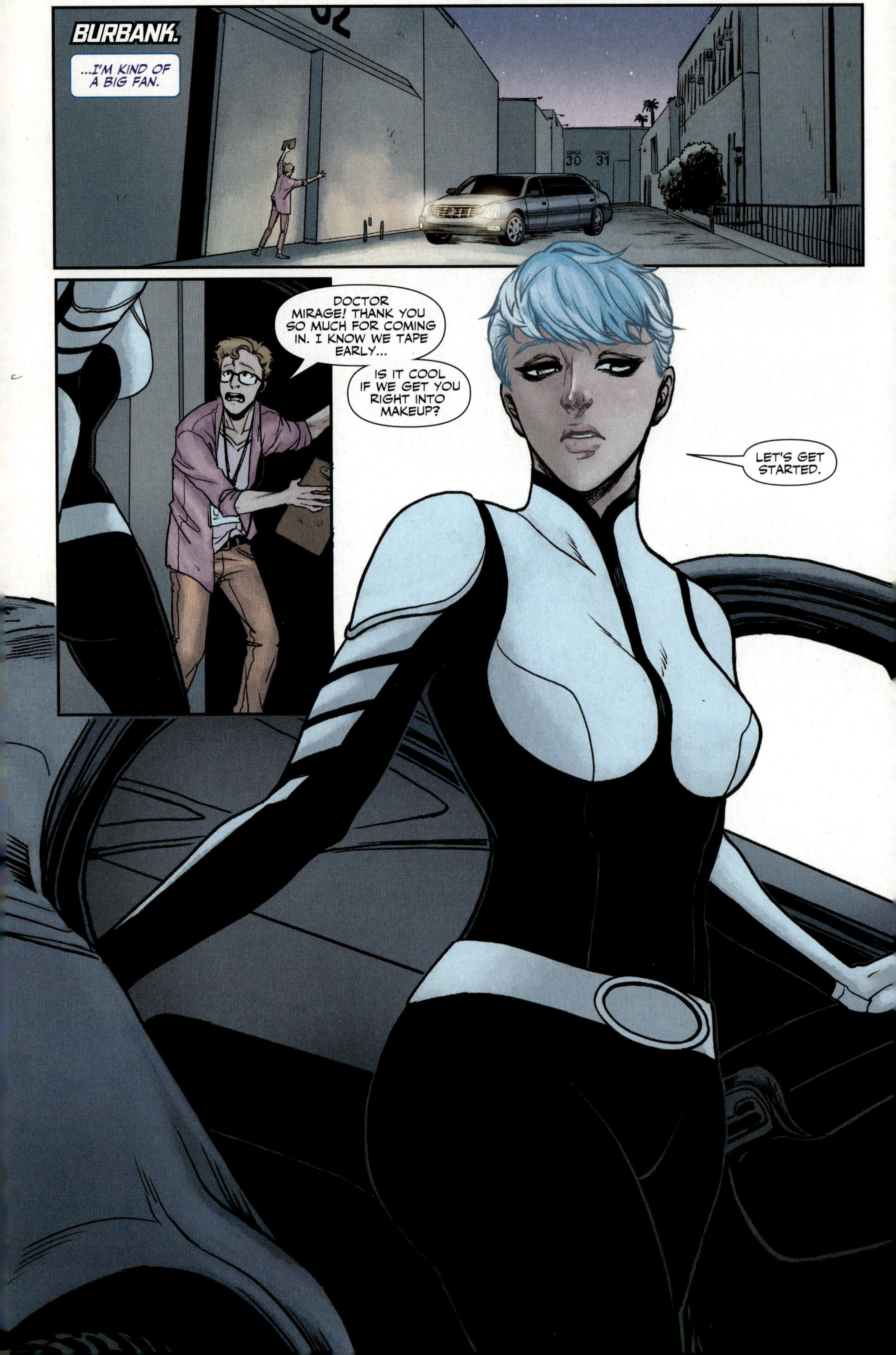
BURBANK.
...I'M KIND OF A BIG FAN.
STAGE 30
STAGE 31
DOCTOR MIRAGE! THANK YOU SO MUCH FOR COMING IN. I KNOW WE TAPE EARLY...
IS IT COOL IF WE GET YOU RIGHT INTO MAKEUP?
LET'S GET STARTED.

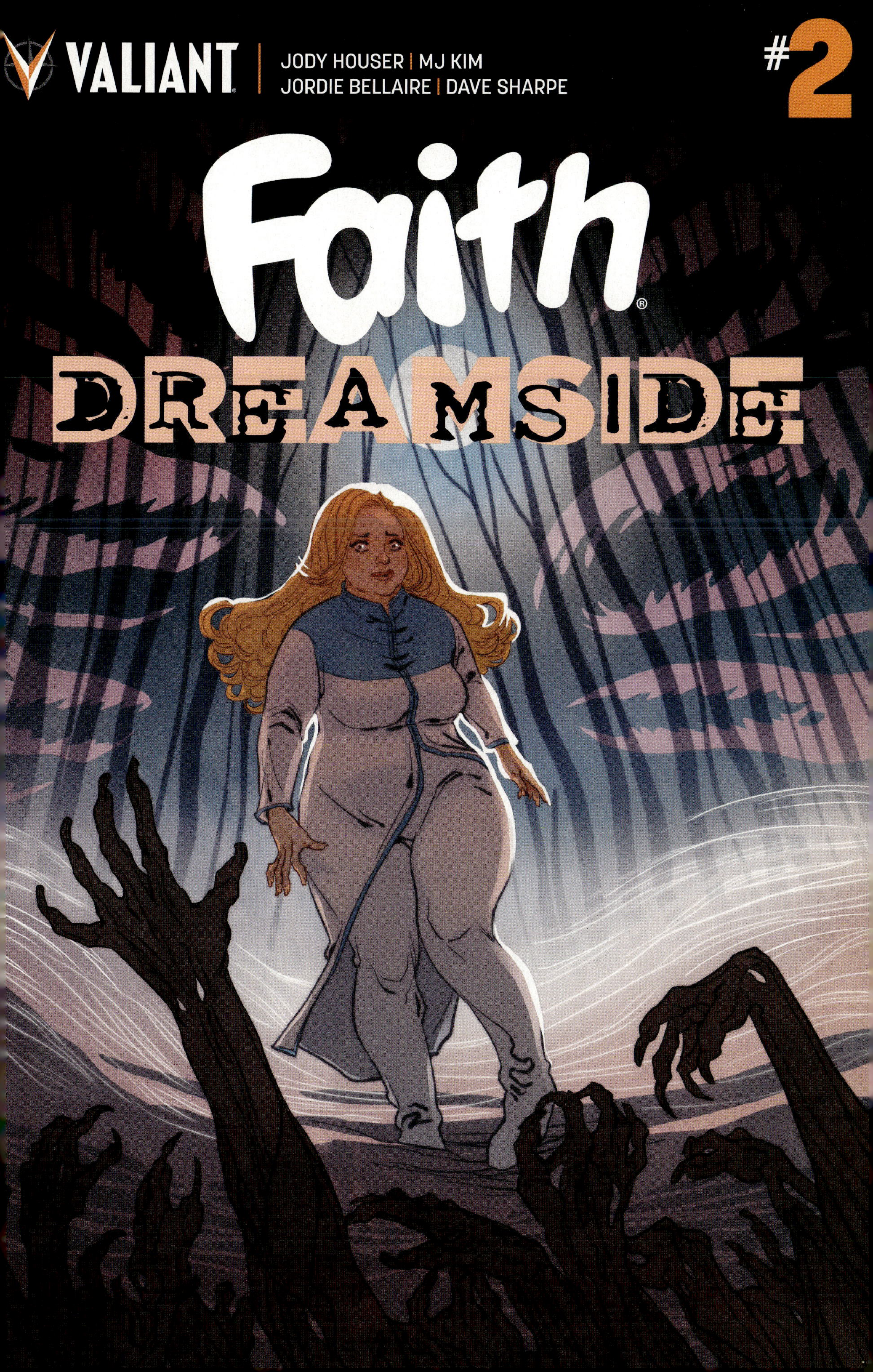
VALIANT
JODY HOUSER | MJ KIM
JORDIE BELLAIRE | DAVE SHARPE
#2
Faith®
DREAMSIDE

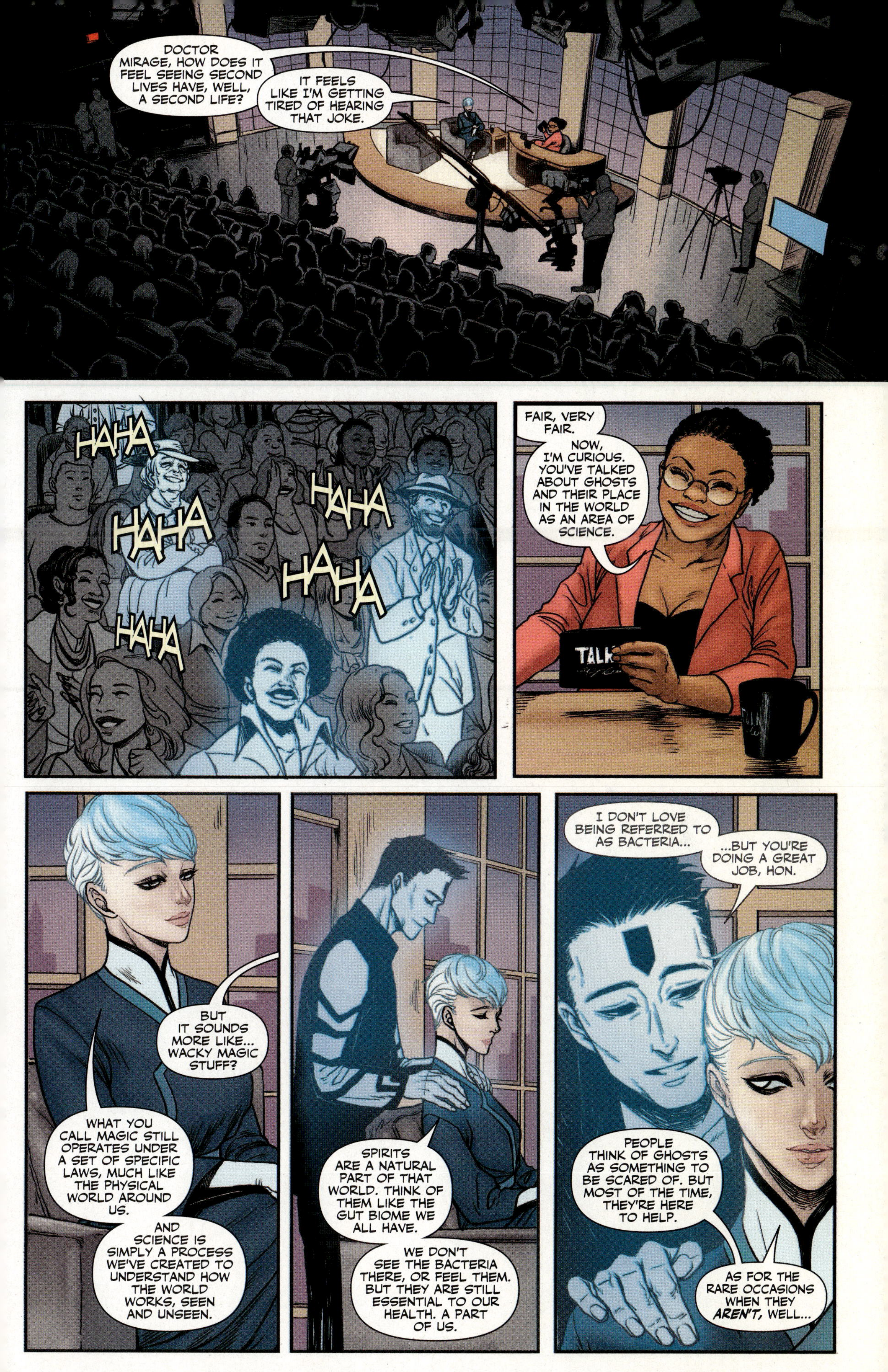
DOCTOR MIRAGE, HOW DOES IT FEEL SEEING SECOND LIVES HAVE, WELL, A SECOND LIFE?
IT FEELS LIKE I'M GETTING TIRED OF HEARING THAT JOKE.
HAHA
HAHA
HAHA
HAHA
HAHA
FAIR, VERY FAIR.
NOW, I'M CURIOUS. YOU'VE TALKED ABOUT GHOSTS AND THEIR PLACE IN THE WORLD AS AN AREA OF SCIENCE.
TALK
BUT IT SOUNDS MORE LIKE... WACKY MAGIC STUFF?
WHAT YOU CALL MAGIC STILL OPERATES UNDER A SET OF SPECIFIC LAWS, MUCH LIKE THE PHYSICAL WORLD AROUND US.
AND SCIENCE IS SIMPLY A PROCESS WE'VE CREATED TO UNDERSTAND HOW THE WORLD WORKS, SEEN AND UNSEEN.
SPIRITS ARE A NATURAL PART OF THAT WORLD. THINK OF THEM LIKE THE GUT BIOME WE ALL HAVE.
WE DON'T SEE THE BACTERIA THERE, OR FEEL THEM. BUT THEY ARE STILL ESSENTIAL TO OUR HEALTH. A PART OF US.
I DON'T LOVE BEING REFERRED TO AS BACTERIA...
...BUT YOU'RE DOING A GREAT JOB, HON.
PEOPLE THINK OF GHOSTS AS SOMETHING TO BE SCARED OF. BUT MOST OF THE TIME, THEY'RE HERE TO HELP.
AS FOR THE RARE OCCASIONS WHEN THEY *AREN'T*, WELL...

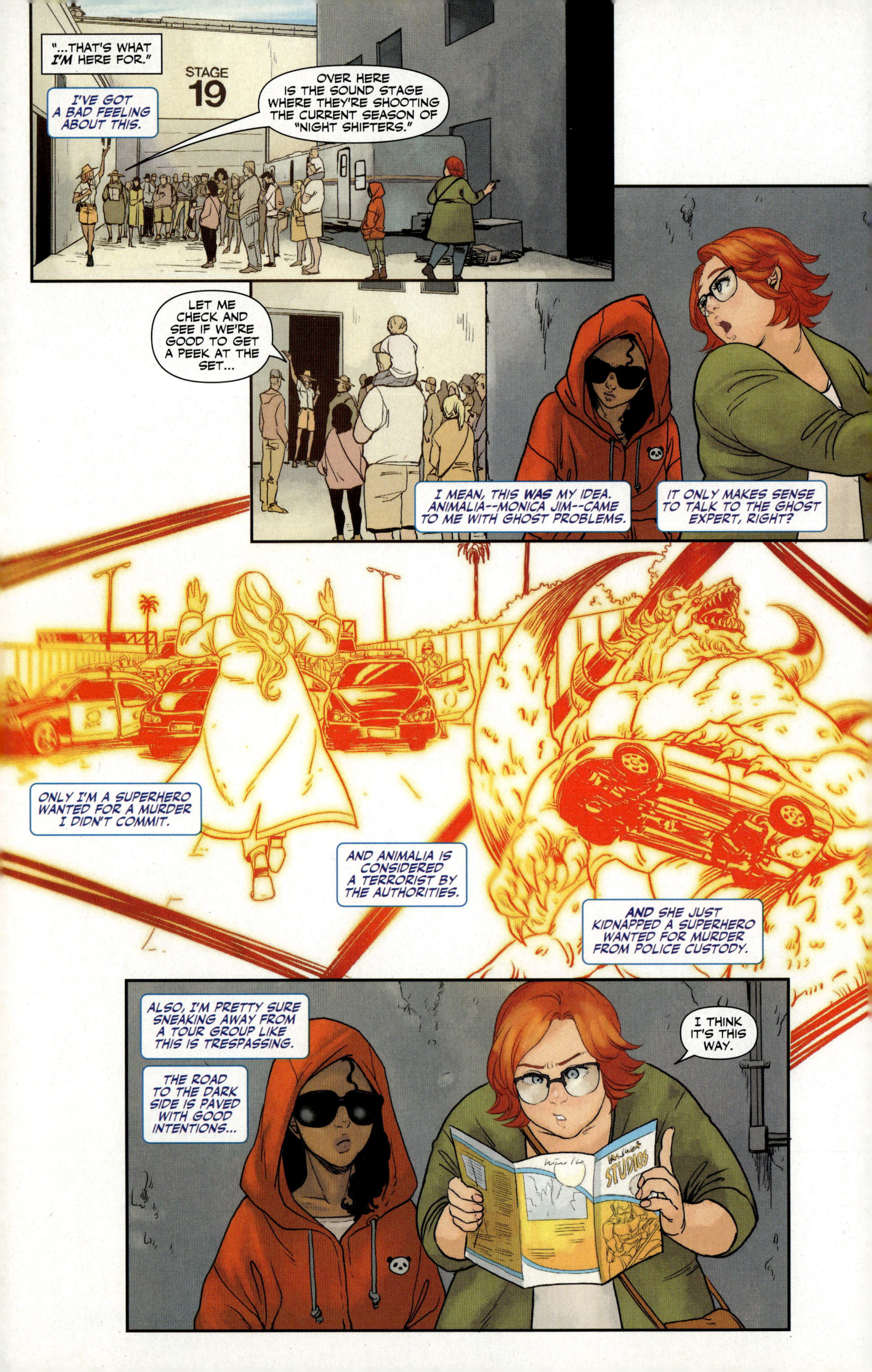
"...THAT'S WHAT I'M HERE FOR."
STAGE 19
I'VE GOT A BAD FEELING ABOUT THIS.
OVER HERE IS THE SOUND STAGE WHERE THEY'RE SHOOTING THE CURRENT SEASON OF "NIGHT SHIFTERS."
LET ME CHECK AND SEE IF WE'RE GOOD TO GET A PEEK AT THE SET...
I MEAN, THIS WAS MY IDEA. ANIMALIA--MONICA JIM--CAME TO ME WITH GHOST PROBLEMS.
IT ONLY MAKES SENSE TO TALK TO THE GHOST EXPERT, RIGHT?
ONLY I'M A SUPERHERO WANTED FOR A MURDER I DIDN'T COMMIT.
AND ANIMALIA IS CONSIDERED A TERRORIST BY THE AUTHORITIES.
AND SHE JUST KIDNAPPED A SUPERHERO WANTED FOR MURDER FROM POLICE CUSTODY.
ALSO, I'M PRETTY SURE SNEAKING AWAY FROM A TOUR GROUP LIKE THIS IS TRESPASSING.
THE ROAD TO THE DARK SIDE IS PAVED WITH GOOD INTENTIONS...
I THINK IT'S THIS WAY.
STUDIOS

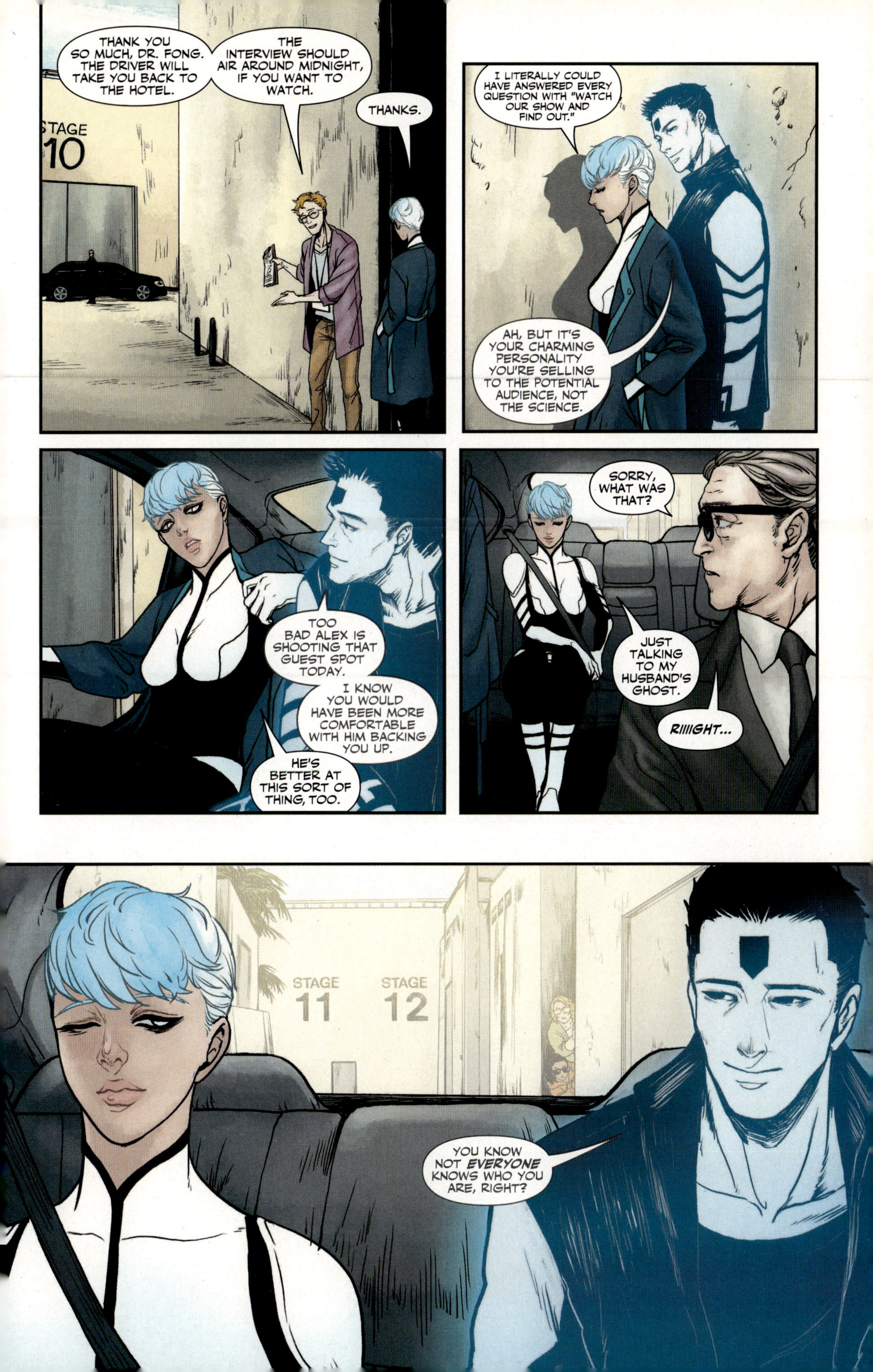

THANK YOU SO MUCH, DR. FONG. THE DRIVER WILL TAKE YOU BACK TO THE HOTEL.
THE INTERVIEW SHOULD AIR AROUND MIDNIGHT, IF YOU WANT TO WATCH.
STAGE 10
THANKS.
I LITERALLY COULD HAVE ANSWERED EVERY QUESTION WITH "WATCH OUR SHOW AND FIND OUT."
AH, BUT IT'S YOUR CHARMING PERSONALITY YOU'RE SELLING TO THE POTENTIAL AUDIENCE, NOT THE SCIENCE.
TOO BAD ALEX IS SHOOTING THAT GUEST SPOT TODAY.
I KNOW YOU WOULD HAVE BEEN MORE COMFORTABLE WITH HIM BACKING YOU UP.
HE'S BETTER AT THIS SORT OF THING, TOO.
SORRY, WHAT WAS THAT?
JUST TALKING TO MY HUSBAND'S GHOST.
RIIIIGHT...
STAGE 11
STAGE 12
YOU KNOW NOT *EVERYONE* KNOWS WHO YOU ARE, RIGHT?

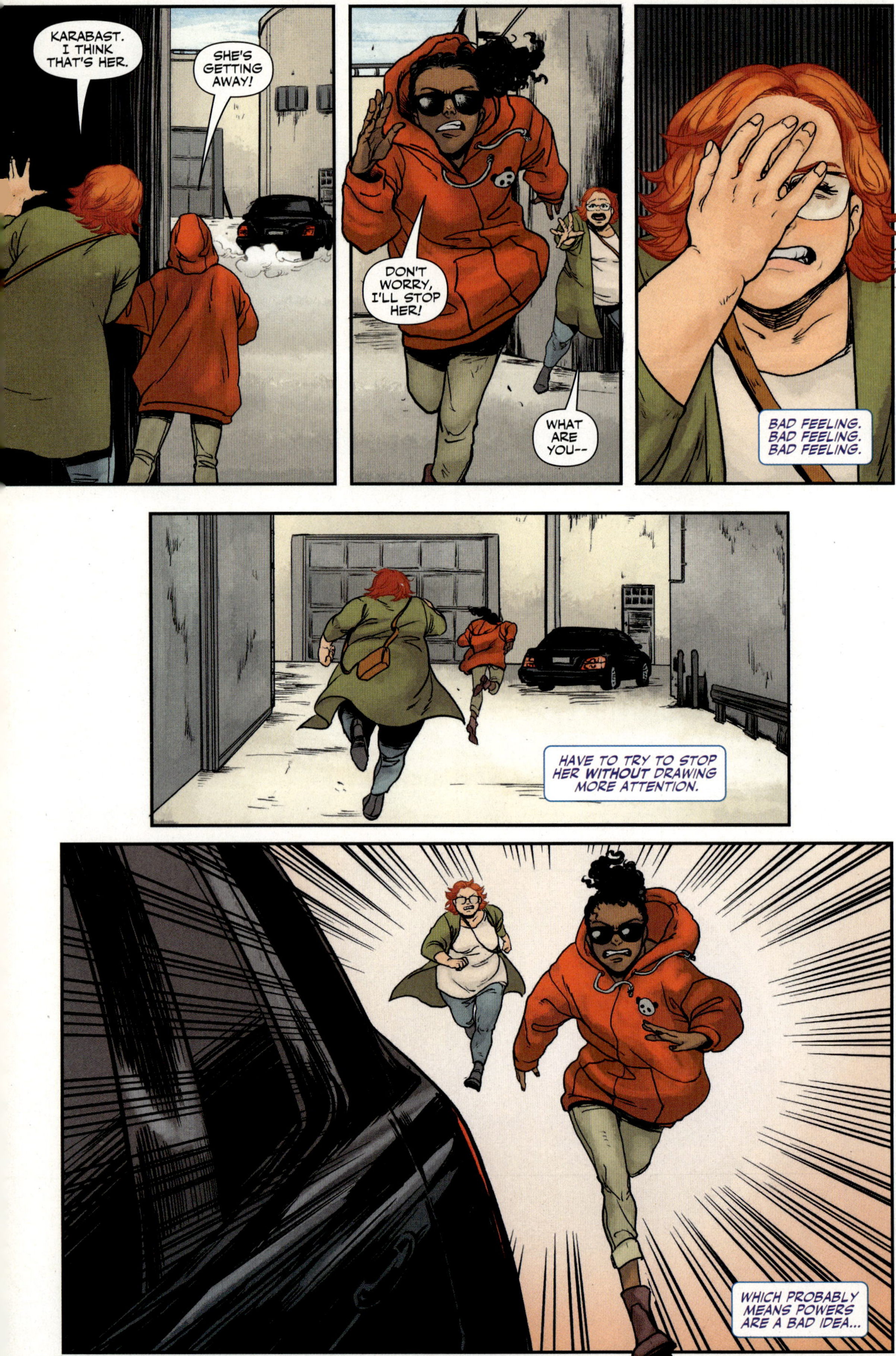
KARABAST. I THINK THAT'S HER.
SHE'S GETTING AWAY!
DON'T WORRY, I'LL STOP HER!
WHAT ARE YOU--
BAD FEELING. BAD FEELING. BAD FEELING.
HAVE TO TRY TO STOP HER WITHOUT DRAWING MORE ATTENTION.
WHICH PROBABLY MEANS POWERS ARE A BAD IDEA...

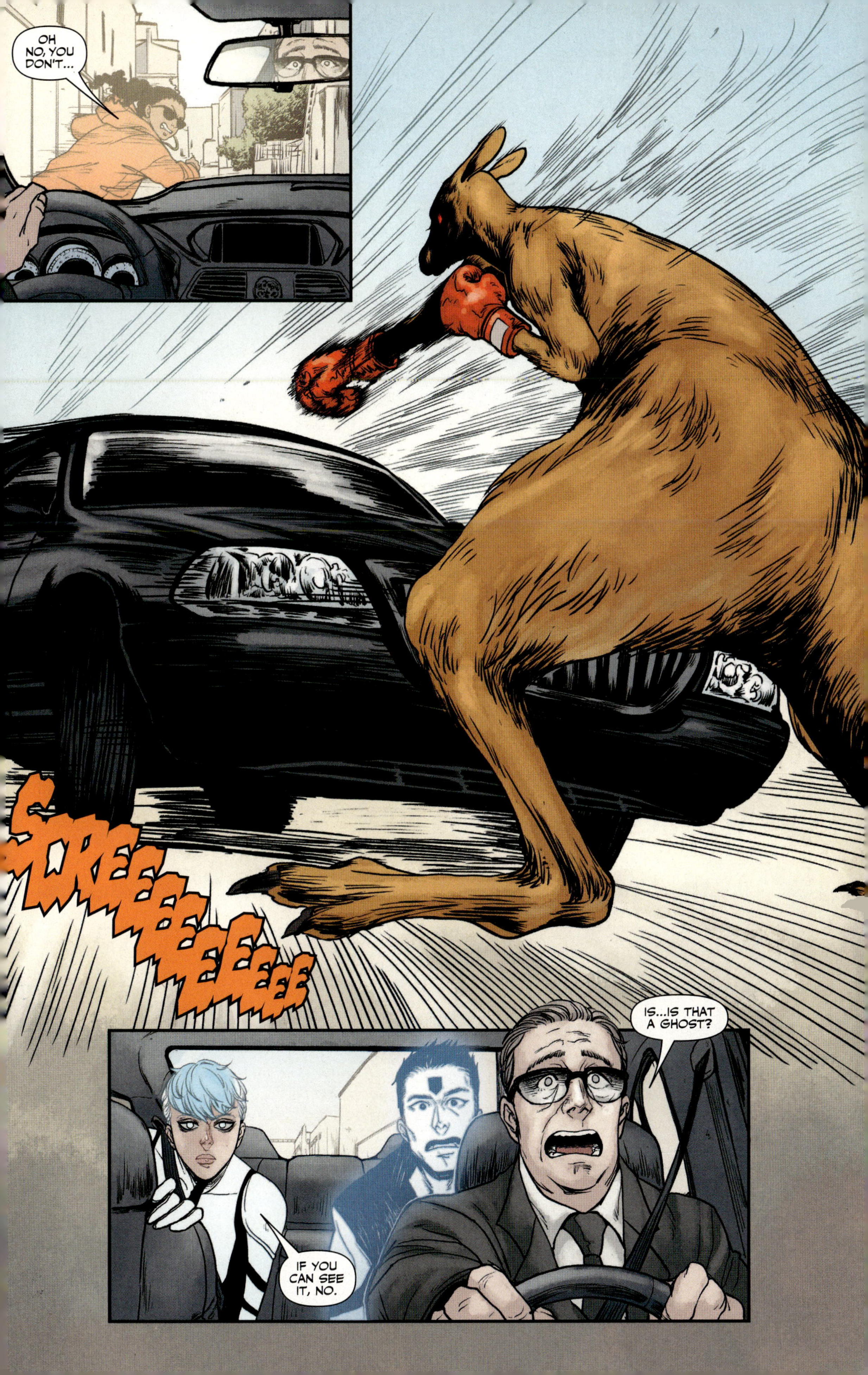
OH NO, YOU DON'T...
SCREEEEEEEEEEEE
IS...IS THAT A GHOST?
IF YOU CAN SEE IT, NO.

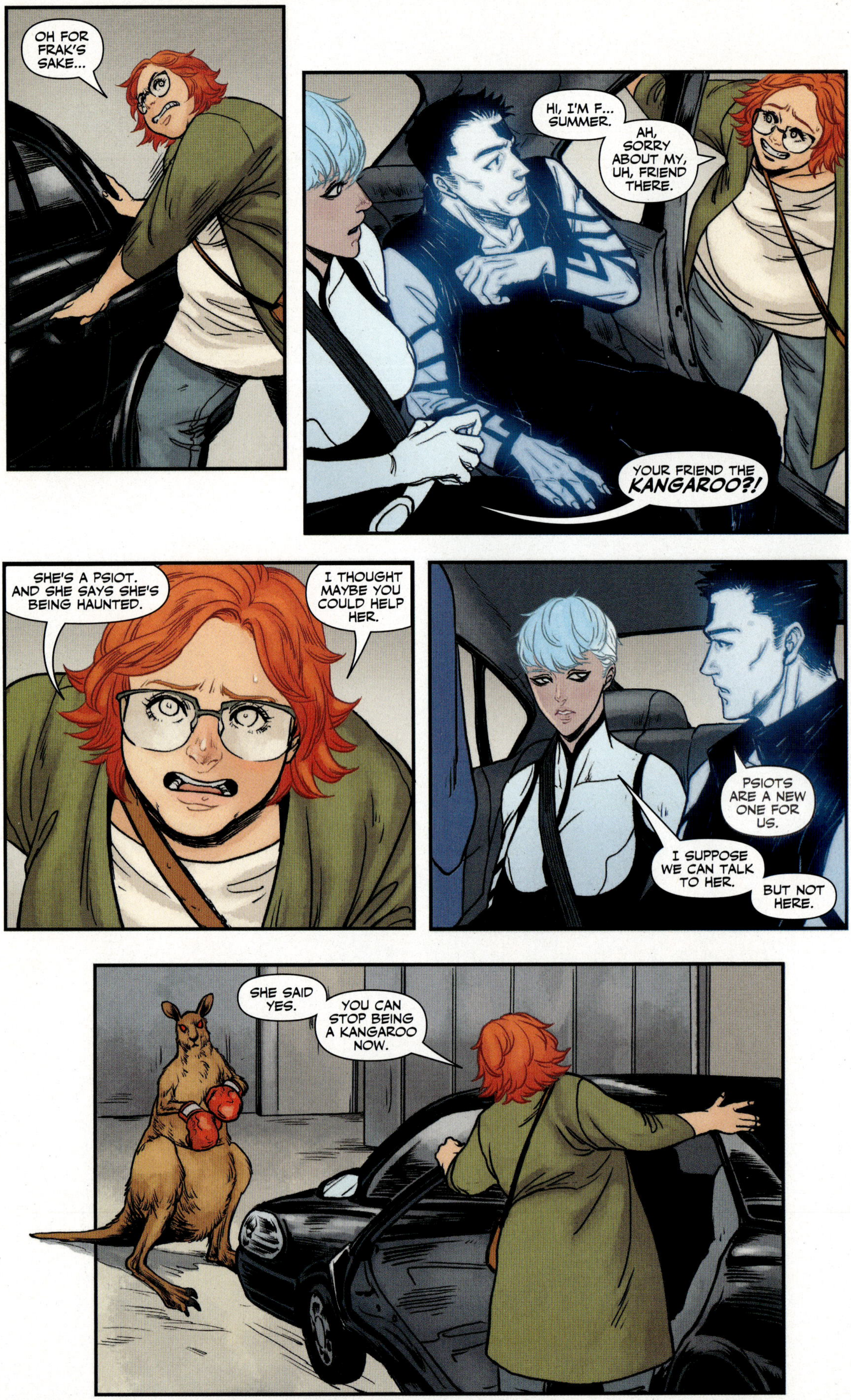
OH FOR FRAK'S SAKE...
HI, I'M F... SUMMER.
AH, SORRY ABOUT MY, UH, FRIEND THERE.
YOUR FRIEND THE *KANGAROO?!*
SHE'S A PSIOT. AND SHE SAYS SHE'S BEING HAUNTED.
I THOUGHT MAYBE YOU COULD HELP HER.
PSIOTS ARE A NEW ONE FOR US.
I SUPPOSE WE CAN TALK TO HER.
BUT NOT HERE.
SHE SAID YES.
YOU CAN STOP BEING A KANGAROO NOW.

"I'M *REALLY* SORRY ABOUT THIS...

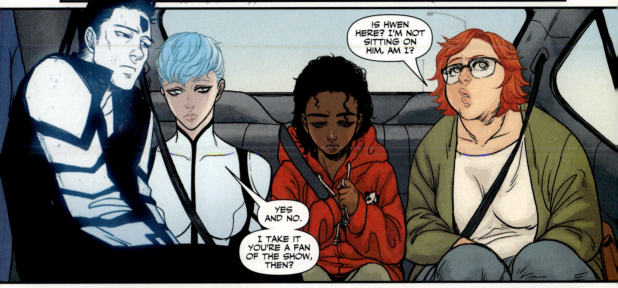

IS HWEN HERE? I'M NOT SITTING ON HIM, AM I?

YES AND NO.

I TAKE IT YOU'RE A FAN OF THE SHOW, THEN?

BIG FAN. OF *BOTH* VERSIONS OF THE SHOW.

WHO'S HWEN?

MY HUSBAND. HE'S A GHOST.

I'M SORRY. ABOUT WHAT HAPPENED TO HWEN.

THAT GOES FOR *BOTH* OF YOU, I GUESS.

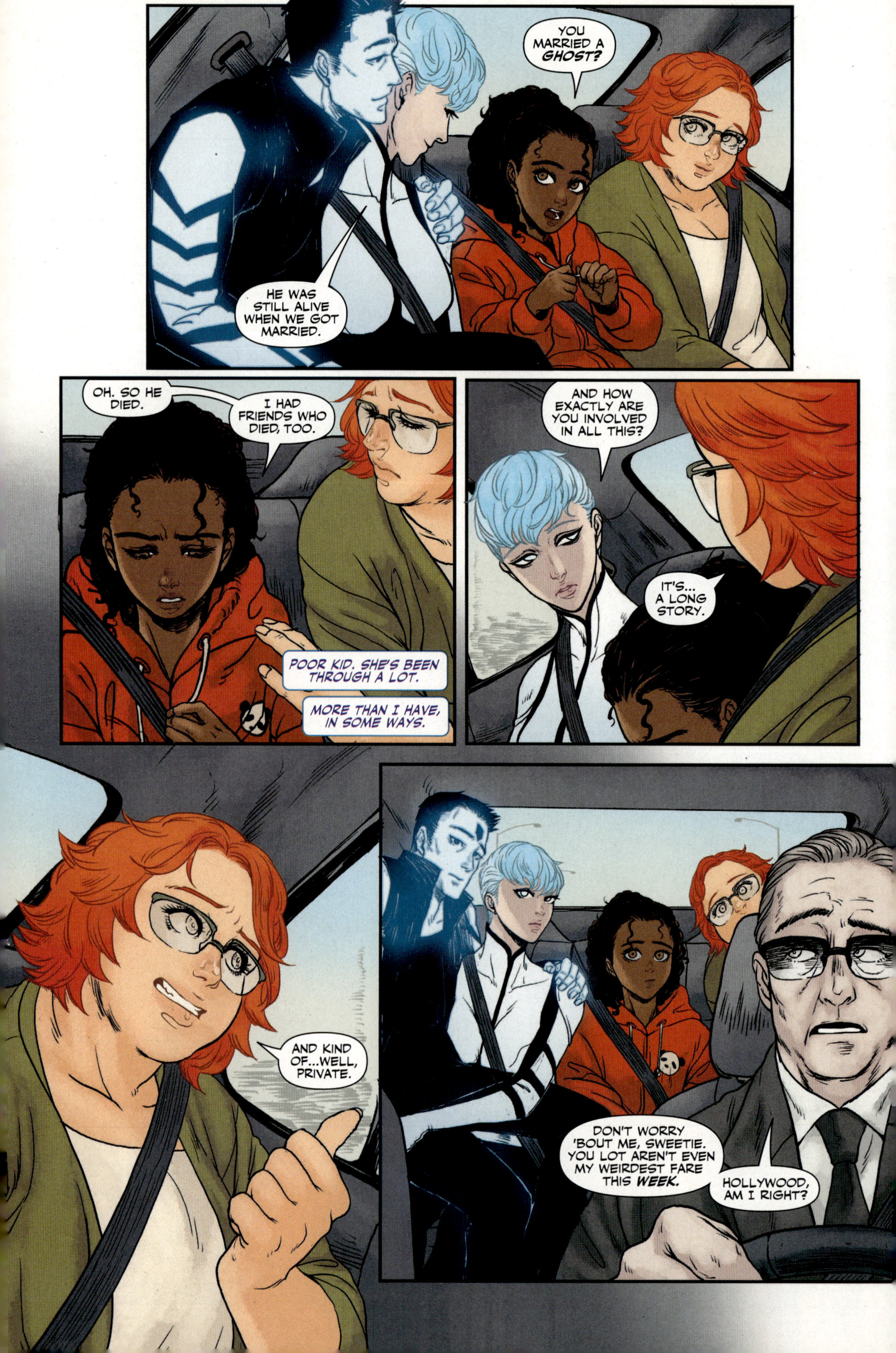

YOU MARRIED A GHOST?
HE WAS STILL ALIVE WHEN WE GOT MARRIED.
OH. SO HE DIED.
I HAD FRIENDS WHO DIED, TOO.
POOR KID. SHE'S BEEN THROUGH A LOT.
MORE THAN I HAVE, IN SOME WAYS.
AND HOW EXACTLY ARE YOU INVOLVED IN ALL THIS?
IT'S... A LONG STORY.
AND KIND OF...WELL, PRIVATE.
DON'T WORRY 'BOUT ME, SWEETIE. YOU LOT AREN'T EVEN MY WEIRDEST FARE THIS WEEK.
HOLLYWOOD, AM I RIGHT?

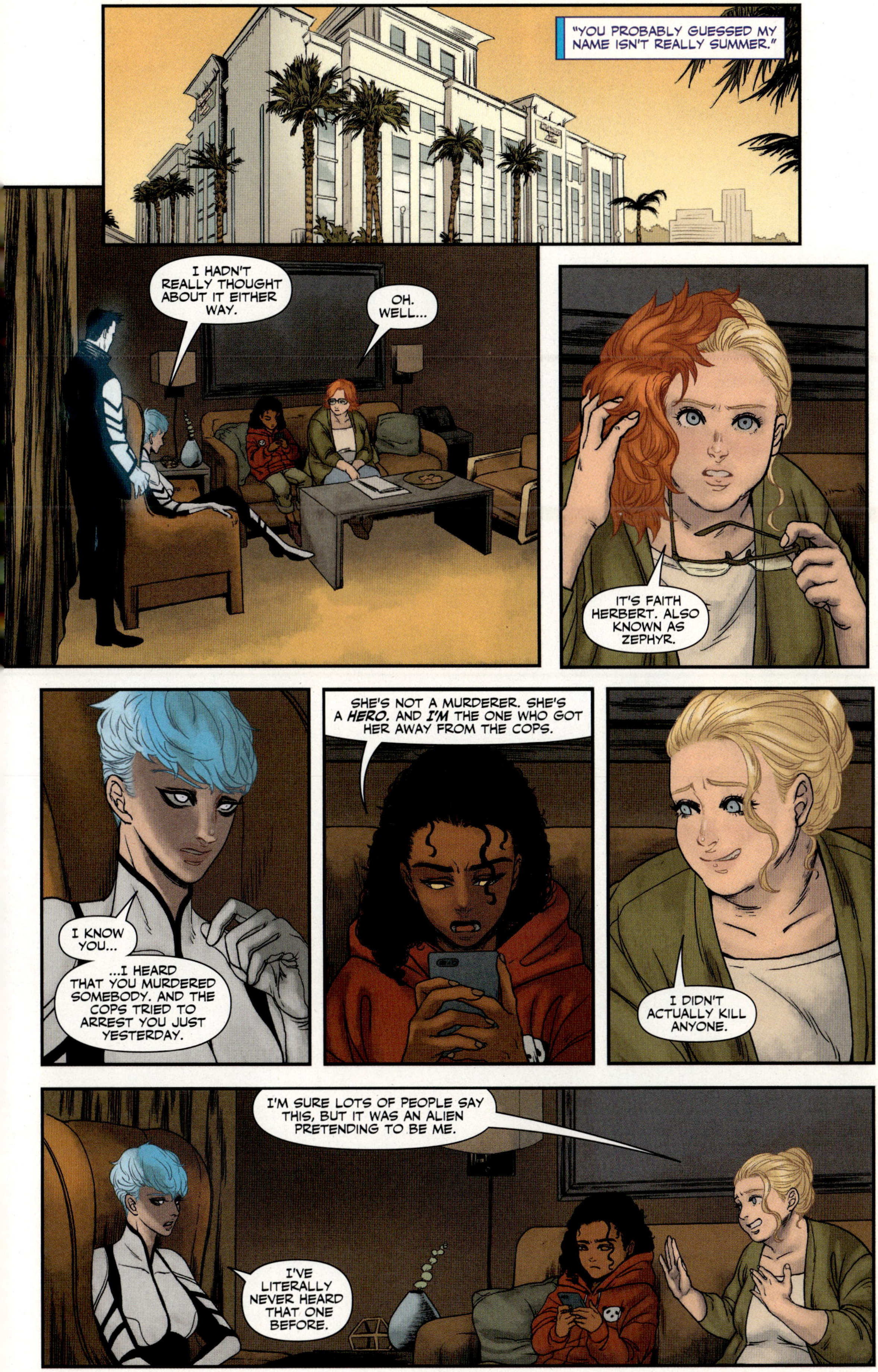
"YOU PROBABLY GUESSED MY NAME ISN'T REALLY SUMMER."
I HADN'T REALLY THOUGHT ABOUT IT EITHER WAY.
OH. WELL...
IT'S FAITH HERBERT. ALSO KNOWN AS ZEPHYR.
I KNOW YOU...
...I HEARD THAT YOU MURDERED SOMEBODY. AND THE COPS TRIED TO ARREST YOU JUST YESTERDAY.
SHE'S NOT A MURDERER. SHE'S A *HERO.* AND *I'M* THE ONE WHO GOT HER AWAY FROM THE COPS.
I DIDN'T ACTUALLY KILL ANYONE.
I'M SURE LOTS OF PEOPLE SAY THIS, BUT IT WAS AN ALIEN PRETENDING TO BE ME.
I'VE LITERALLY NEVER HEARD THAT ONE BEFORE.

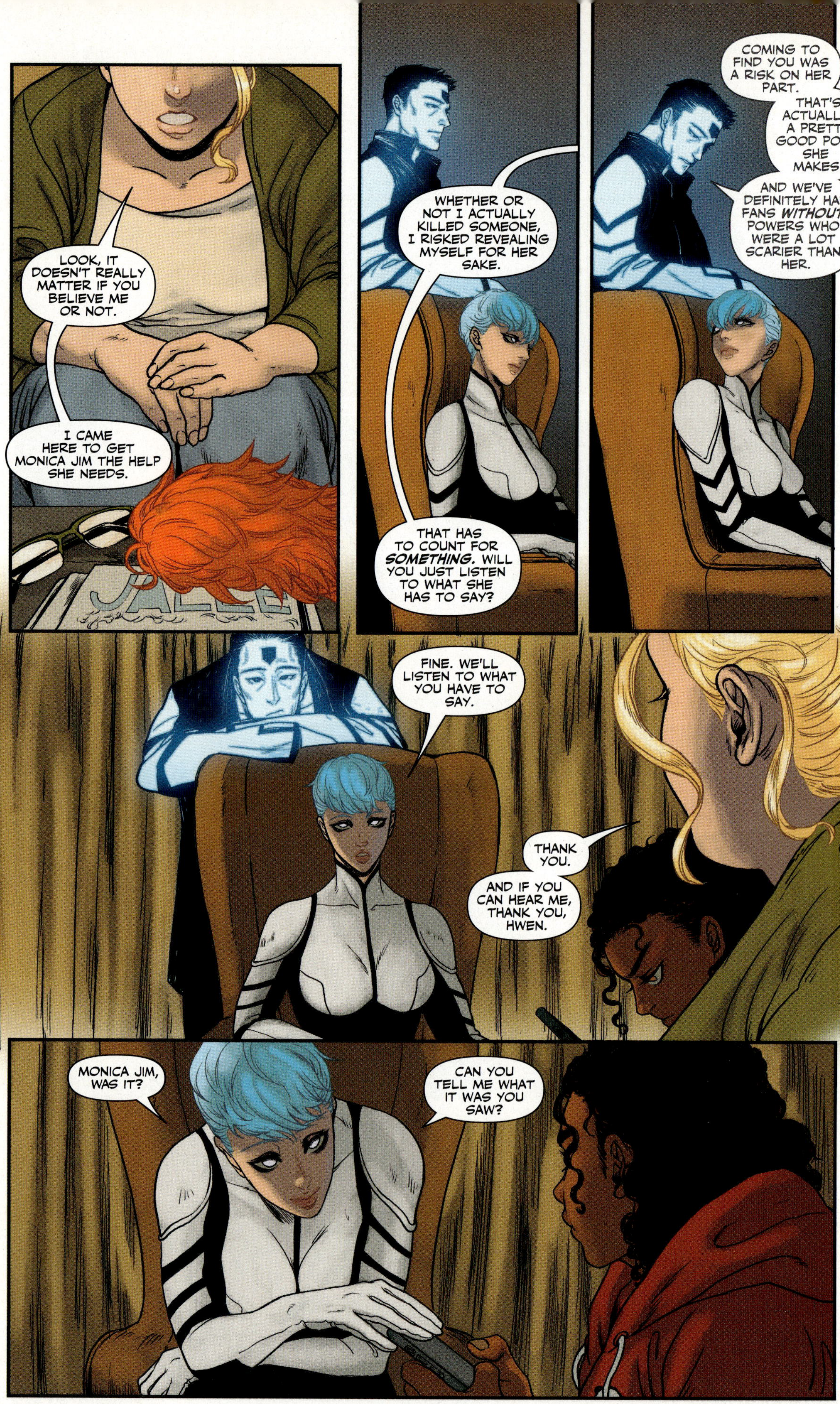
LOOK, IT DOESN'T REALLY MATTER IF YOU BELIEVE ME OR NOT.
I CAME HERE TO GET MONICA JIM THE HELP SHE NEEDS.
WHETHER OR NOT I ACTUALLY KILLED SOMEONE, I RISKED REVEALING MYSELF FOR HER SAKE.
THAT HAS TO COUNT FOR *SOMETHING.* WILL YOU JUST LISTEN TO WHAT SHE HAS TO SAY?
COMING TO FIND YOU WAS A RISK ON HER PART.
THAT'S ACTUALLY A PRETTY GOOD POINT SHE MAKES.
AND WE'VE DEFINITELY HAD FANS *WITHOUT* POWERS WHO WERE A LOT SCARIER THAN HER.
FINE. WE'LL LISTEN TO WHAT YOU HAVE TO SAY.
THANK YOU.
AND IF YOU CAN HEAR ME, THANK YOU, HWEN.
MONICA JIM, WAS IT?
CAN YOU TELL ME WHAT IT WAS YOU SAW?

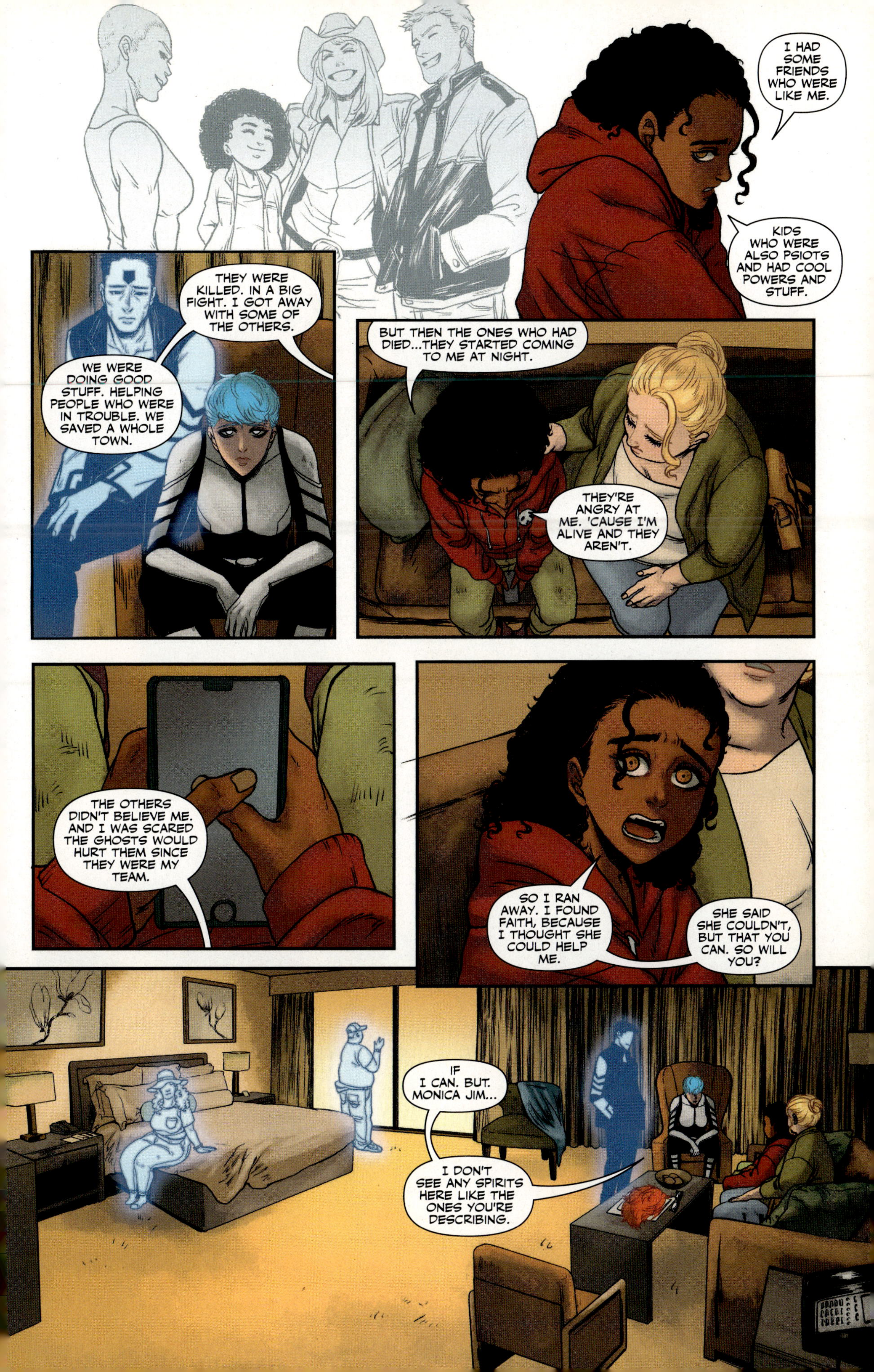
I HAD SOME FRIENDS WHO WERE LIKE ME.
KIDS WHO WERE ALSO PSIOTS AND HAD COOL POWERS AND STUFF.
WE WERE DOING GOOD STUFF. HELPING PEOPLE WHO WERE IN TROUBLE. WE SAVED A WHOLE TOWN.
THEY WERE KILLED. IN A BIG FIGHT. I GOT AWAY WITH SOME OF THE OTHERS.
BUT THEN THE ONES WHO HAD DIED...THEY STARTED COMING TO ME AT NIGHT.
THEY'RE ANGRY AT ME. 'CAUSE I'M ALIVE AND THEY AREN'T.
THE OTHERS DIDN'T BELIEVE ME. AND I WAS SCARED THE GHOSTS WOULD HURT THEM SINCE THEY WERE MY TEAM.
SO I RAN AWAY. I FOUND FAITH, BECAUSE I THOUGHT SHE COULD HELP ME.
SHE SAID SHE COULDN'T, BUT THAT YOU CAN. SO WILL YOU?
IF I CAN. BUT. MONICA JIM...
I DON'T SEE ANY SPIRITS HERE LIKE THE ONES YOU'RE DESCRIBING.

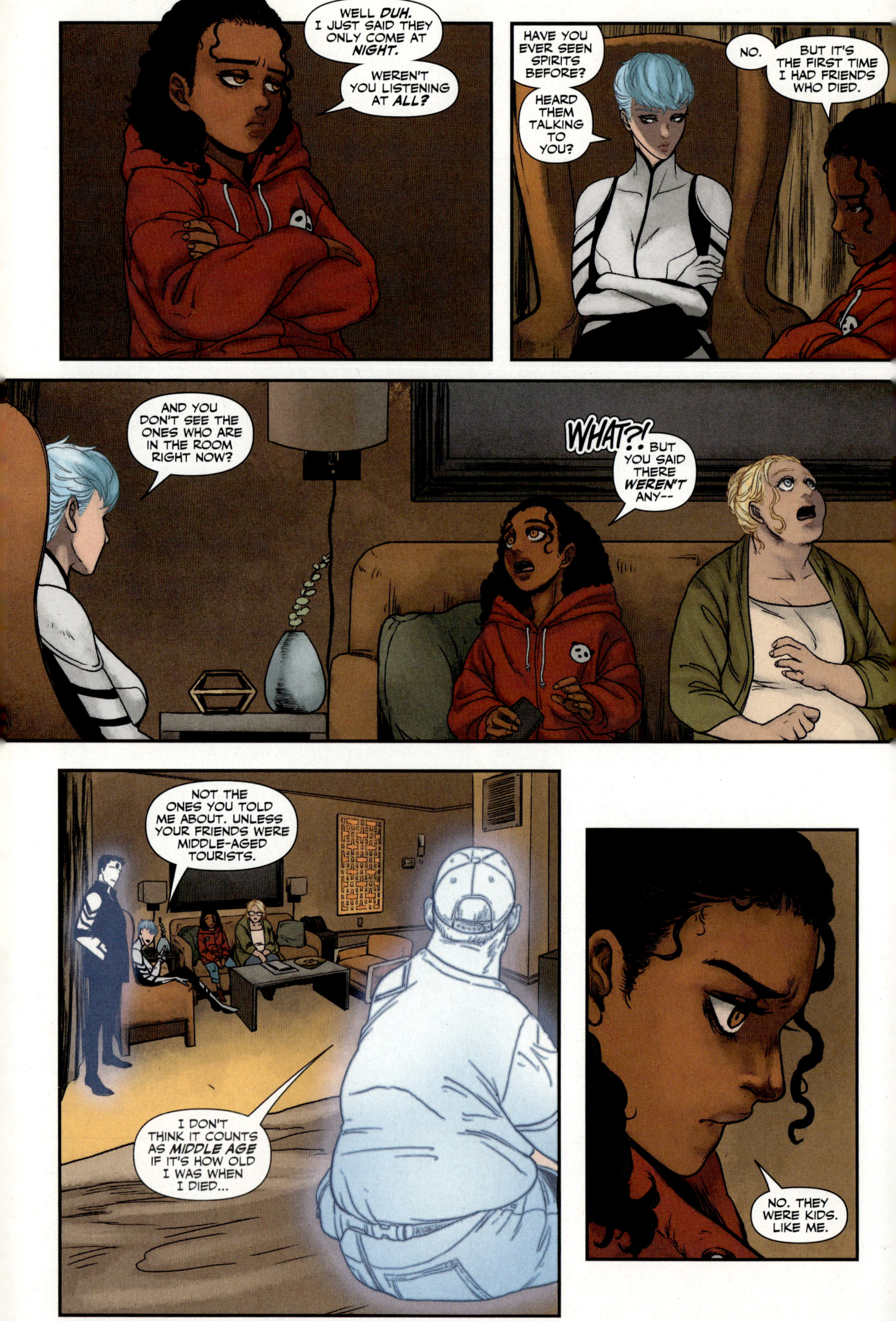
WELL *DUH.* I JUST SAID THEY ONLY COME AT *NIGHT.*
WEREN'T YOU LISTENING AT *ALL?*
HAVE YOU EVER SEEN SPIRITS BEFORE?
HEARD THEM TALKING TO YOU?
NO.
BUT IT'S THE FIRST TIME I HAD FRIENDS WHO DIED.
AND YOU DON'T SEE THE ONES WHO ARE IN THE ROOM RIGHT NOW?
WHAT?!
BUT YOU SAID THERE *WEREN'T* ANY--
NOT THE ONES YOU TOLD ME ABOUT. UNLESS YOUR FRIENDS WERE MIDDLE-AGED TOURISTS.
I DON'T THINK IT COUNTS AS *MIDDLE AGE* IF IT'S HOW OLD I WAS WHEN I DIED...
NO. THEY WERE KIDS. LIKE ME.

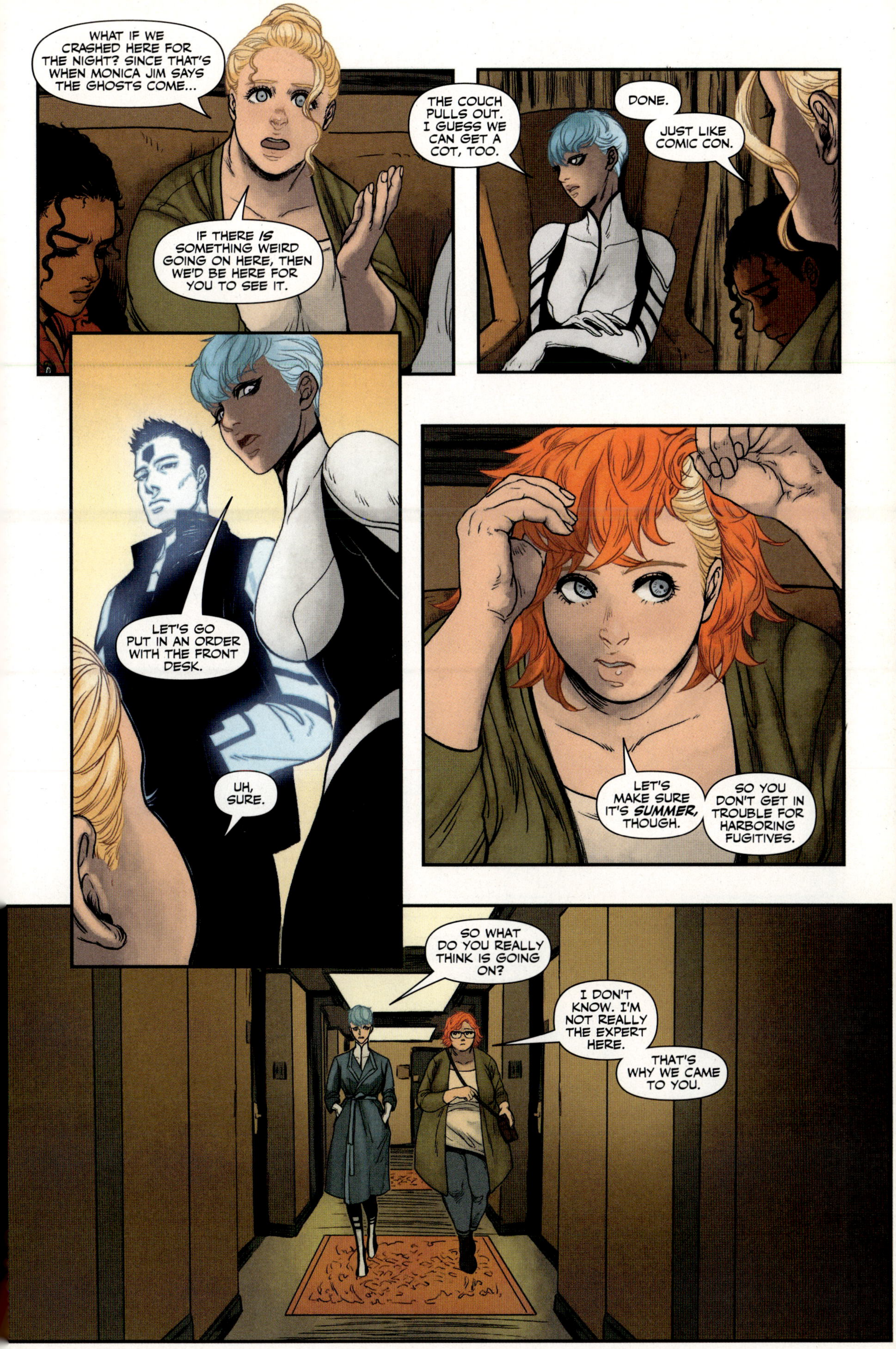
WHAT IF WE CRASHED HERE FOR THE NIGHT? SINCE THAT'S WHEN MONICA JIM SAYS THE GHOSTS COME...
IF THERE *IS* SOMETHING WEIRD GOING ON HERE, THEN WE'D BE HERE FOR YOU TO SEE IT.
THE COUCH PULLS OUT. I GUESS WE CAN GET A COT, TOO.
DONE.
JUST LIKE COMIC CON.
LET'S GO PUT IN AN ORDER WITH THE FRONT DESK.
UH, SURE.
LET'S MAKE SURE IT'S ***SUMMER,*** THOUGH.
SO YOU DON'T GET IN TROUBLE FOR HARBORING FUGITIVES.
SO WHAT DO YOU REALLY THINK IS GOING ON?
I DON'T KNOW. I'M NOT REALLY THE EXPERT HERE.
THAT'S WHY WE CAME TO YOU.

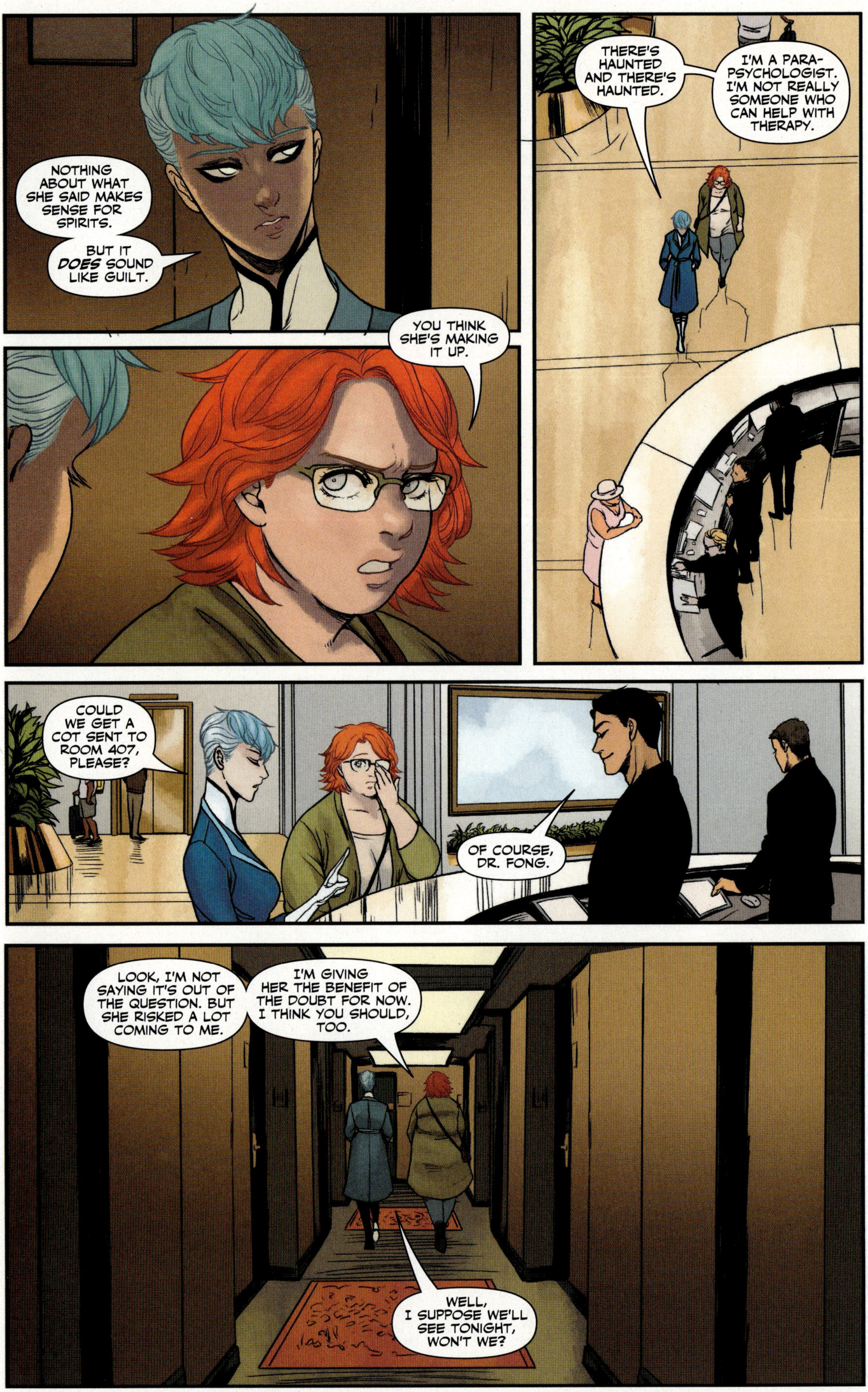
NOTHING ABOUT WHAT SHE SAID MAKES SENSE FOR SPIRITS.
BUT IT *DOES* SOUND LIKE GUILT.
YOU THINK SHE'S MAKING IT UP.
THERE'S HAUNTED AND THERE'S HAUNTED.
I'M A PARA-PSYCHOLOGIST. I'M NOT REALLY SOMEONE WHO CAN HELP WITH THERAPY.
COULD WE GET A COT SENT TO ROOM 407, PLEASE?
OF COURSE, DR. FONG.
LOOK, I'M NOT SAYING IT'S OUT OF THE QUESTION. BUT SHE RISKED A LOT COMING TO ME.
I'M GIVING HER THE BENEFIT OF THE DOUBT FOR NOW. I THINK YOU SHOULD, TOO.
WELL, I SUPPOSE WE'LL SEE TONIGHT, WON'T WE?

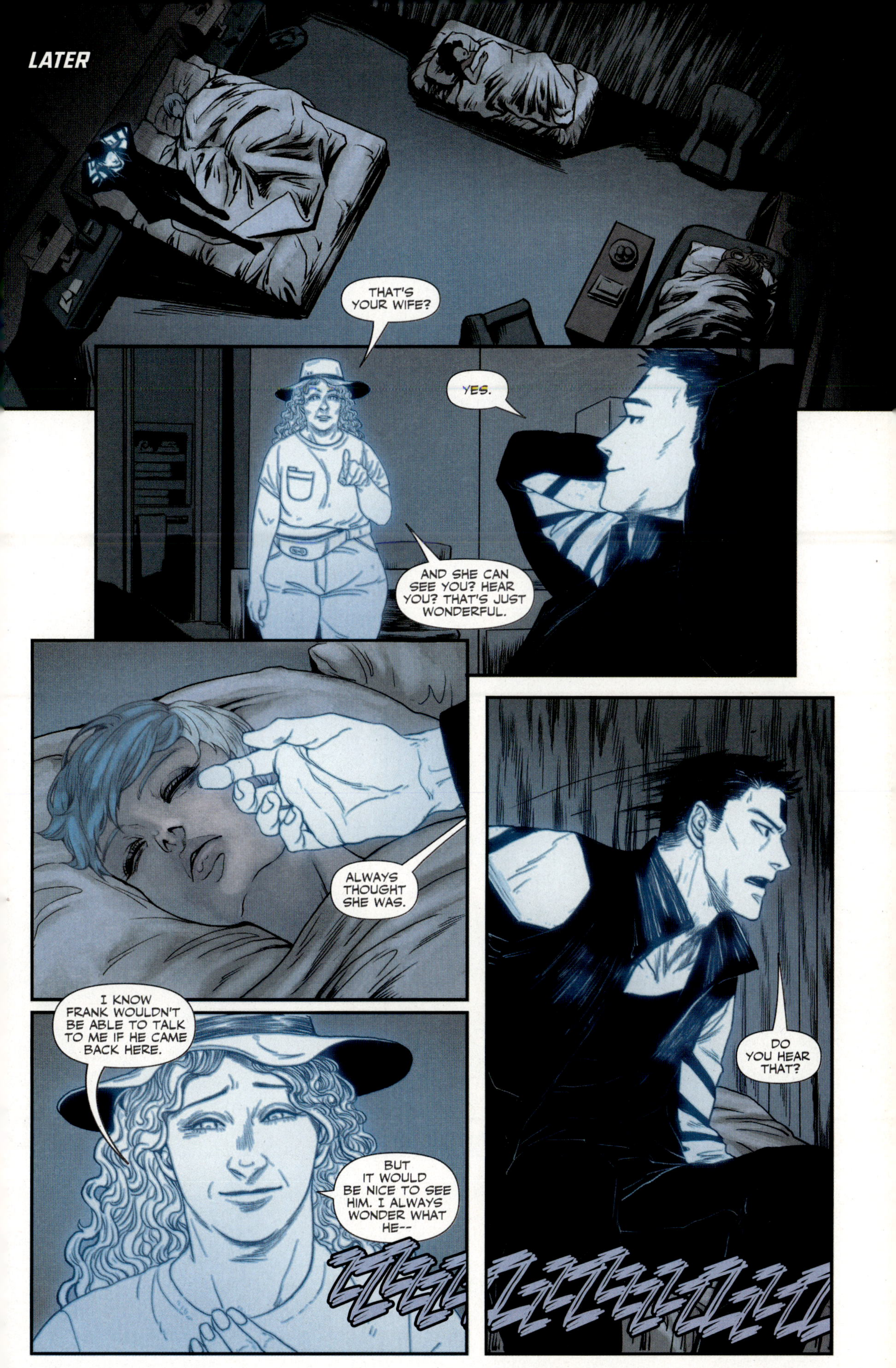
LATER
THAT'S YOUR WIFE?
YES.
AND SHE CAN SEE YOU? HEAR YOU? THAT'S JUST WONDERFUL.
ALWAYS THOUGHT SHE WAS.
I KNOW FRANK WOULDN'T BE ABLE TO TALK TO ME IF HE CAME BACK HERE.
BUT IT WOULD BE NICE TO SEE HIM. I ALWAYS WONDER WHAT HE--
DO YOU HEAR THAT?
ZZZZZZZZZZZZZZZZZZ

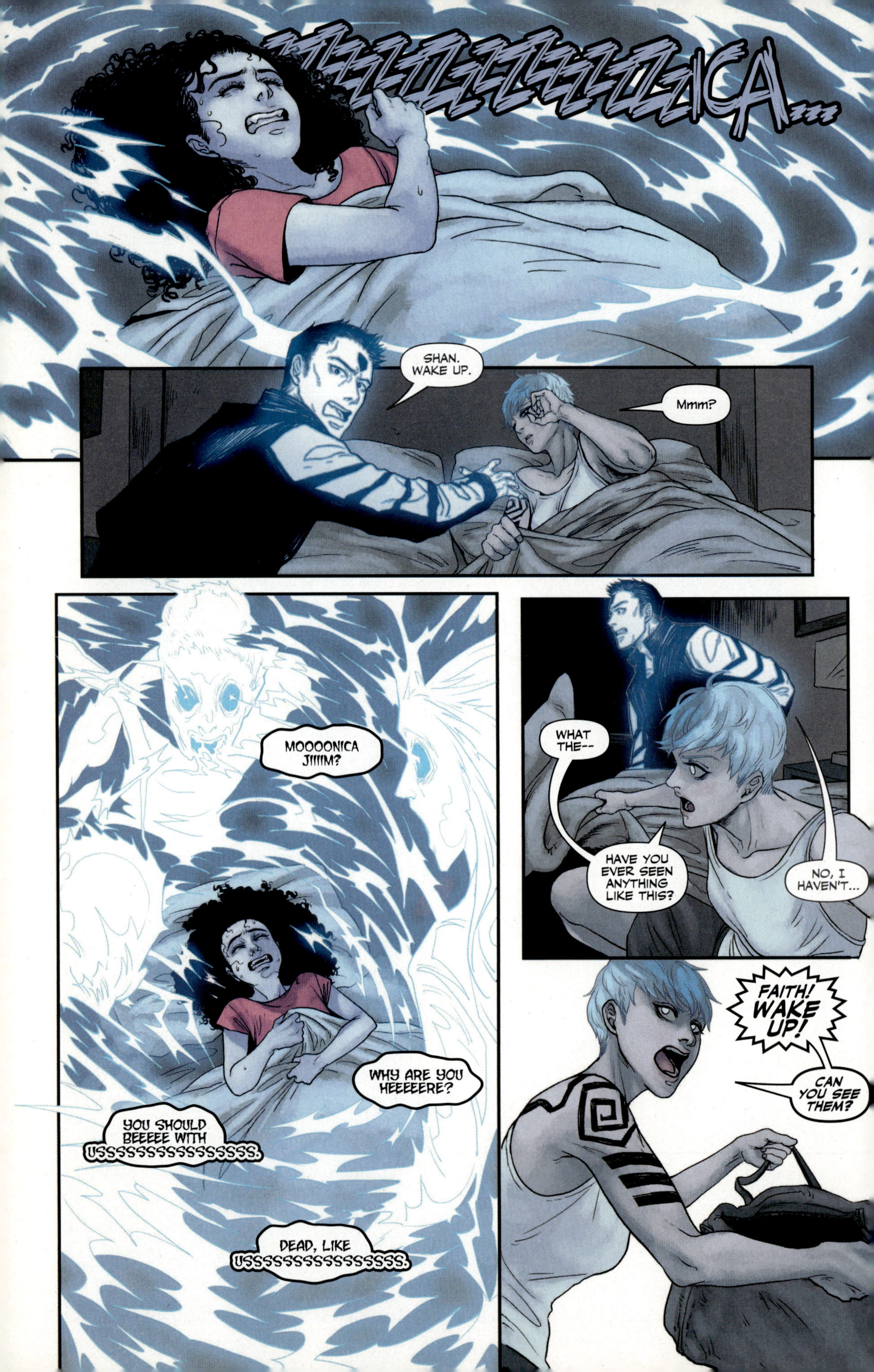
ZZZZZZZZZZZZZZZZICA...
SHAN. WAKE UP.
Mmm?
MOOOONICA JIIIIM?
WHY ARE YOU HEEEEERE?
YOU SHOULD BEEEEE WITH USSSSSSSSSSSSSSSS.
DEAD, LIKE USSSSSSSSSSSSSSSS.
WHAT THE--
HAVE YOU EVER SEEN ANYTHING LIKE THIS?
NO, I HAVEN'T...
FAITH! WAKE UP!
CAN YOU SEE THEM?

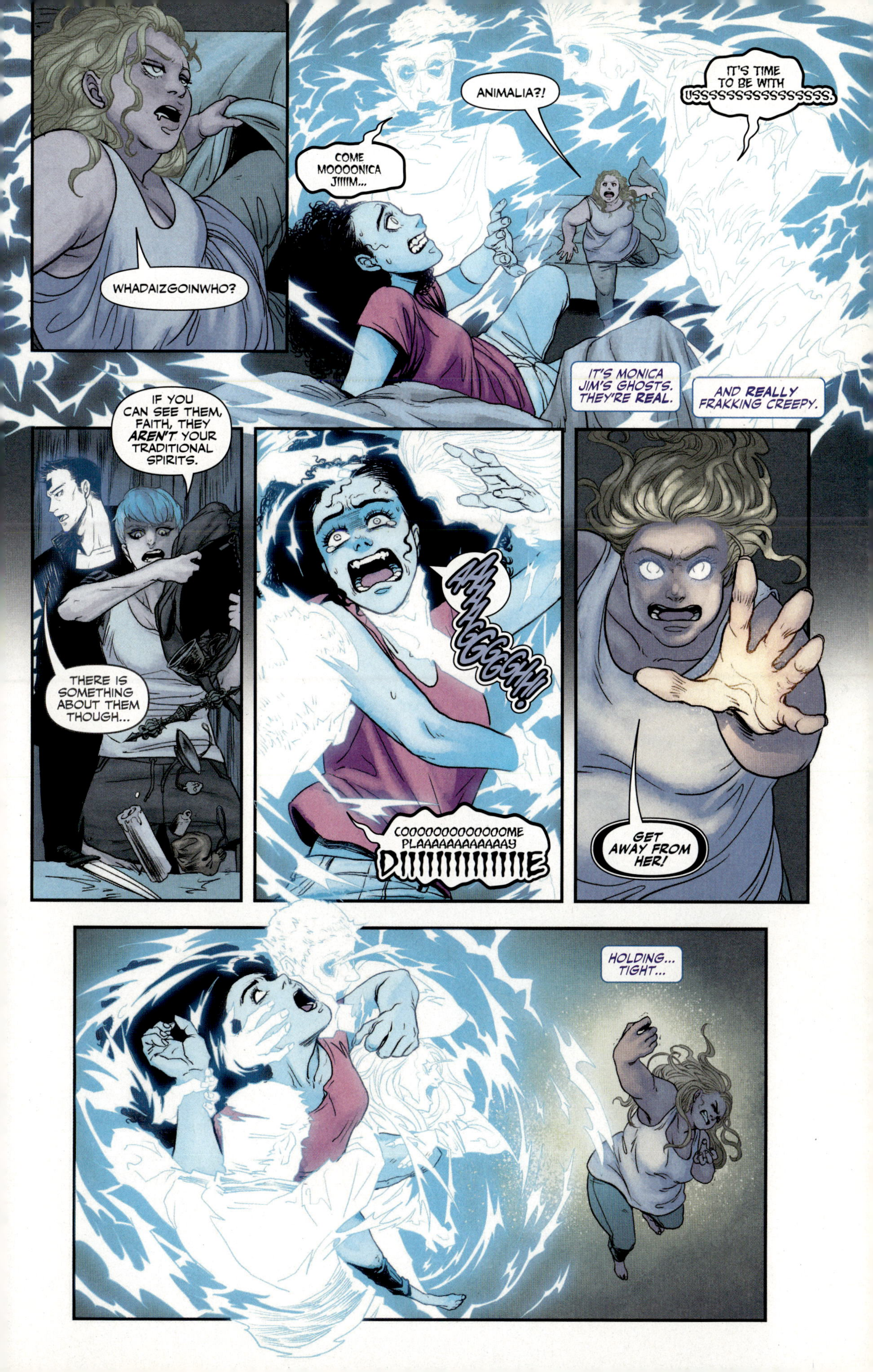
WHADAIZGOINWHO?
COME MOOOONICA JIIIIM...
ANIMALIA?!
IT'S TIME TO BE WITH USSSSSSSSSSSSSSSS.
IT'S MONICA JIM'S GHOSTS. THEY'RE REAL.
AND REALLY FRAKKING CREEPY.
IF YOU CAN SEE THEM, FAITH, THEY AREN'T YOUR TRADITIONAL SPIRITS.
THERE IS SOMETHING ABOUT THEM THOUGH...
AAAGGGGH!
COOOOOOOOOOOOOME PLAAAAAAAAAAAAY DIIIIIIIIIIIIIIE
GET AWAY FROM HER!
HOLDING... TIGHT...

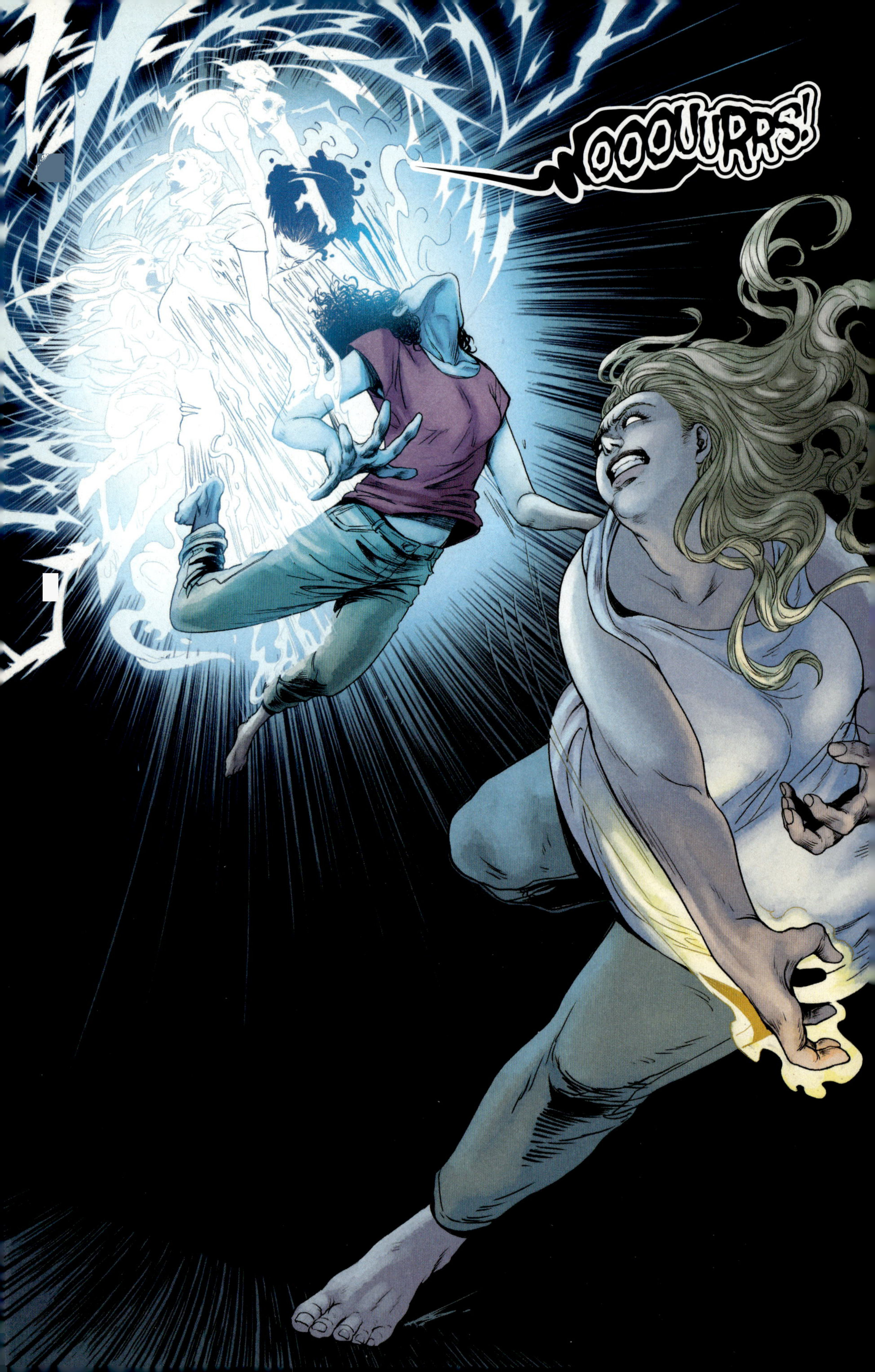
OOOUURRS!

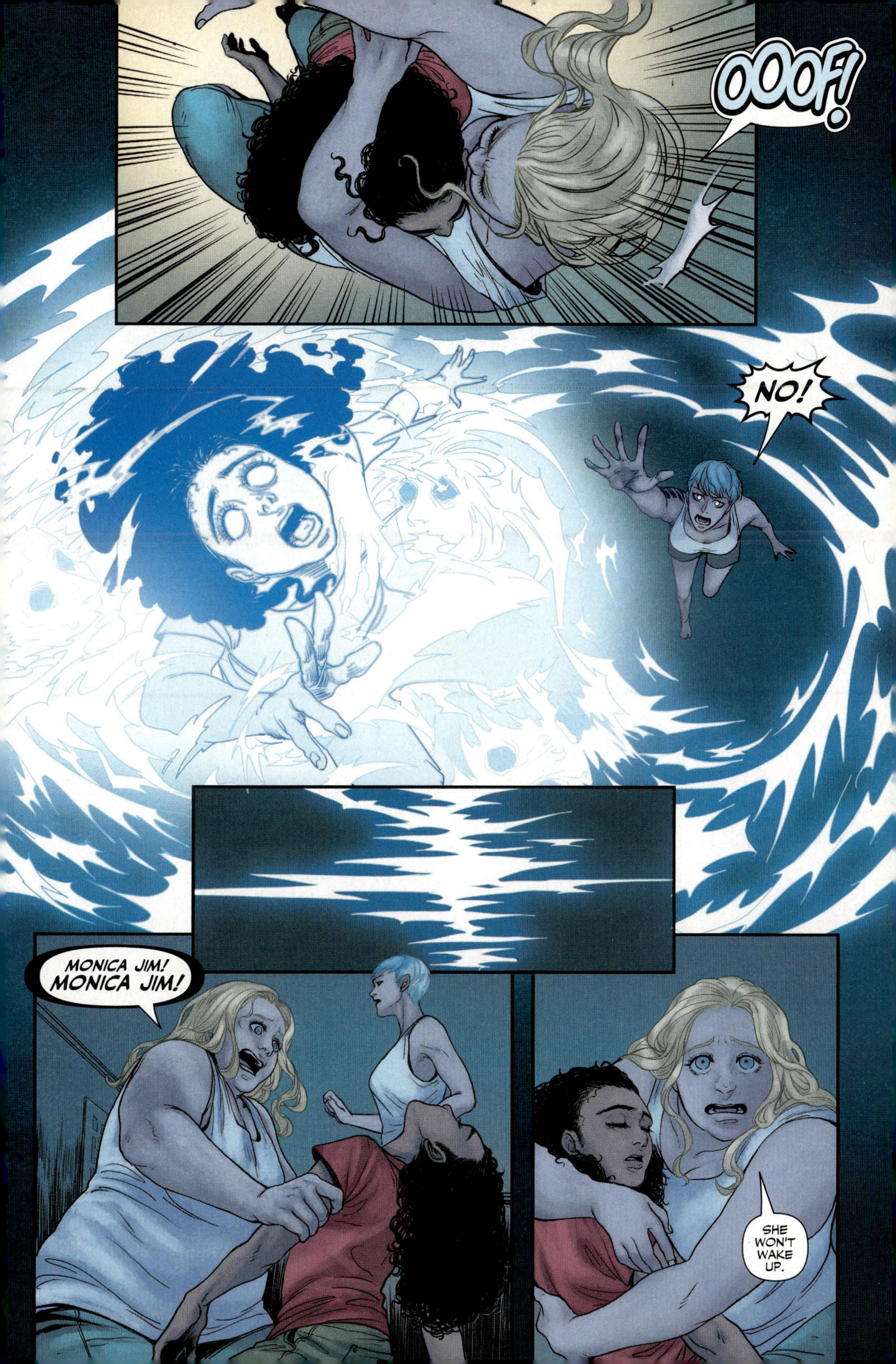
OOOF!
NO!
MONICA JIM! MONICA JIM!
SHE WON'T WAKE UP.

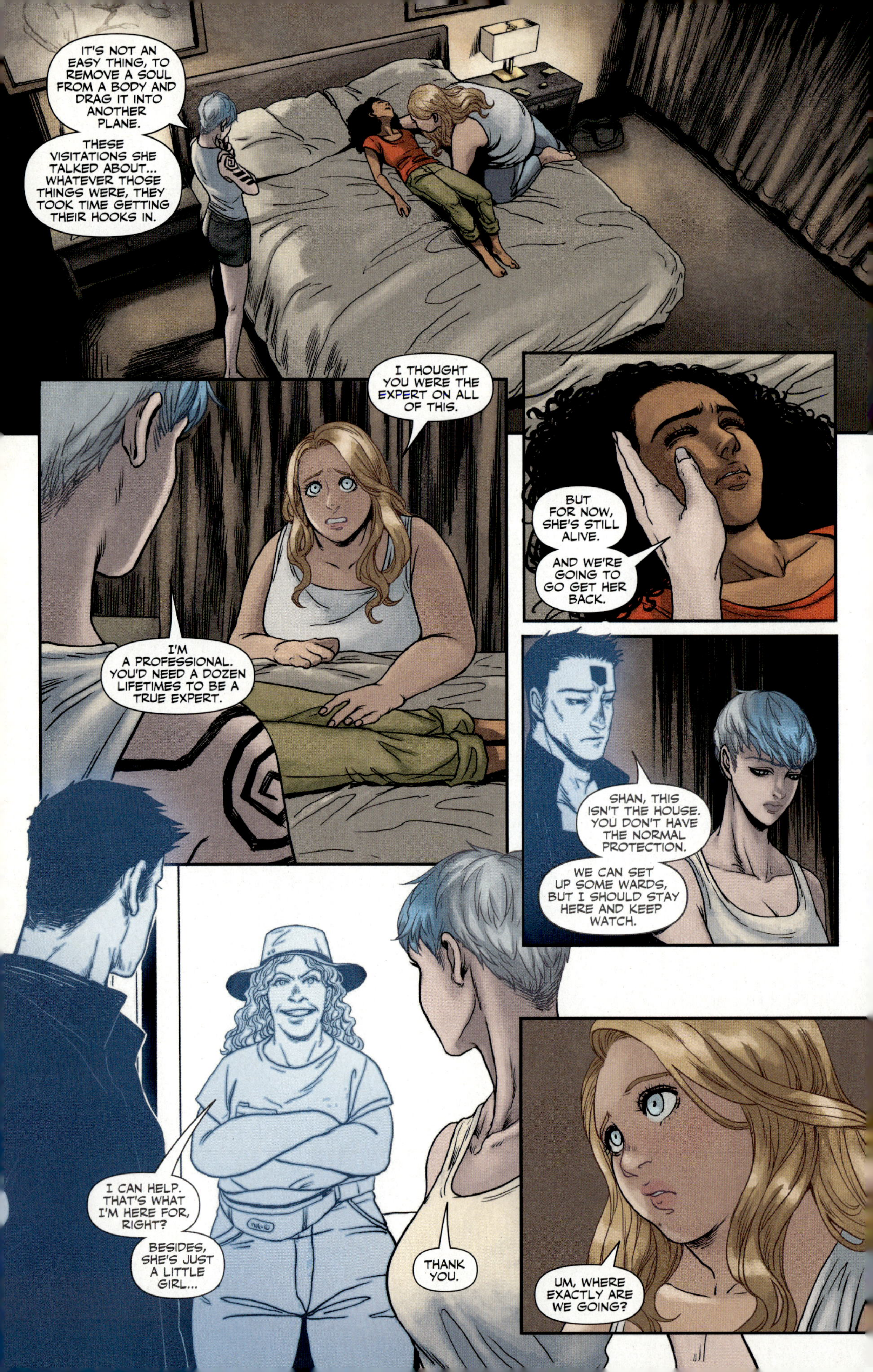
IT'S NOT AN EASY THING, TO REMOVE A SOUL FROM A BODY AND DRAG IT INTO ANOTHER PLANE.
THESE VISITATIONS SHE TALKED ABOUT... WHATEVER THOSE THINGS WERE, THEY TOOK TIME GETTING THEIR HOOKS IN.
I THOUGHT YOU WERE THE EXPERT ON ALL OF THIS.
I'M A PROFESSIONAL. YOU'D NEED A DOZEN LIFETIMES TO BE A TRUE EXPERT.
BUT FOR NOW, SHE'S STILL ALIVE.
AND WE'RE GOING TO GO GET HER BACK.
SHAN, THIS ISN'T THE HOUSE. YOU DON'T HAVE THE NORMAL PROTECTION.
WE CAN SET UP SOME WARDS, BUT I SHOULD STAY HERE AND KEEP WATCH.
I CAN HELP. THAT'S WHAT I'M HERE FOR, RIGHT?
BESIDES, SHE'S JUST A LITTLE GIRL...
THANK YOU.
UM, WHERE EXACTLY ARE WE GOING?

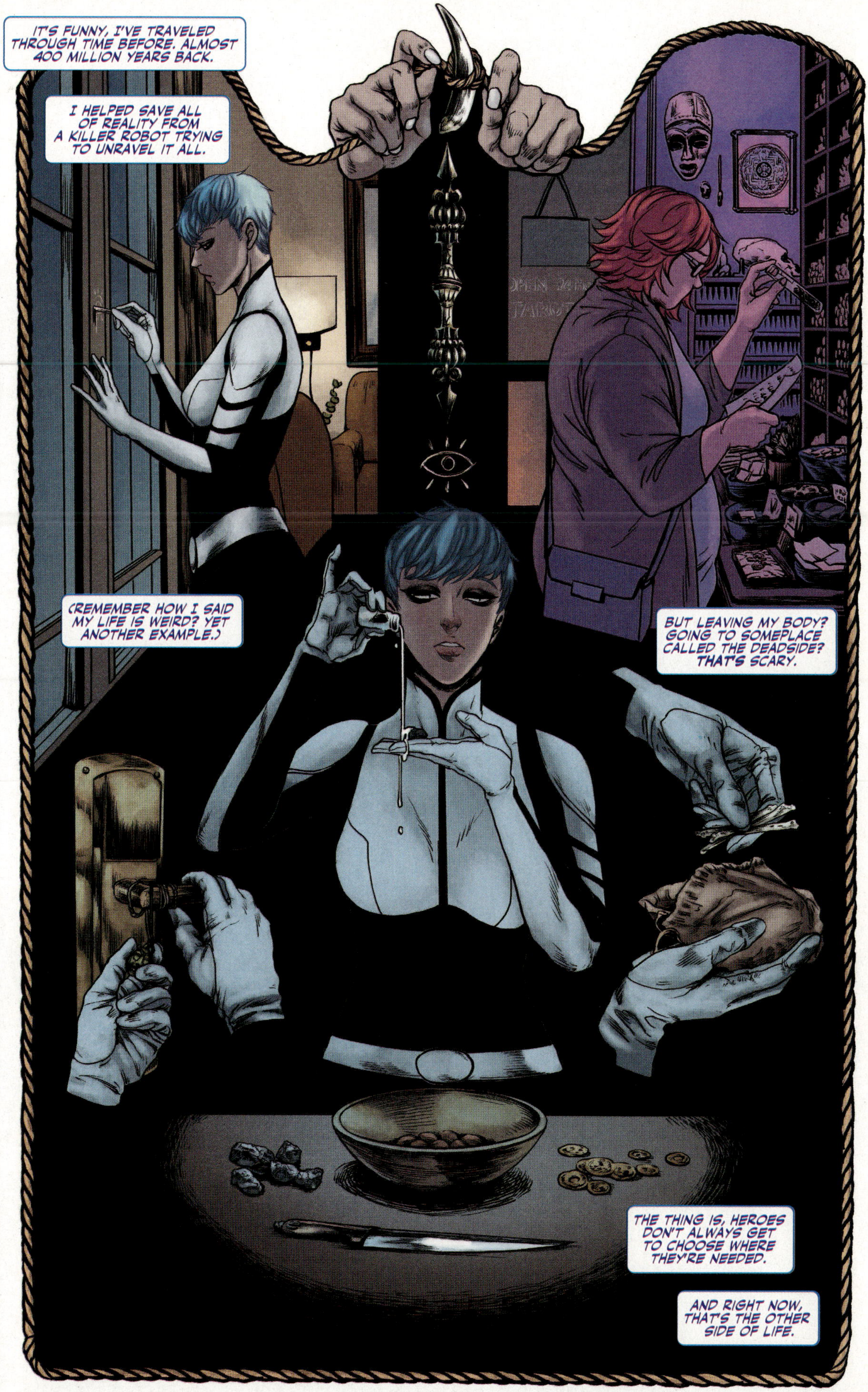
IT'S FUNNY, I'VE TRAVELED THROUGH TIME BEFORE. ALMOST 400 MILLION YEARS BACK.
I HELPED SAVE ALL OF REALITY FROM A KILLER ROBOT TRYING TO UNRAVEL IT ALL.
(REMEMBER HOW I SAID MY LIFE IS WEIRD? YET ANOTHER EXAMPLE.)
BUT LEAVING MY BODY? GOING TO SOMEPLACE CALLED THE DEADSIDE? THAT'S SCARY.
THE THING IS, HEROES DON'T ALWAYS GET TO CHOOSE WHERE THEY'RE NEEDED.
AND RIGHT NOW, THAT'S THE OTHER SIDE OF LIFE.

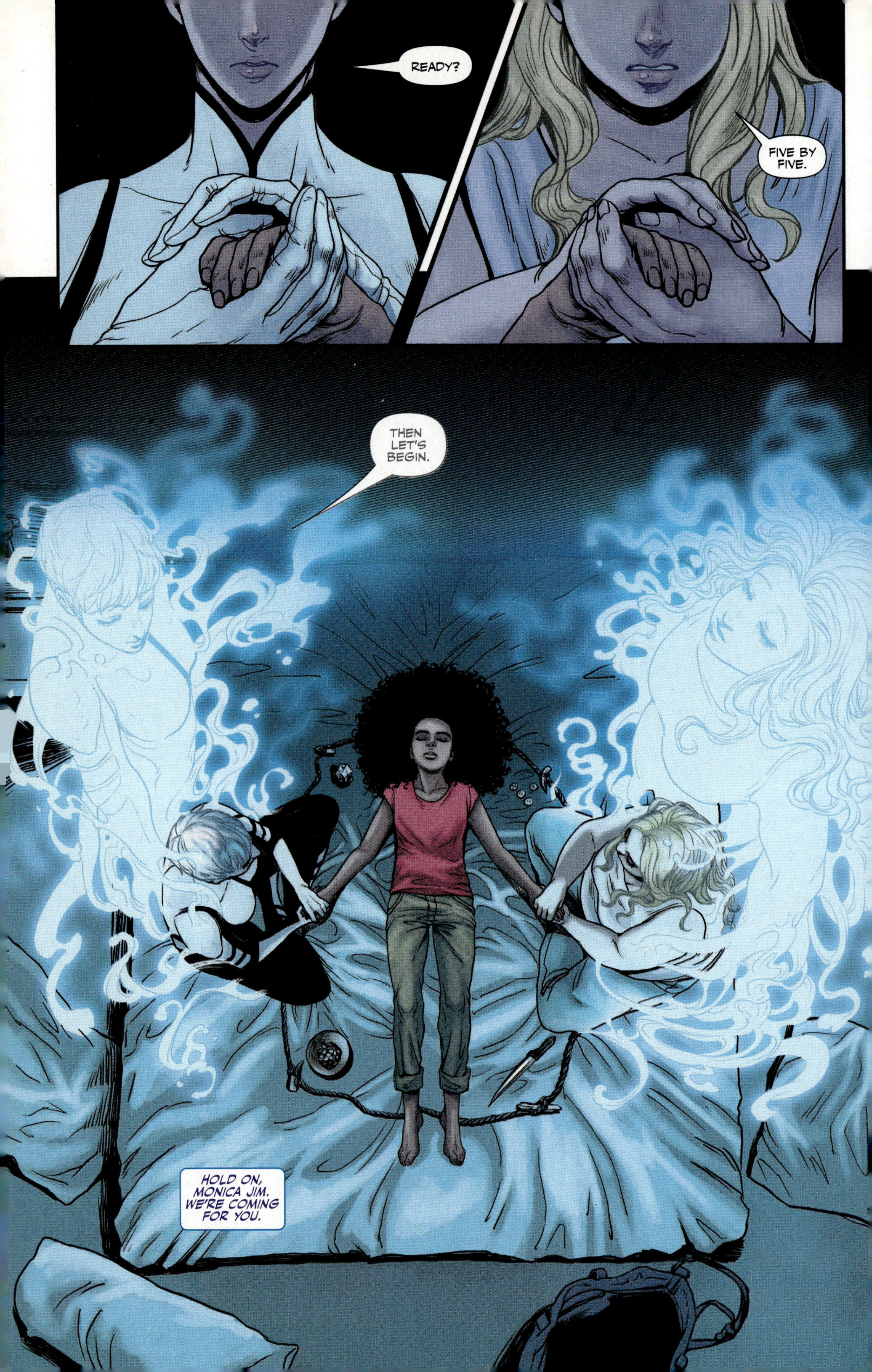
READY?
FIVE BY FIVE.
THEN LET'S BEGIN.
HOLD ON, MONICA JIM. WE'RE COMING FOR YOU.

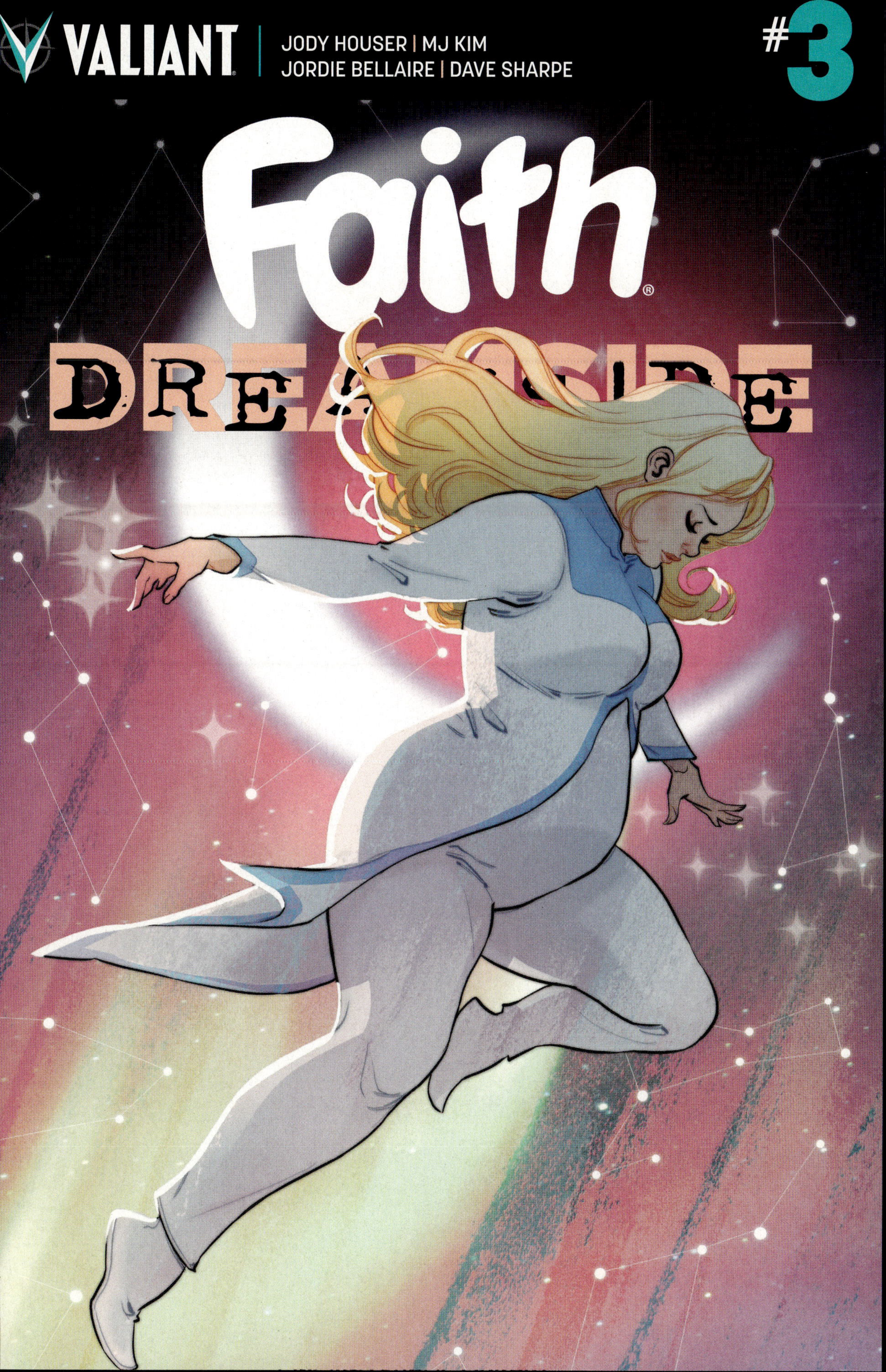
VALIANT
JODY HOUSER | MJ KIM
JORDIE BELLAIRE | DAVE SHARPE
#3
Faith®
DREAMSIDE

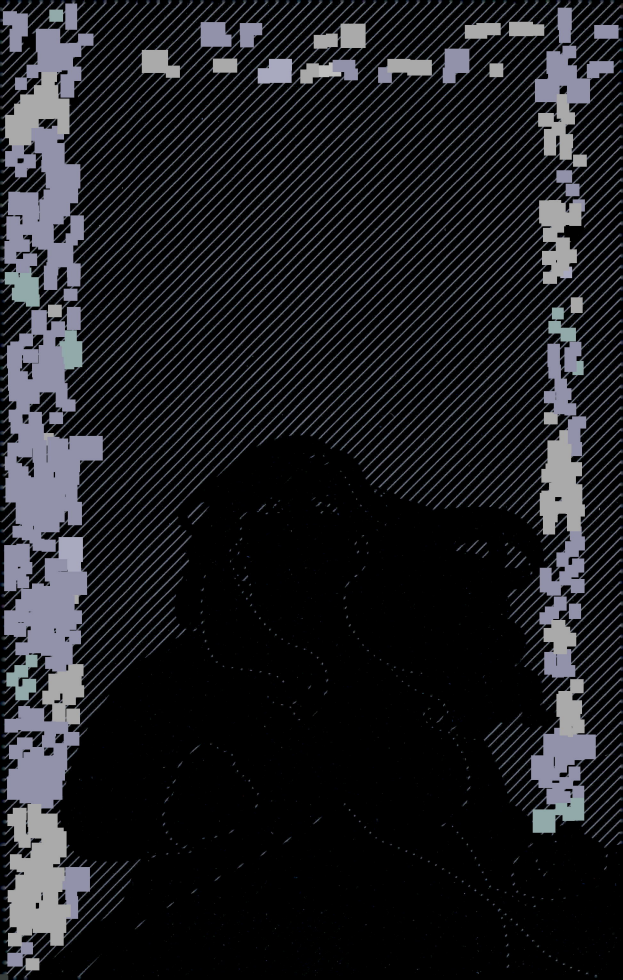

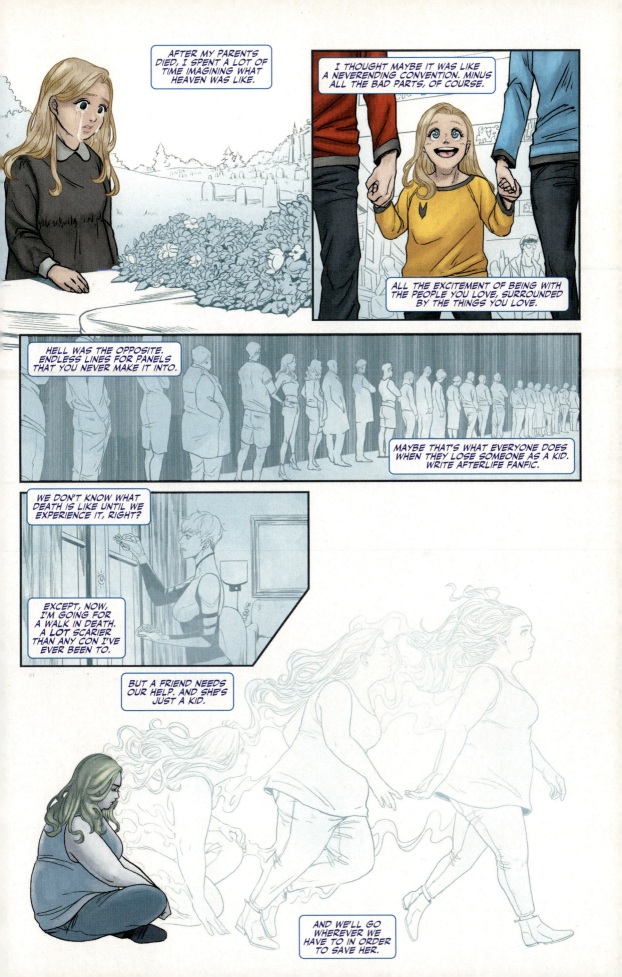

AFTER MY PARENTS DIED, I SPENT A LOT OF TIME IMAGINING WHAT HEAVEN WAS LIKE.

I THOUGHT MAYBE IT WAS LIKE A NEVERENDING CONVENTION. MINUS ALL THE BAD PARTS, OF COURSE.

ALL THE EXCITEMENT OF BEING WITH THE PEOPLE YOU LOVE, SURROUNDED BY THE THINGS YOU LOVE.

HELL WAS THE OPPOSITE. ENDLESS LINES FOR PANELS THAT YOU NEVER MAKE IT INTO.

MAYBE THAT'S WHAT EVERYONE DOES WHEN THEY LOSE SOMEONE AS A KID. WRITE AFTERLIFE FANFIC.

WE DON'T KNOW WHAT DEATH IS LIKE UNTIL WE EXPERIENCE IT, RIGHT?

EXCEPT, NOW, I'M GOING FOR A WALK IN DEATH. A LOT SCARIER THAN ANY CON I'VE EVER BEEN TO.

BUT A FRIEND NEEDS OUR HELP. AND SHE'S JUST A KID.

AND WE'LL GO WHEREVER WE HAVE TO IN ORDER TO SAVE HER.

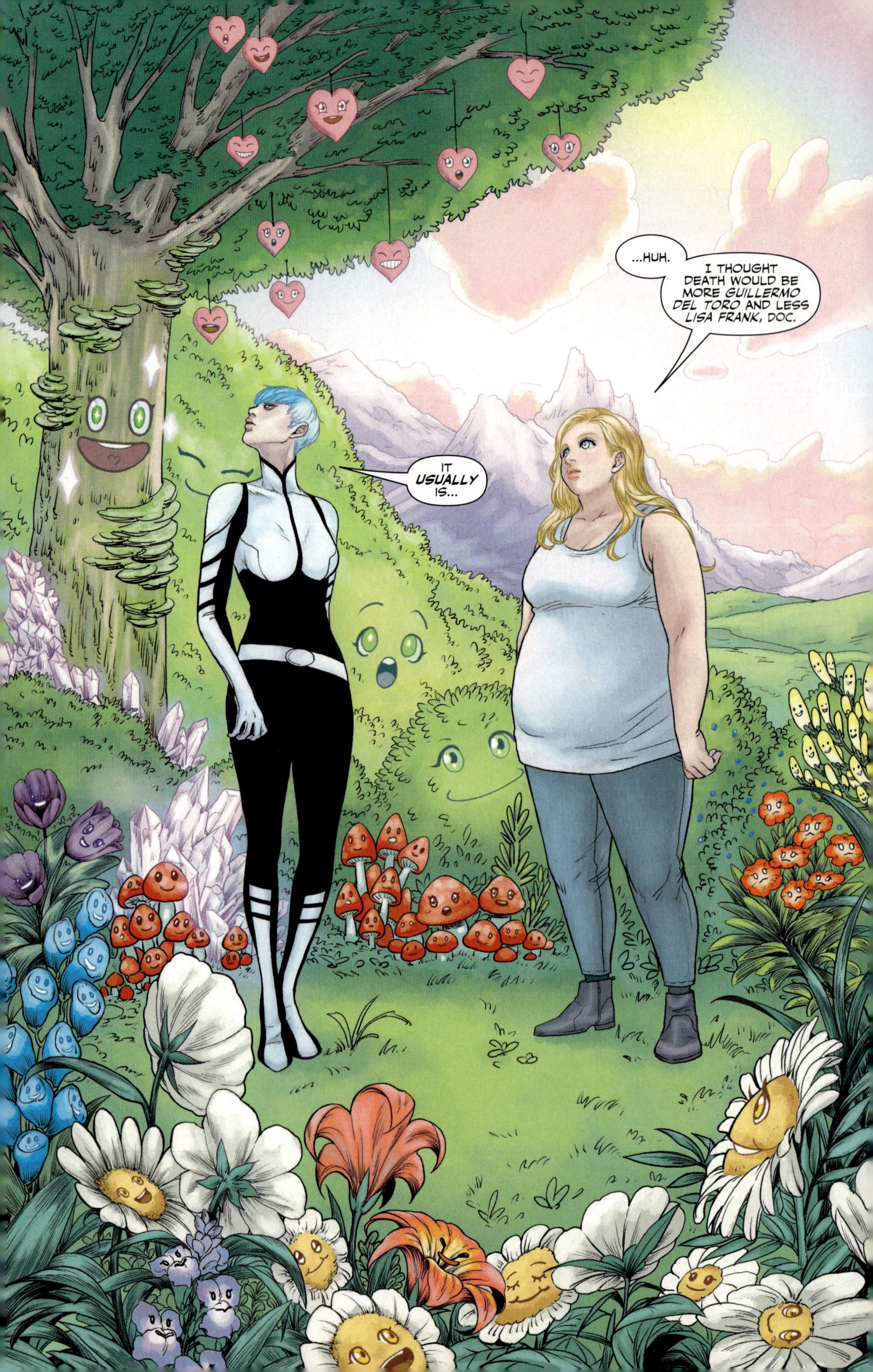
...HUH.
I THOUGHT DEATH WOULD BE MORE GUILLERMO DEL TORO AND LESS LISA FRANK, DOC.
IT USUALLY IS...

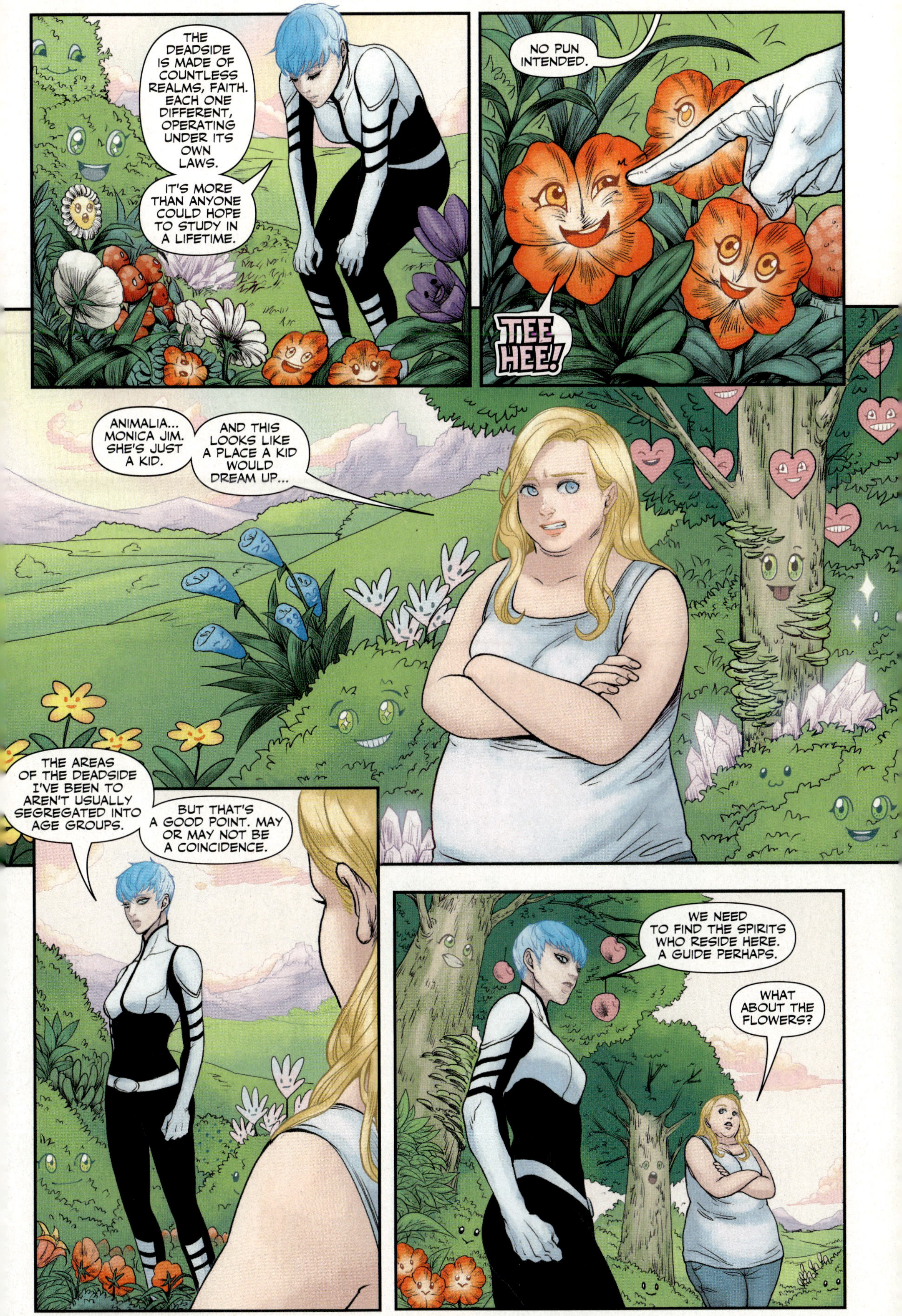
THE DEADSIDE IS MADE OF COUNTLESS REALMS, FAITH. EACH ONE DIFFERENT, OPERATING UNDER ITS OWN LAWS.
IT'S MORE THAN ANYONE COULD HOPE TO STUDY IN A LIFETIME.
NO PUN INTENDED.
TEE HEE!
ANIMALIA... MONICA JIM. SHE'S JUST A KID.
AND THIS LOOKS LIKE A PLACE A KID WOULD DREAM UP...
THE AREAS OF THE DEADSIDE I'VE BEEN TO AREN'T USUALLY SEGREGATED INTO AGE GROUPS.
BUT THAT'S A GOOD POINT. MAY OR MAY NOT BE A COINCIDENCE.
WE NEED TO FIND THE SPIRITS WHO RESIDE HERE. A GUIDE PERHAPS.
WHAT ABOUT THE FLOWERS?

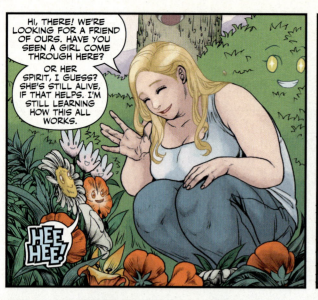

HI, THERE! WE'RE LOOKING FOR A FRIEND OF OURS. HAVE YOU SEEN A GIRL COME THROUGH HERE?

OR HER SPIRIT, I GUESS? SHE'S STILL ALIVE, IF THAT HELPS. I'M STILL LEARNING HOW THIS ALL WORKS.

HEE HEE!

DO YOU KNOW WHICH WAY WE SHOULD HEAD TO FIND HELP? OR WHERE PEOPLE AROUND HERE LIVE?

...SORRY, IS IT RUDE TO USE THE WORD "LIVE" HERE?

HA HAHA!

OKAY, SO I DON'T THINK THE FLOWERS ARE HELPFUL.

THEY AREN'T SPIRITS, AT LEAST NOT IN A FORM I'M FAMILIAR WITH.

AND THEY SEEM A LITTLE... SIMPLE TO BE DEMONS.

I FOUND A PATH, AT LEAST. OR A CLICHÉD APPROXIMATION OF ONE.

ARE YOU SURE WE DIDN'T ACCIDENTLY END UP IN OZ?

OZ ISN'T REAL.

BUT DEMONS ARE?

UNFORTUNATELY...

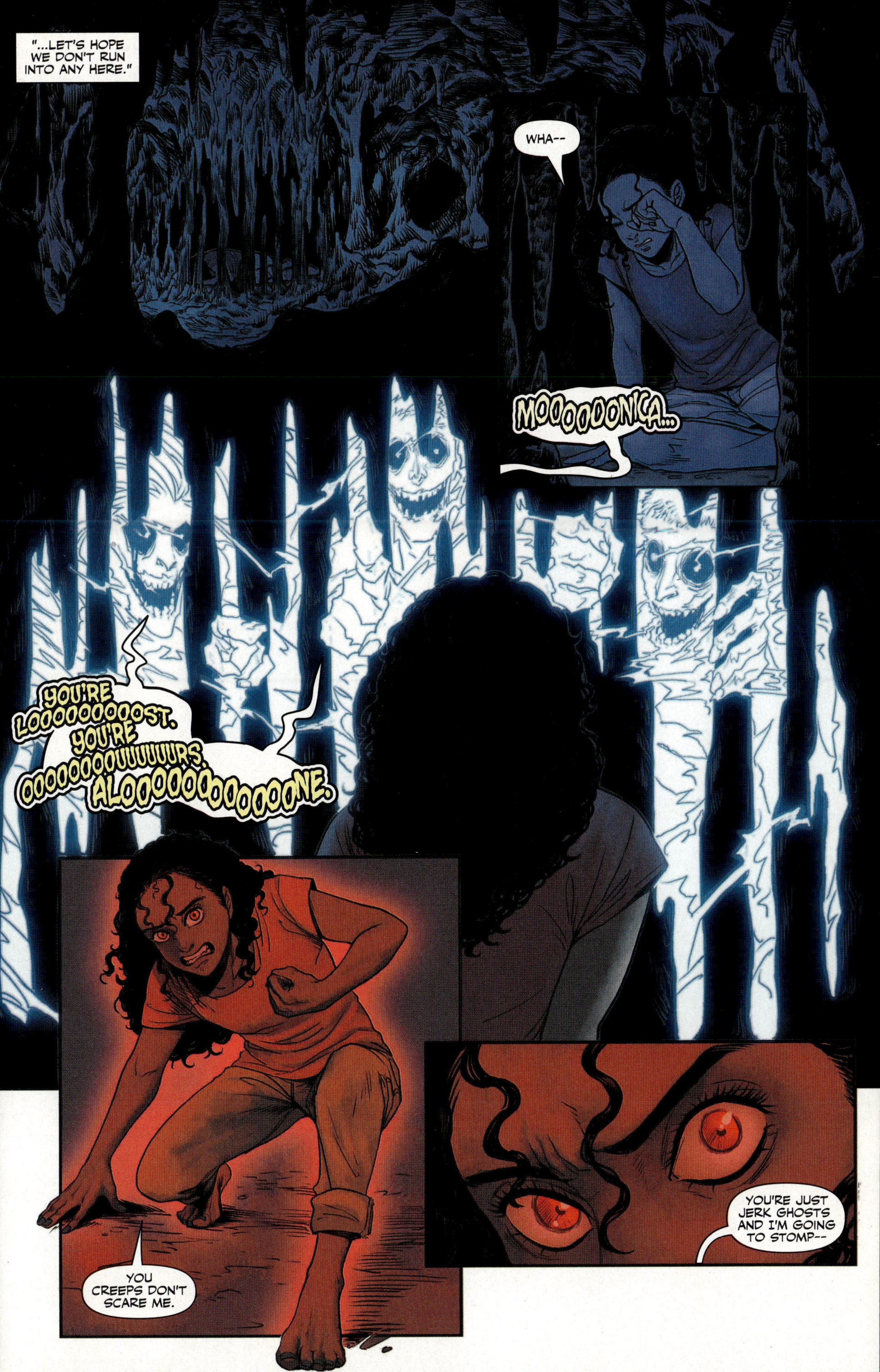
"...LET'S HOPE WE DON'T RUN INTO ANY HERE."
WHA--
MOOOOOONICA...
YOU'RE LOOOOOOOOOST. YOU'RE OOOOOOOOUUUUUURS. ALOOOOOOOOOOOONE.
YOU CREEPS DON'T SCARE ME.
YOU'RE JUST JERK GHOSTS AND I'M GOING TO STOMP--

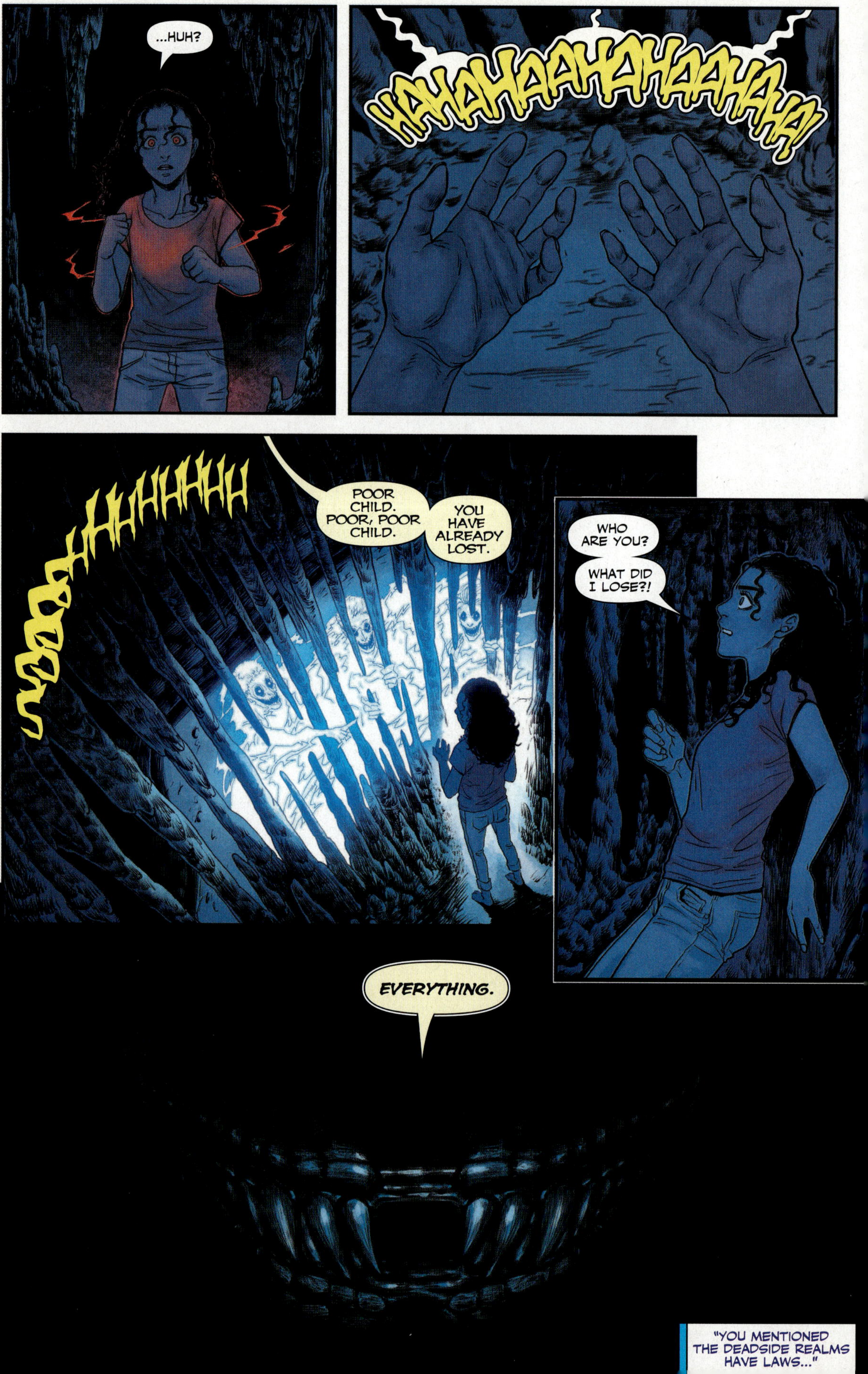
...HUH?
HAHAHAAHAHAAHAHAHA!
POOR CHILD. POOR, POOR CHILD.
YOU HAVE ALREADY LOST.
WHO ARE YOU?
WHAT DID I LOSE?!
EVERYTHING.
"YOU MENTIONED THE DEADSIDE REALMS HAVE LAWS..."

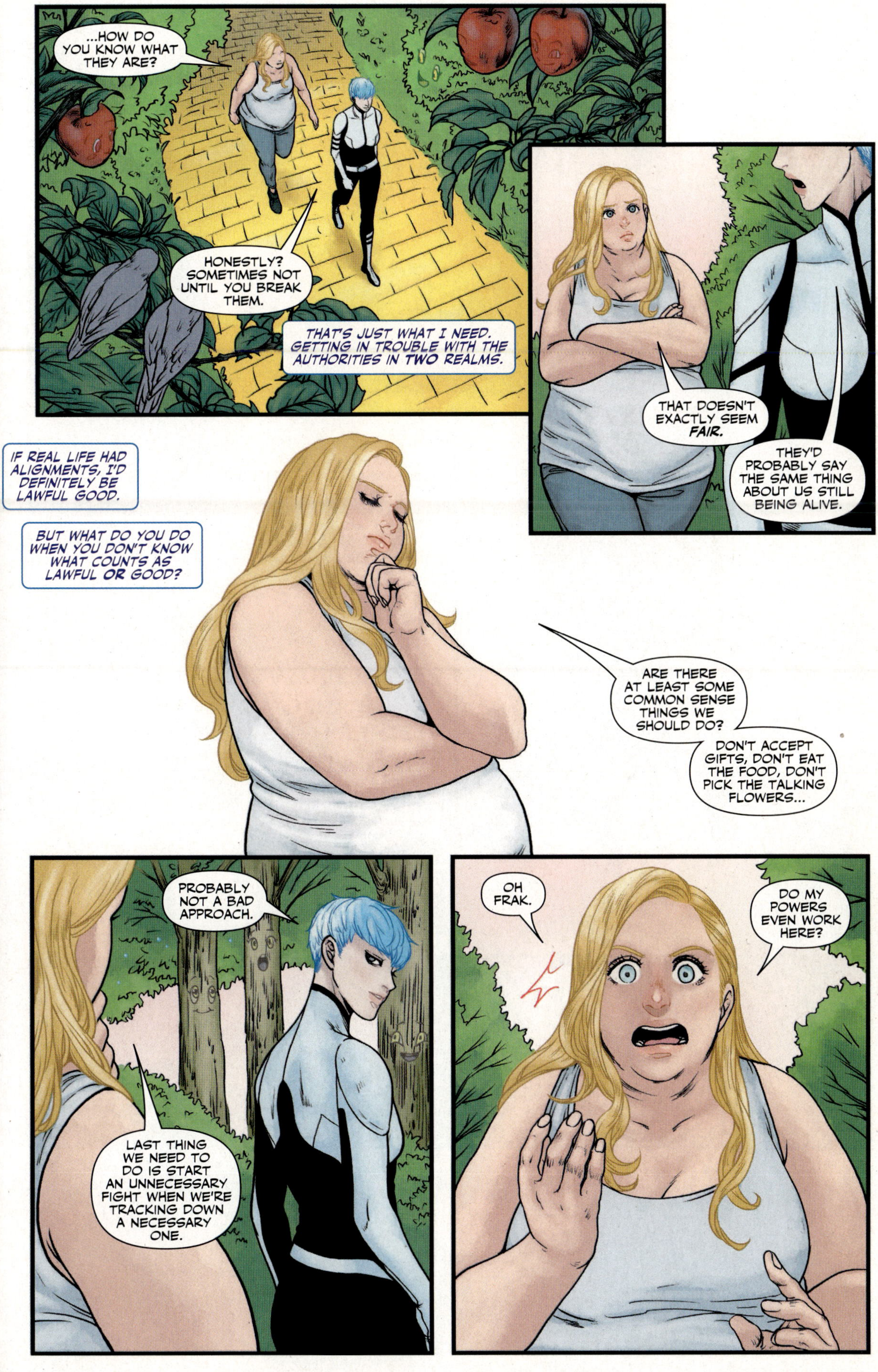
...HOW DO YOU KNOW WHAT THEY ARE?
HONESTLY? SOMETIMES NOT UNTIL YOU BREAK THEM.
THAT'S JUST WHAT I NEED. GETTING IN TROUBLE WITH THE AUTHORITIES IN TWO REALMS.
THAT DOESN'T EXACTLY SEEM FAIR.
THEY'D PROBABLY SAY THE SAME THING ABOUT US STILL BEING ALIVE.
IF REAL LIFE HAD ALIGNMENTS, I'D DEFINITELY BE LAWFUL GOOD.
BUT WHAT DO YOU DO WHEN YOU DON'T KNOW WHAT COUNTS AS LAWFUL OR GOOD?
ARE THERE AT LEAST SOME COMMON SENSE THINGS WE SHOULD DO?
DON'T ACCEPT GIFTS, DON'T EAT THE FOOD, DON'T PICK THE TALKING FLOWERS...
PROBABLY NOT A BAD APPROACH.
LAST THING WE NEED TO DO IS START AN UNNECESSARY FIGHT WHEN WE'RE TRACKING DOWN A NECESSARY ONE.
OH FRAK.
DO MY POWERS EVEN WORK HERE?

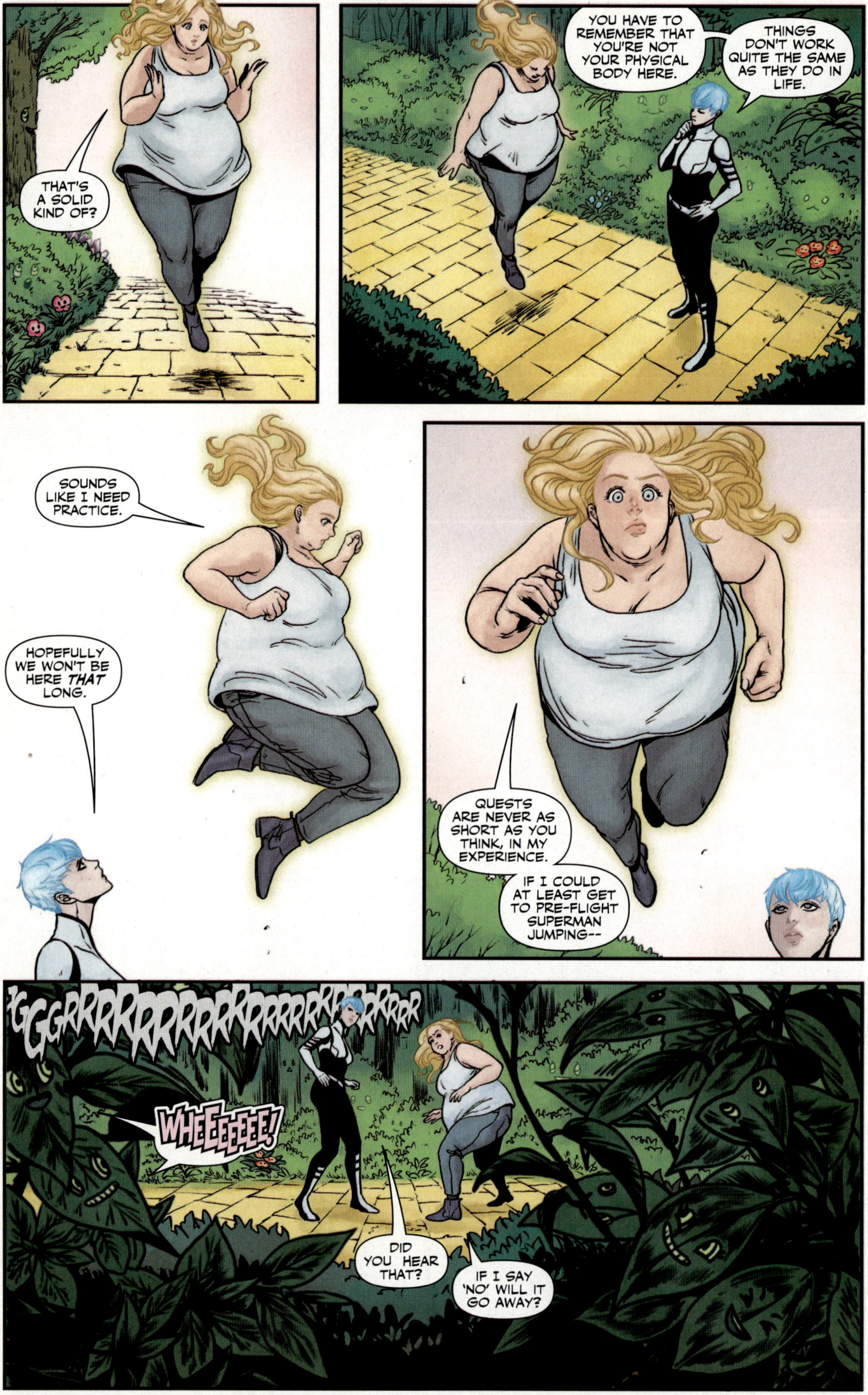
THAT'S A SOLID KIND OF?
YOU HAVE TO REMEMBER THAT YOU'RE NOT YOUR PHYSICAL BODY HERE.
THINGS DON'T WORK QUITE THE SAME AS THEY DO IN LIFE.
SOUNDS LIKE I NEED PRACTICE.
HOPEFULLY WE WON'T BE HERE *THAT* LONG.
QUESTS ARE NEVER AS SHORT AS YOU THINK, IN MY EXPERIENCE.
IF I COULD AT LEAST GET TO PRE-FLIGHT SUPERMAN JUMPING--
GGGRRRRRRRRRRRRRRRRRRRRRR
WHEEEEEEE!
DID YOU HEAR THAT?
IF I SAY 'NO' WILL IT GO AWAY?

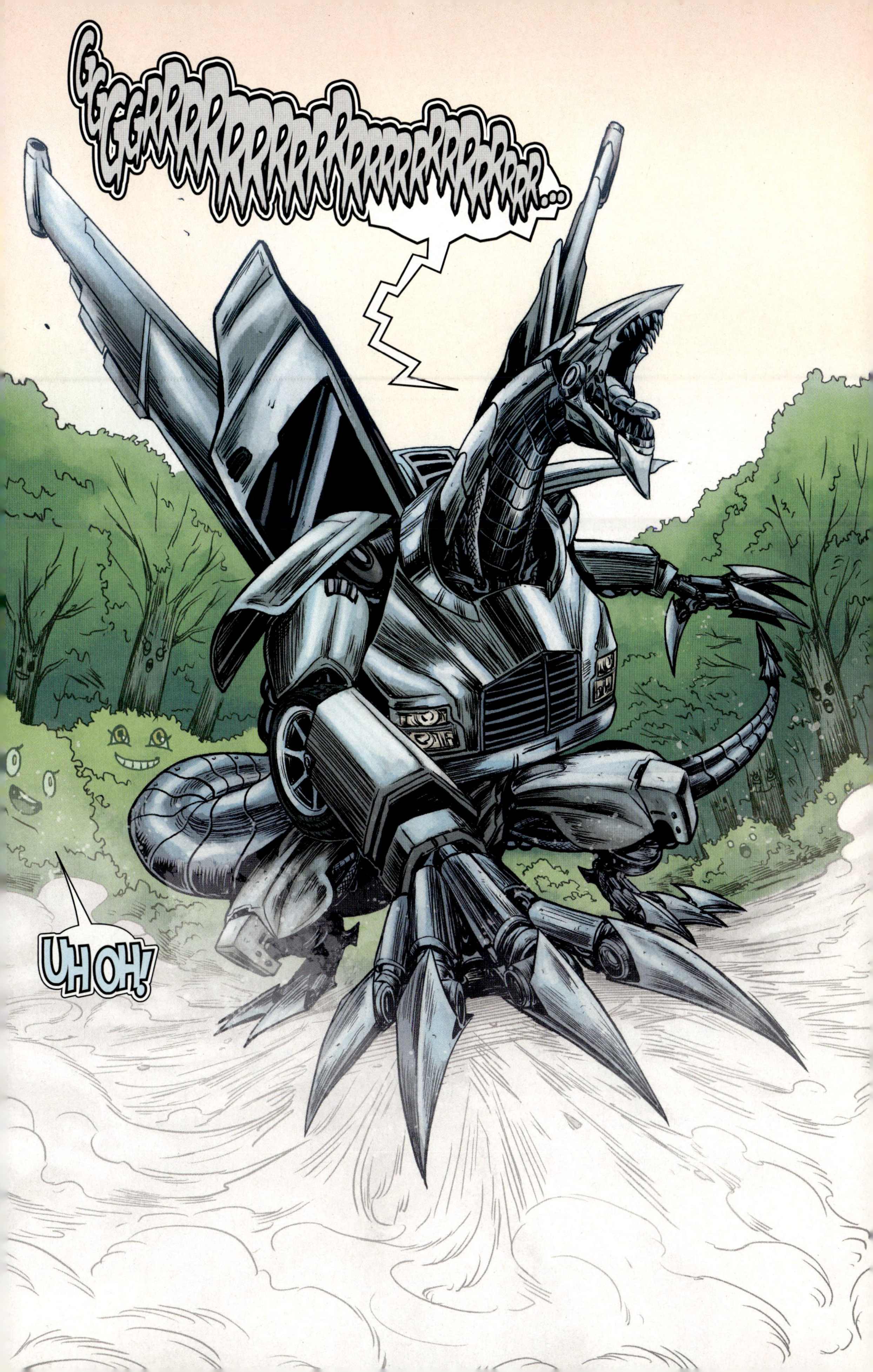
GGGGRRRRRRRRRRRRRRRRRRRRRRRRR...
UH OH!

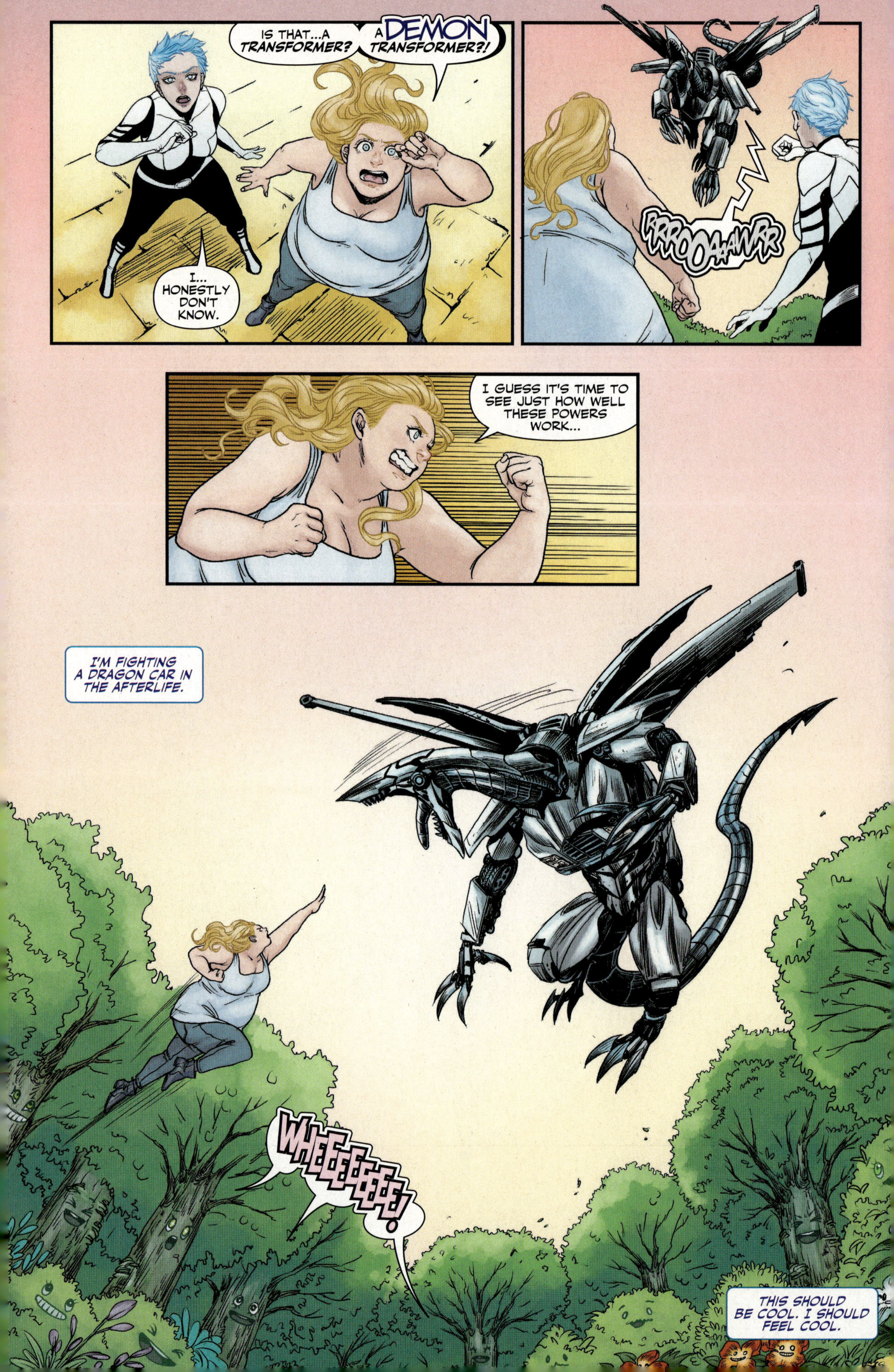

IS THAT...A TRANSFORMER?
A DEMON TRANSFORMER?!
I... HONESTLY DON'T KNOW.
RRROOAAAWRR
I GUESS IT'S TIME TO SEE JUST HOW WELL THESE POWERS WORK...
I'M FIGHTING A DRAGON CAR IN THE AFTERLIFE.
WHEEEEEEEE!
THIS SHOULD BE COOL. I SHOULD FEEL COOL.

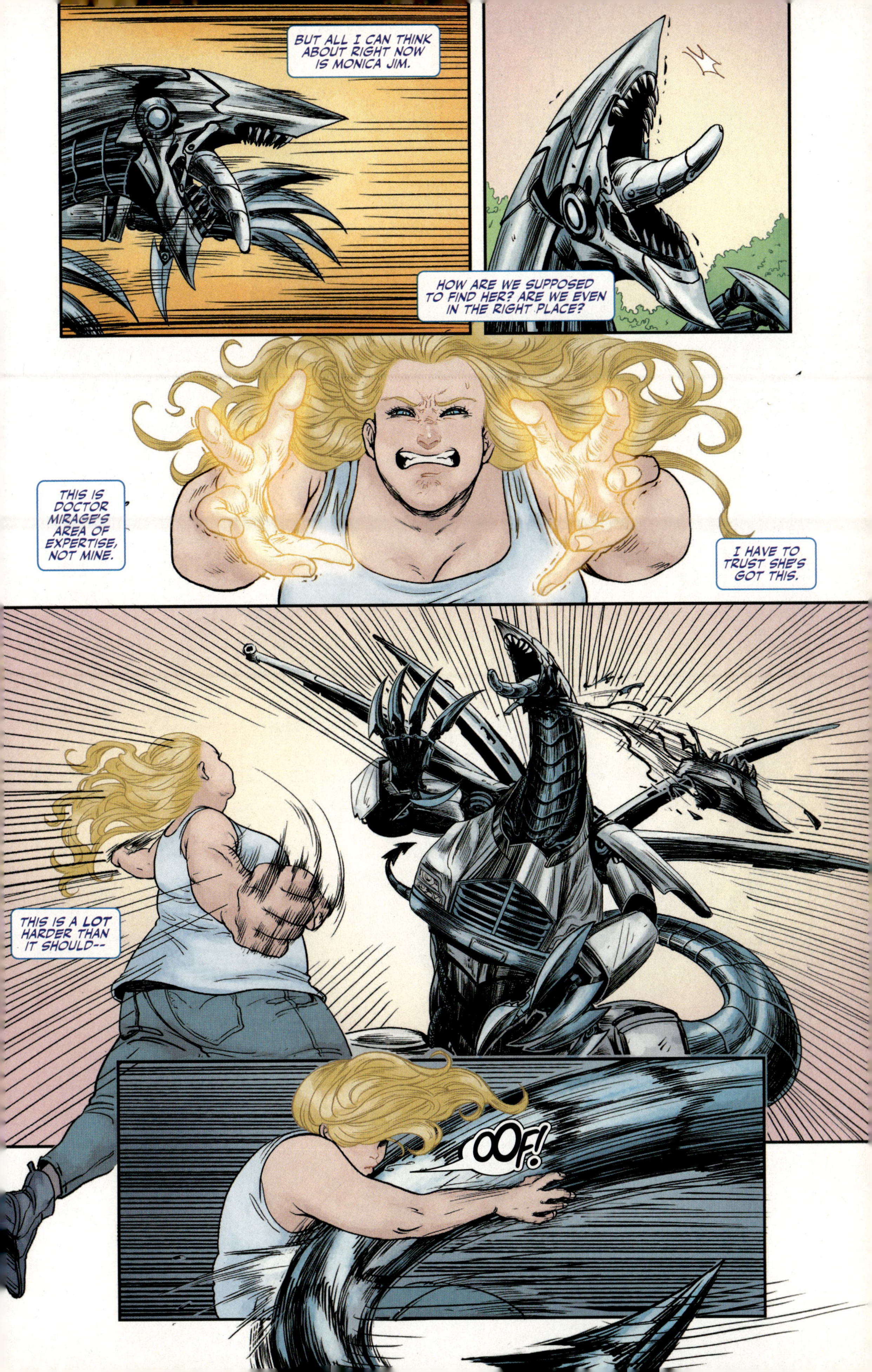
BUT ALL I CAN THINK ABOUT RIGHT NOW IS MONICA JIM.
HOW ARE WE SUPPOSED TO FIND HER? ARE WE EVEN IN THE RIGHT PLACE?
THIS IS DOCTOR MIRAGE'S AREA OF EXPERTISE, NOT MINE.
I HAVE TO TRUST SHE'S GOT THIS.
THIS IS A LOT HARDER THAN IT SHOULD--
OOF!

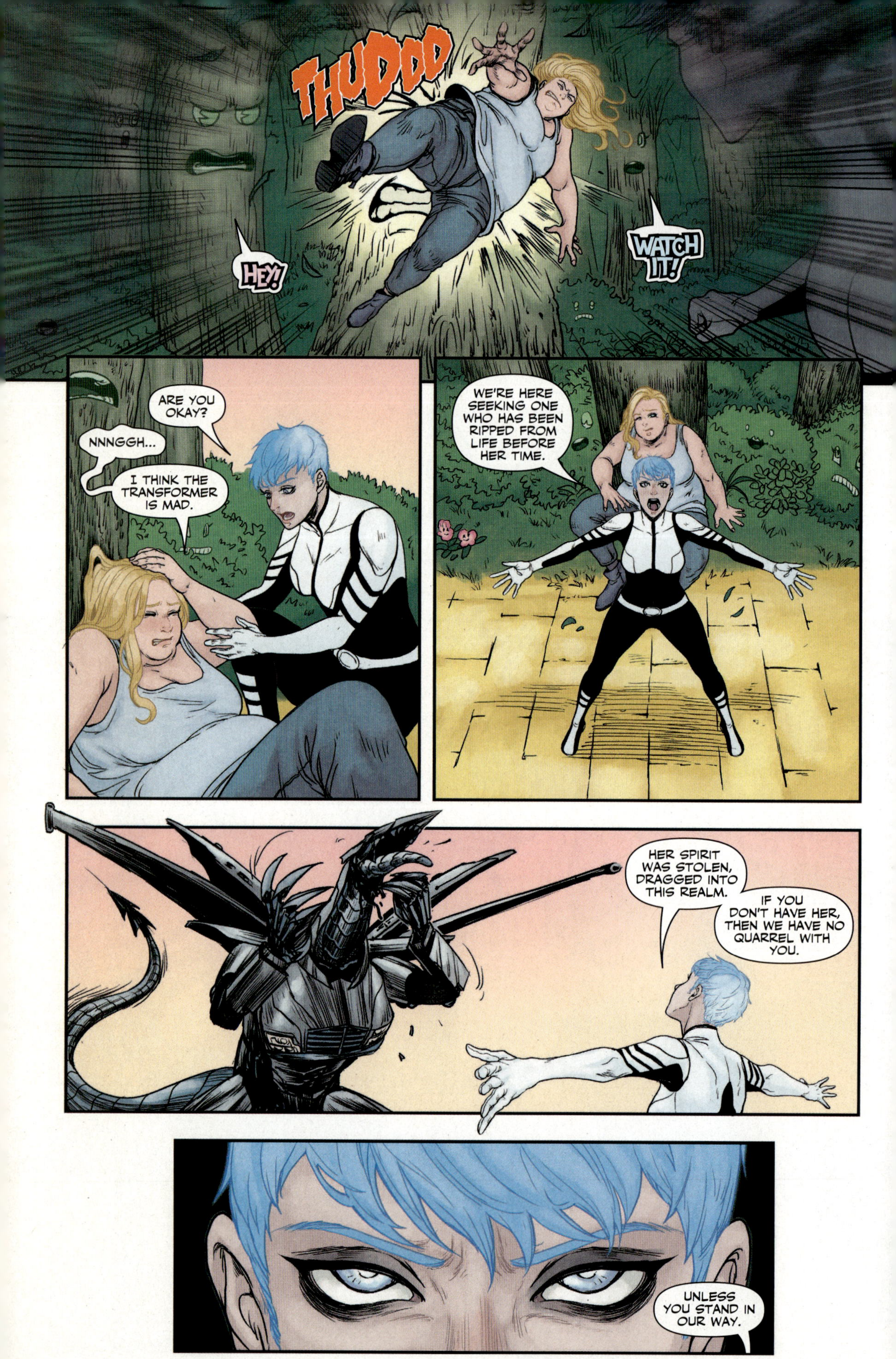
THUDDD
HEY!
WATCH IT!
ARE YOU OKAY?
NNNGGH...
I THINK THE TRANSFORMER IS MAD.
WE'RE HERE SEEKING ONE WHO HAS BEEN RIPPED FROM LIFE BEFORE HER TIME.
HER SPIRIT WAS STOLEN, DRAGGED INTO THIS REALM.
IF YOU DON'T HAVE HER, THEN WE HAVE NO QUARREL WITH YOU.
UNLESS YOU STAND IN OUR WAY.

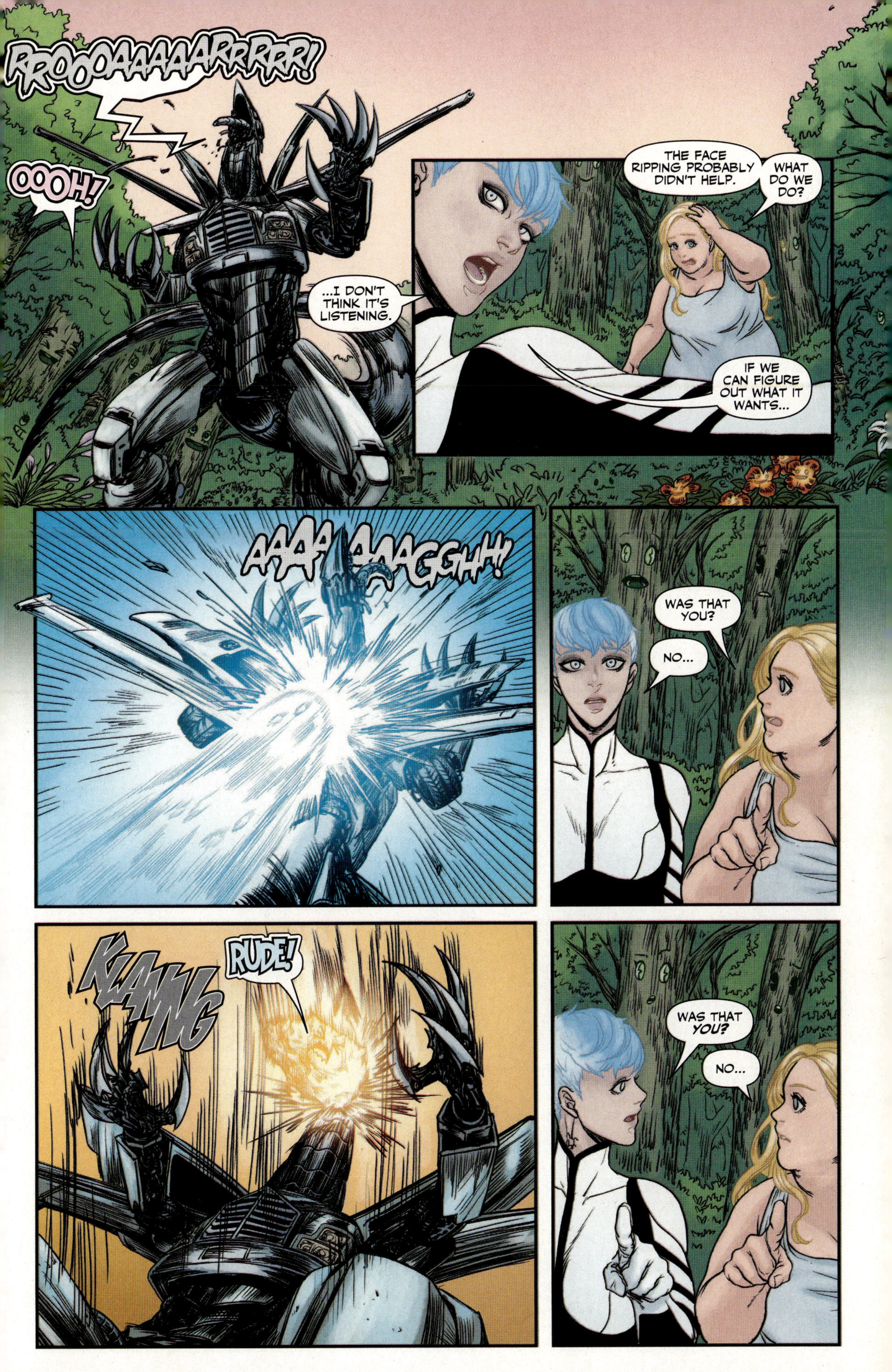
RROOOAAAAARRRRR!
OOOH!
...I DON'T THINK IT'S LISTENING.
THE FACE RIPPING PROBABLY DIDN'T HELP.
WHAT DO WE DO?
IF WE CAN FIGURE OUT WHAT IT WANTS...
AAAAAAAAGGHH!
WAS THAT YOU?
NO...
KLANNG
RUDE!
WAS THAT *YOU?*
NO...

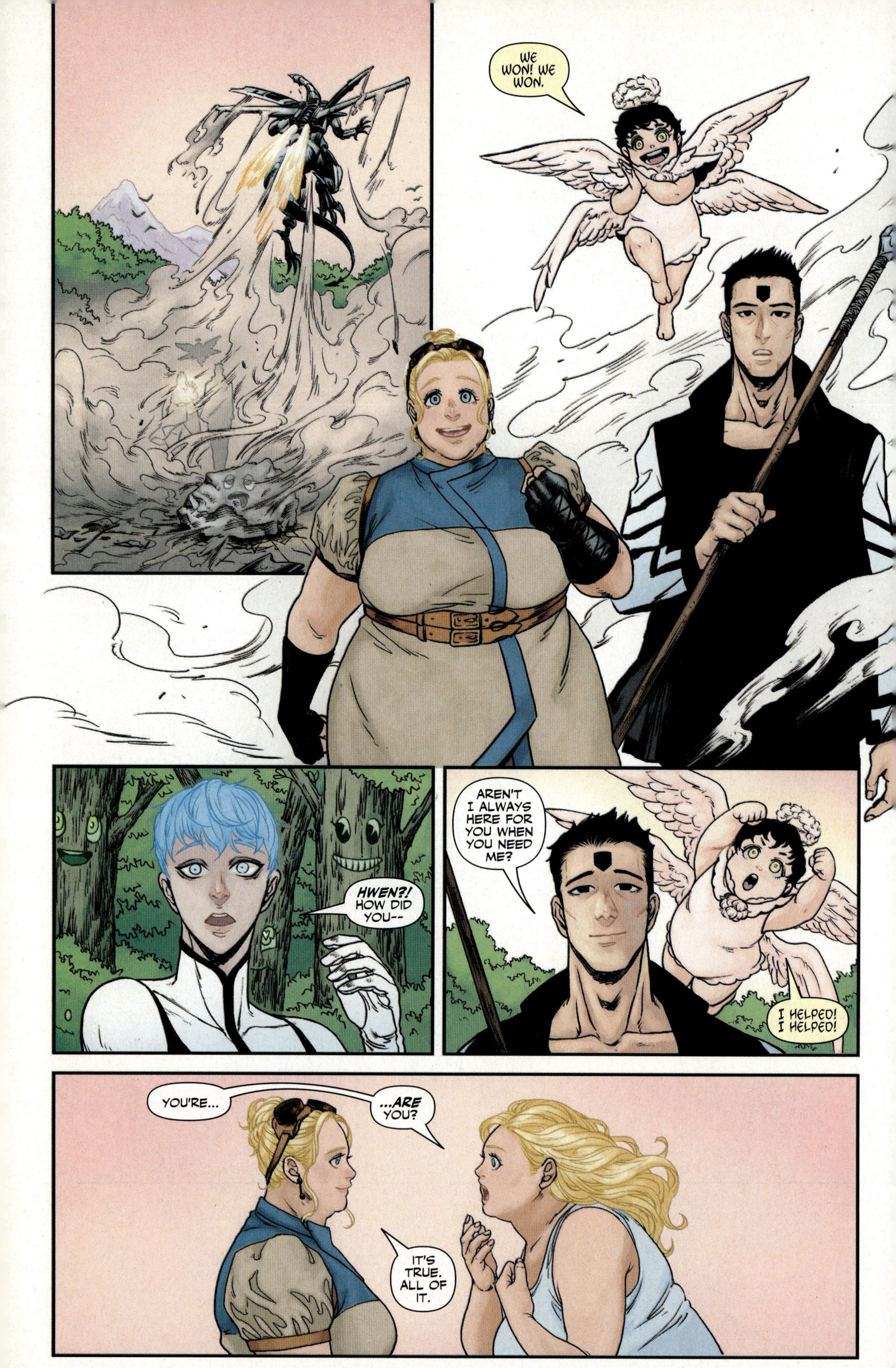
WE WON! WE WON.
HWEN?! HOW DID YOU--
AREN'T I ALWAYS HERE FOR YOU WHEN YOU NEED ME?
I HELPED! I HELPED!
YOU'RE...
...ARE YOU?
IT'S TRUE. ALL OF IT.

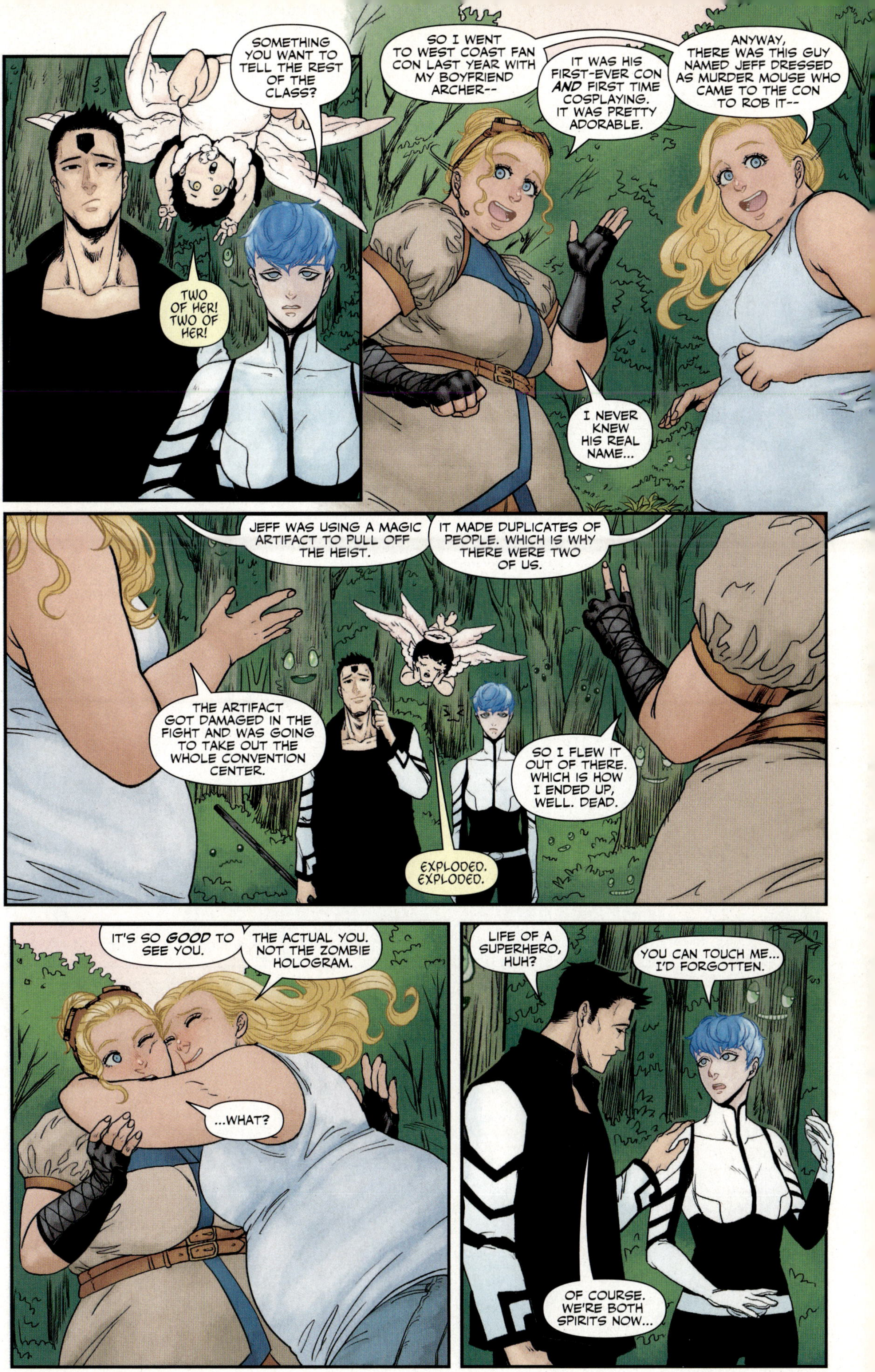
SOMETHING YOU WANT TO TELL THE REST OF THE CLASS?
TWO OF HER! TWO OF HER!
SO I WENT TO WEST COAST FAN CON LAST YEAR WITH MY BOYFRIEND ARCHER--
IT WAS HIS FIRST-EVER CON AND FIRST TIME COSPLAYING. IT WAS PRETTY ADORABLE.
ANYWAY, THERE WAS THIS GUY NAMED JEFF DRESSED AS MURDER MOUSE WHO CAME TO THE CON TO ROB IT--
I NEVER KNEW HIS REAL NAME...
JEFF WAS USING A MAGIC ARTIFACT TO PULL OFF THE HEIST.
IT MADE DUPLICATES OF PEOPLE. WHICH IS WHY THERE WERE TWO OF US.
THE ARTIFACT GOT DAMAGED IN THE FIGHT AND WAS GOING TO TAKE OUT THE WHOLE CONVENTION CENTER.
SO I FLEW IT OUT OF THERE. WHICH IS HOW I ENDED UP, WELL. DEAD.
EXPLODED. EXPLODED.
IT'S SO GOOD TO SEE YOU.
THE ACTUAL YOU. NOT THE ZOMBIE HOLOGRAM.
...WHAT?
LIFE OF A SUPERHERO, HUH?
YOU CAN TOUCH ME... I'D FORGOTTEN.
OF COURSE. WE'RE BOTH SPIRITS NOW...

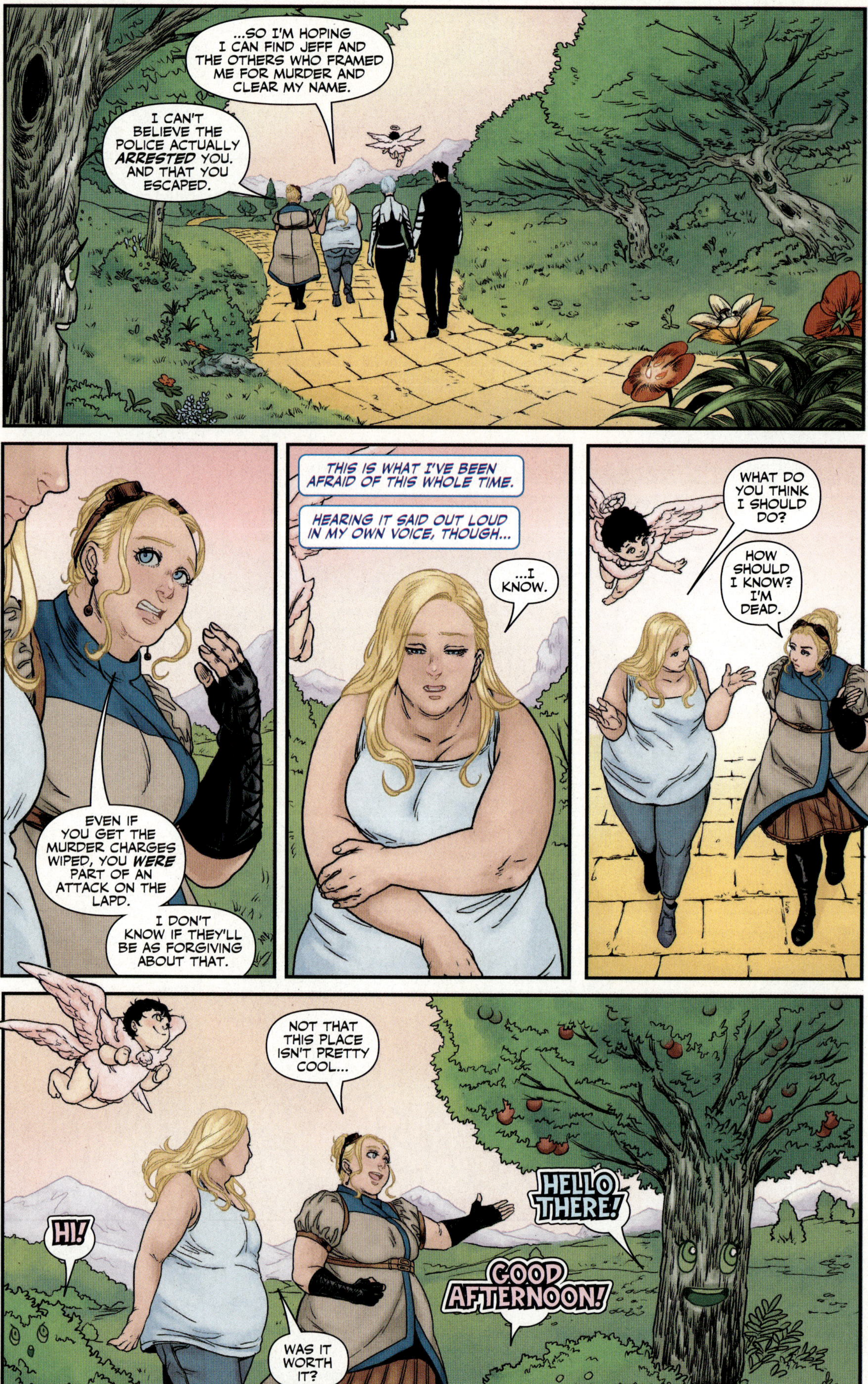

...SO I'M HOPING I CAN FIND JEFF AND THE OTHERS WHO FRAMED ME FOR MURDER AND CLEAR MY NAME.
I CAN'T BELIEVE THE POLICE ACTUALLY ARRESTED YOU. AND THAT YOU ESCAPED.
EVEN IF YOU GET THE MURDER CHARGES WIPED, YOU WERE PART OF AN ATTACK ON THE LAPD.
I DON'T KNOW IF THEY'LL BE AS FORGIVING ABOUT THAT.
THIS IS WHAT I'VE BEEN AFRAID OF THIS WHOLE TIME.
HEARING IT SAID OUT LOUD IN MY OWN VOICE, THOUGH...
...I KNOW.
WHAT DO YOU THINK I SHOULD DO?
HOW SHOULD I KNOW? I'M DEAD.
NOT THAT THIS PLACE ISN'T PRETTY COOL...
HI!
HELLO THERE!
GOOD AFTERNOON!
WAS IT WORTH IT?

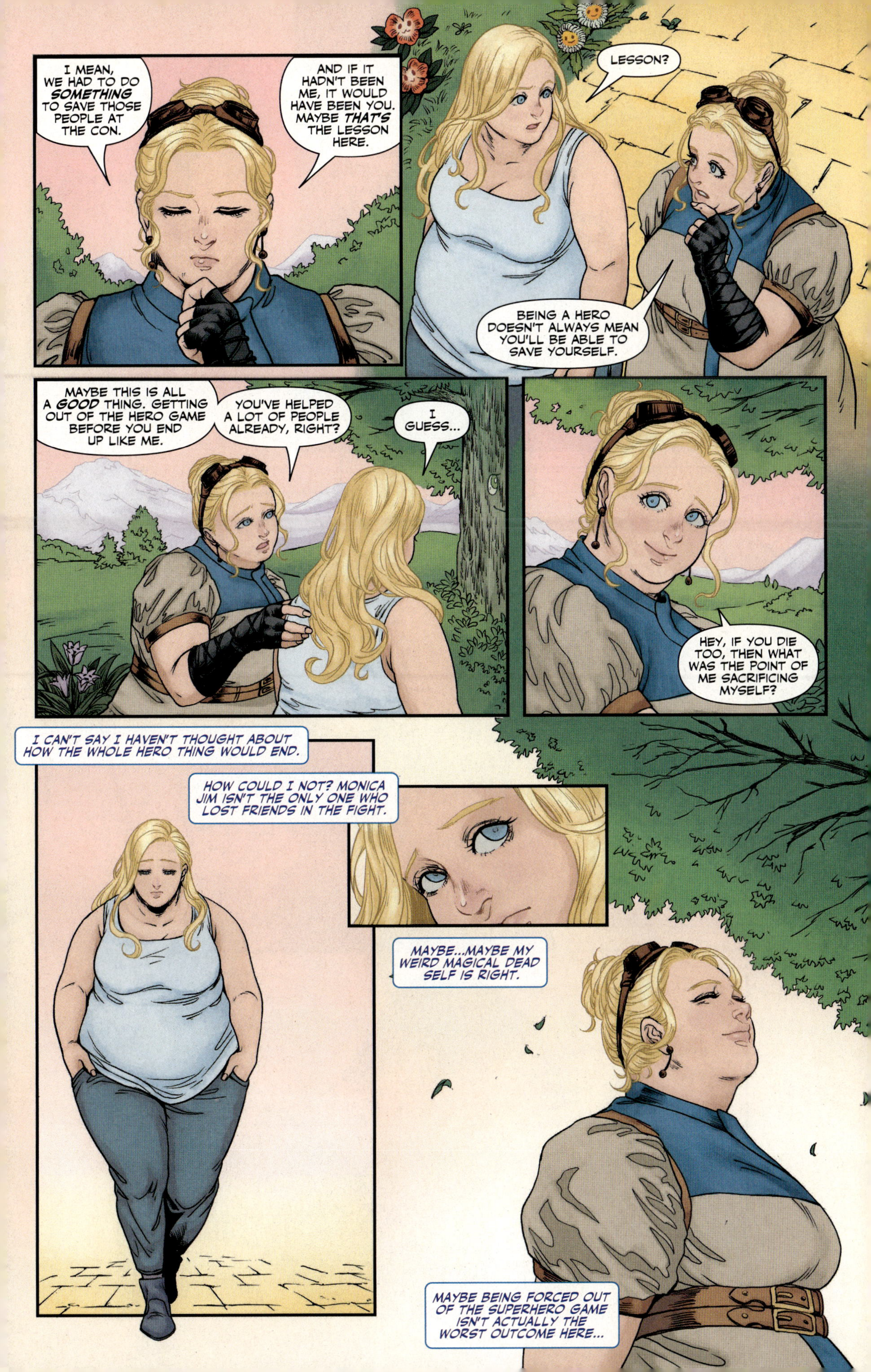
I MEAN, WE HAD TO DO *SOMETHING* TO SAVE THOSE PEOPLE AT THE CON.
AND IF IT HADN'T BEEN ME, IT WOULD HAVE BEEN YOU. MAYBE *THAT'S* THE LESSON HERE.
LESSON?
BEING A HERO DOESN'T ALWAYS MEAN YOU'LL BE ABLE TO SAVE YOURSELF.
MAYBE THIS IS ALL A *GOOD* THING. GETTING OUT OF THE HERO GAME BEFORE YOU END UP LIKE ME.
YOU'VE HELPED A LOT OF PEOPLE ALREADY, RIGHT?
I GUESS...
HEY, IF YOU DIE TOO, THEN WHAT WAS THE POINT OF ME SACRIFICING MYSELF?
I CAN'T SAY I HAVEN'T THOUGHT ABOUT HOW THE WHOLE HERO THING WOULD END.
HOW COULD I NOT? MONICA JIM ISN'T THE ONLY ONE WHO LOST FRIENDS IN THE FIGHT.
MAYBE...MAYBE MY WEIRD MAGICAL DEAD SELF IS RIGHT.
MAYBE BEING FORCED OUT OF THE SUPERHERO GAME ISN'T ACTUALLY THE WORST OUTCOME HERE...

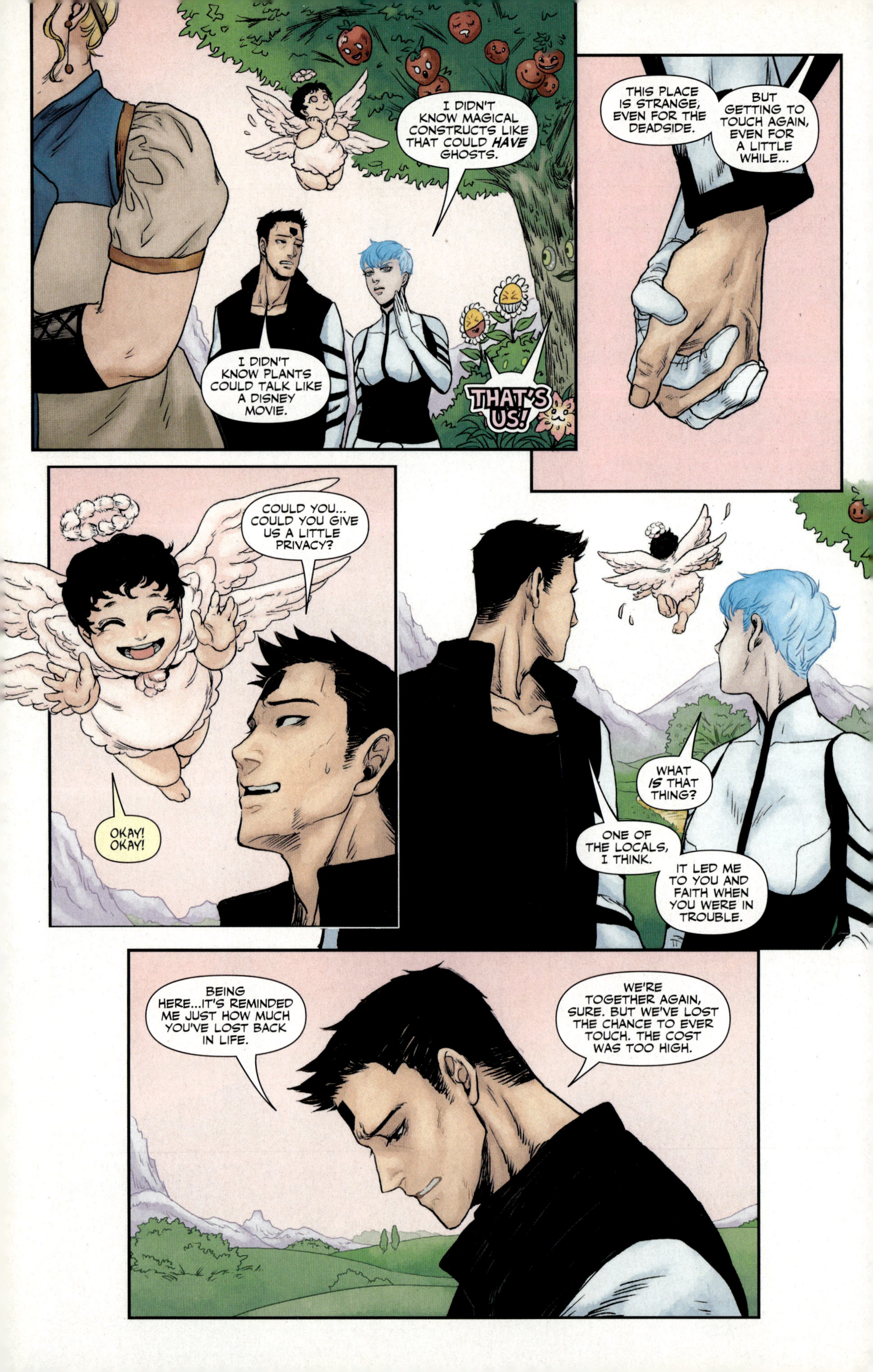
I DIDN'T KNOW MAGICAL CONSTRUCTS LIKE THAT COULD HAVE GHOSTS.
I DIDN'T KNOW PLANTS COULD TALK LIKE A DISNEY MOVIE.
THAT'S US!
THIS PLACE IS STRANGE, EVEN FOR THE DEADSIDE.
BUT GETTING TO TOUCH AGAIN, EVEN FOR A LITTLE WHILE...
COULD YOU... COULD YOU GIVE US A LITTLE PRIVACY?
OKAY! OKAY!
WHAT IS THAT THING?
ONE OF THE LOCALS, I THINK.
IT LED ME TO YOU AND FAITH WHEN YOU WERE IN TROUBLE.
BEING HERE...IT'S REMINDED ME JUST HOW MUCH YOU'VE LOST BACK IN LIFE.
WE'RE TOGETHER AGAIN, SURE. BUT WE'VE LOST THE CHANCE TO EVER TOUCH. THE COST WAS TOO HIGH.

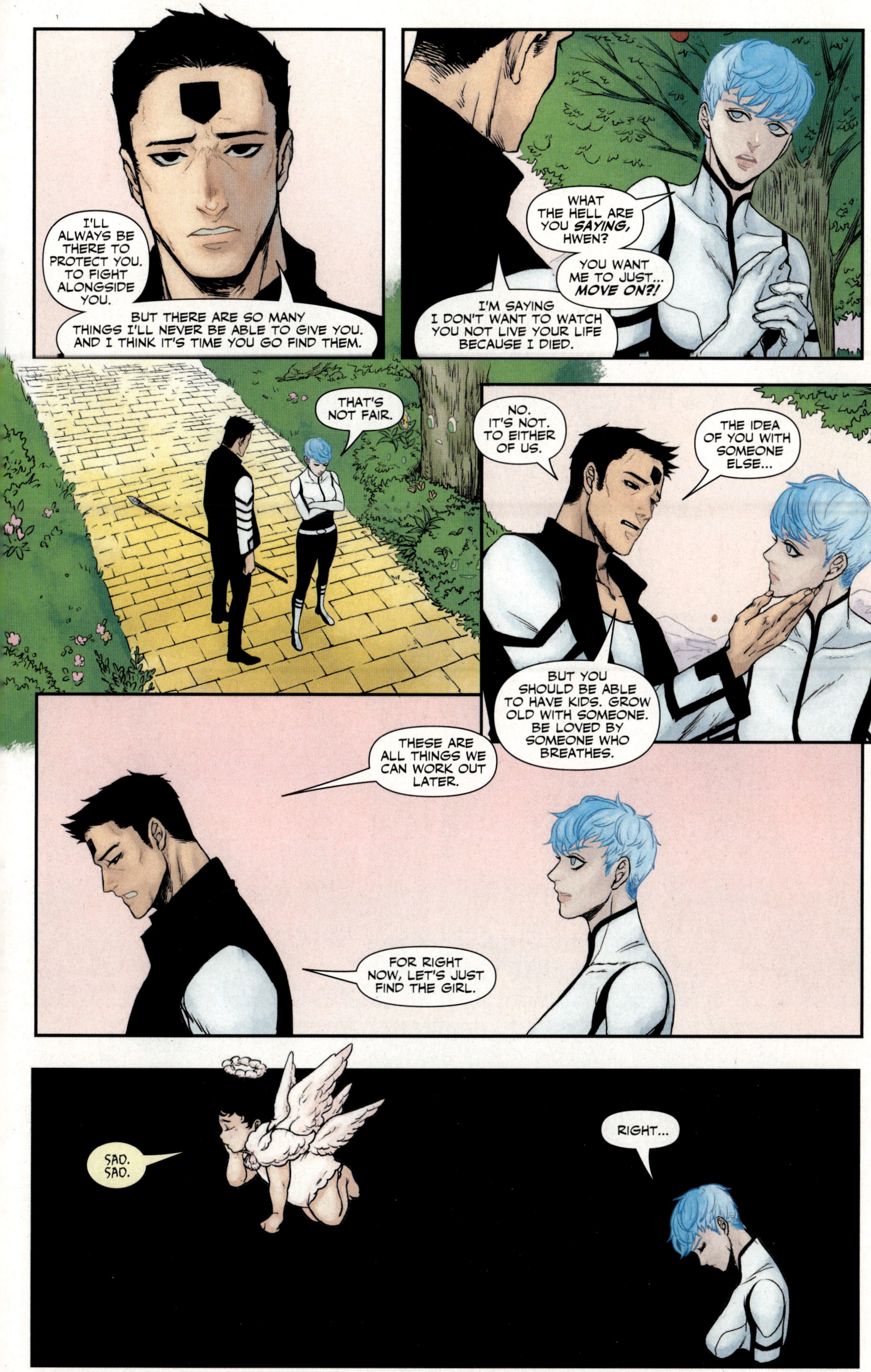
I'LL ALWAYS BE THERE TO PROTECT YOU. TO FIGHT ALONGSIDE YOU.
BUT THERE ARE SO MANY THINGS I'LL NEVER BE ABLE TO GIVE YOU. AND I THINK IT'S TIME YOU GO FIND THEM.
WHAT THE HELL ARE YOU *SAYING,* HWEN?
YOU WANT ME TO JUST... *MOVE ON?!*
I'M SAYING I DON'T WANT TO WATCH YOU NOT LIVE YOUR LIFE BECAUSE I DIED.
THAT'S NOT FAIR.
NO. IT'S NOT. TO EITHER OF US.
THE IDEA OF YOU WITH SOMEONE ELSE...
BUT YOU SHOULD BE ABLE TO HAVE KIDS. GROW OLD WITH SOMEONE. BE LOVED BY SOMEONE WHO BREATHES.
THESE ARE ALL THINGS WE CAN WORK OUT LATER.
FOR RIGHT NOW, LET'S JUST FIND THE GIRL.
SAD. SAD.
RIGHT...

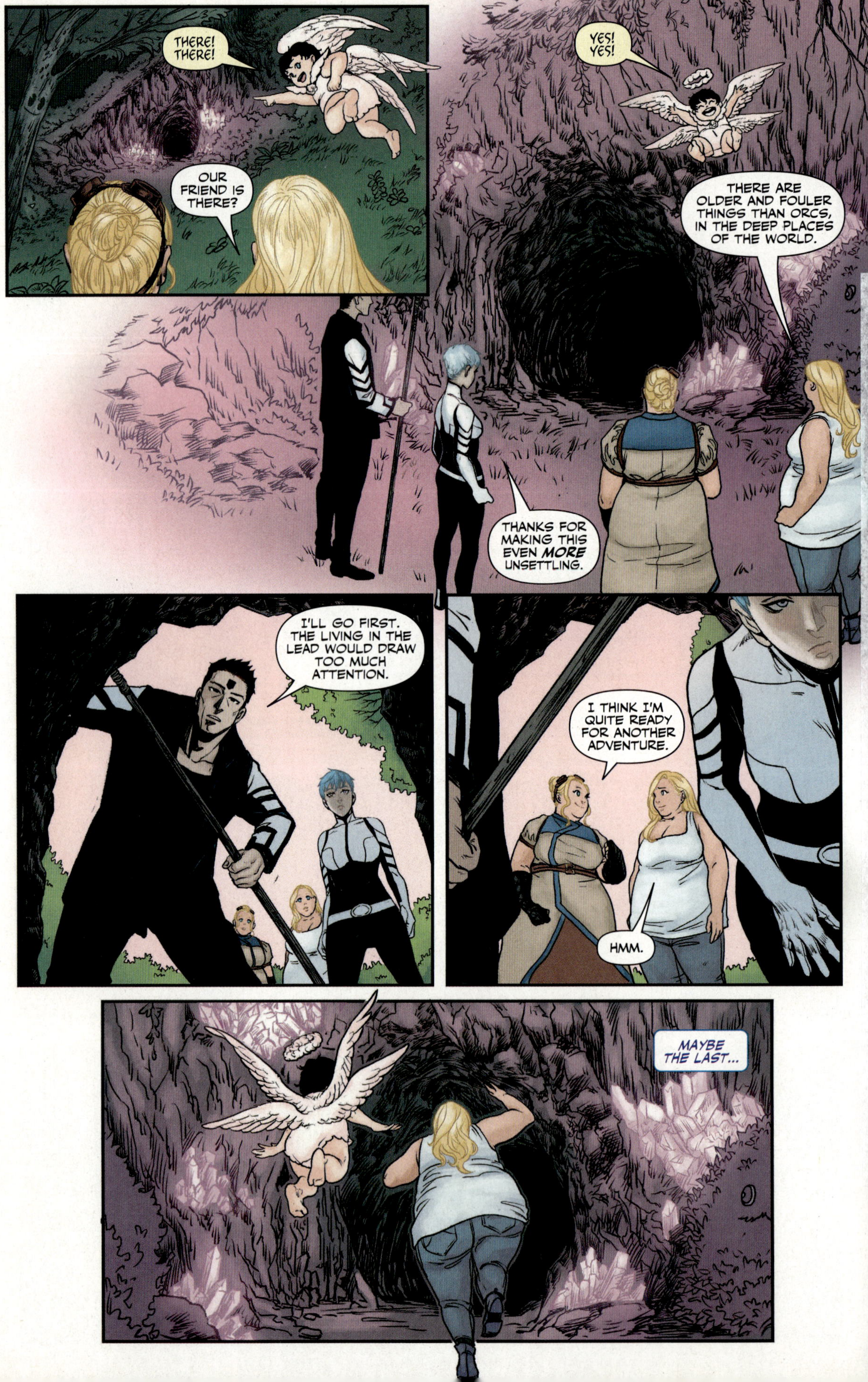
THERE! THERE!
OUR FRIEND IS THERE?
YES! YES!
THERE ARE OLDER AND FOULER THINGS THAN ORCS, IN THE DEEP PLACES OF THE WORLD.
THANKS FOR MAKING THIS EVEN MORE UNSETTLING.
I'LL GO FIRST. THE LIVING IN THE LEAD WOULD DRAW TOO MUCH ATTENTION.
I THINK I'M QUITE READY FOR ANOTHER ADVENTURE.
HMM.
MAYBE THE LAST...

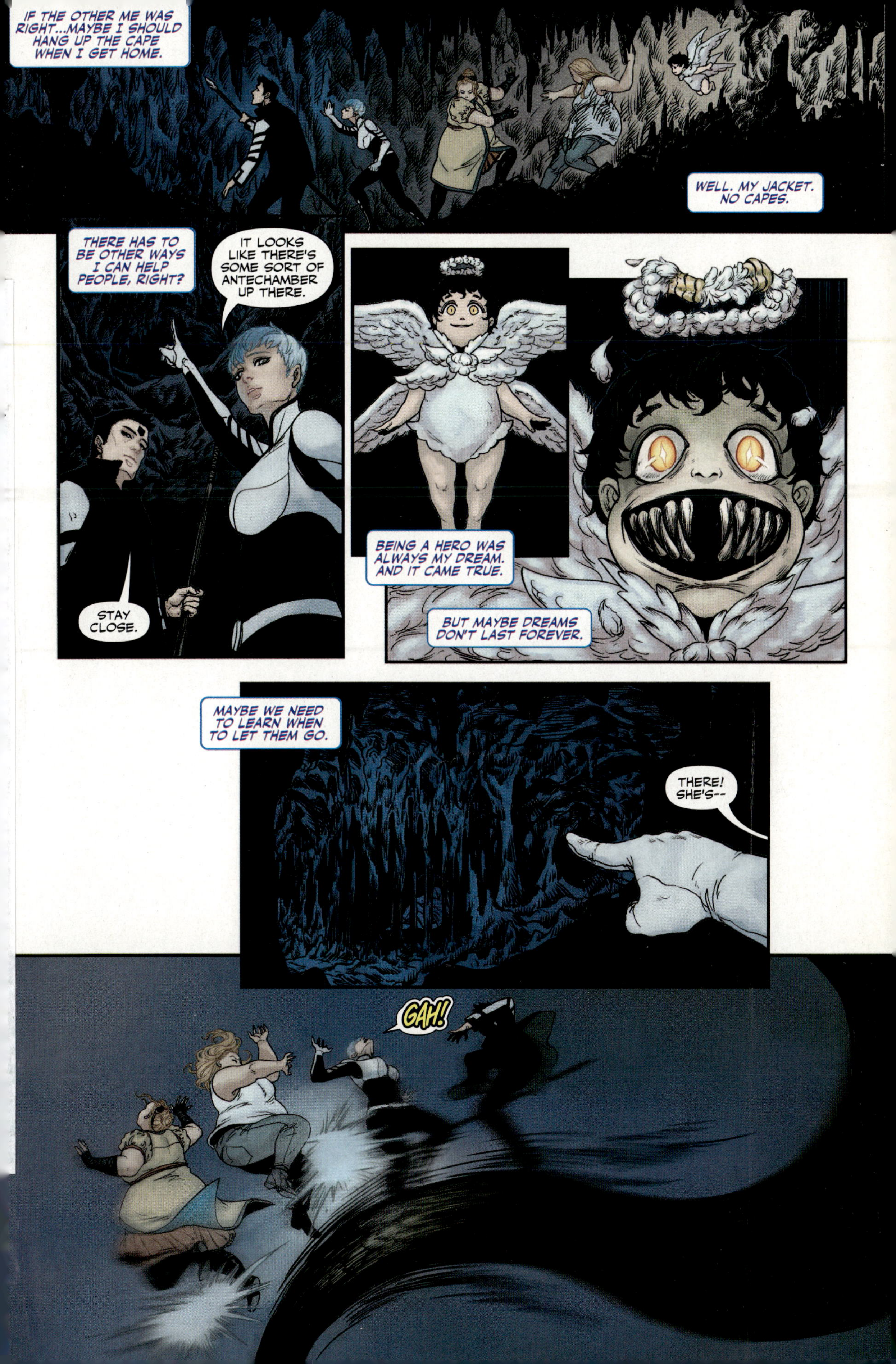
IF THE OTHER ME WAS RIGHT...MAYBE I SHOULD HANG UP THE CAPE WHEN I GET HOME.
WELL. MY JACKET. NO CAPES.
THERE HAS TO BE OTHER WAYS I CAN HELP PEOPLE, RIGHT?
IT LOOKS LIKE THERE'S SOME SORT OF ANTECHAMBER UP THERE.
STAY CLOSE.
BEING A HERO WAS ALWAYS MY DREAM. AND IT CAME TRUE.
BUT MAYBE DREAMS DON'T LAST FOREVER.
MAYBE WE NEED TO LEARN WHEN TO LET THEM GO.
THERE! SHE'S--
GAH!

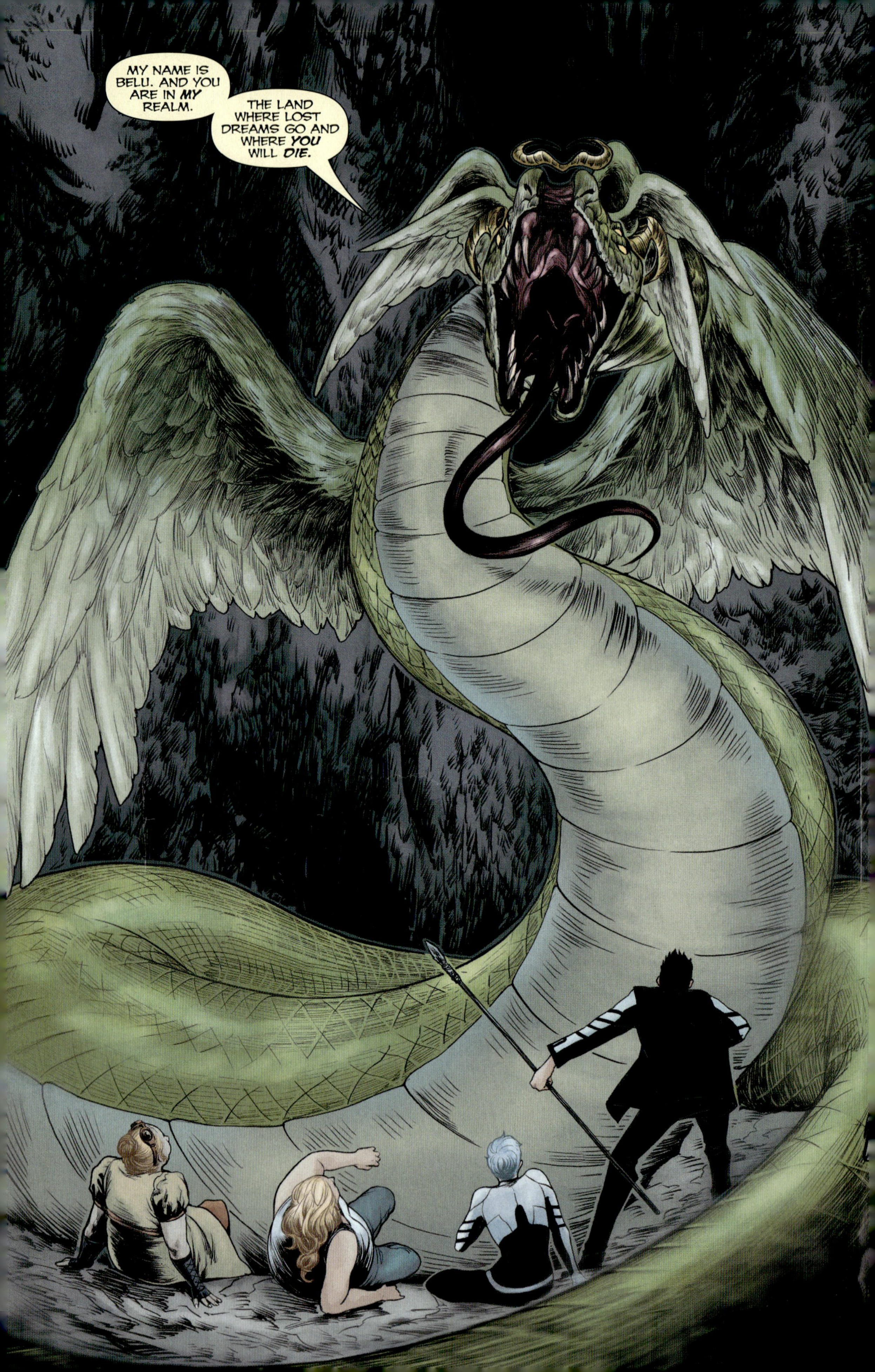
MY NAME IS BELU. AND YOU ARE IN *MY* REALM.
THE LAND WHERE LOST DREAMS GO AND WHERE *YOU* WILL *DIE*.

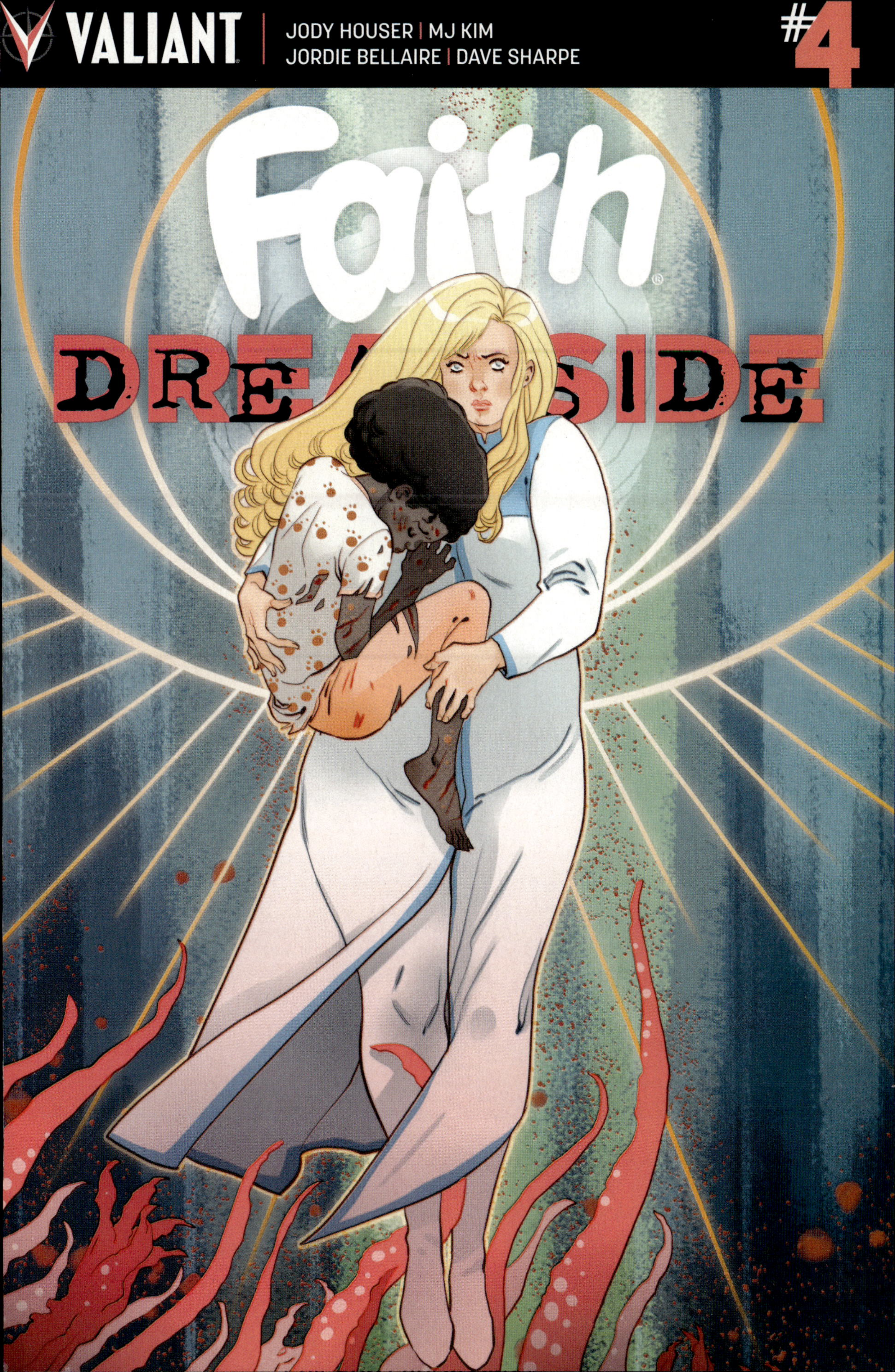
VALIANT
JODY HOUSER | MJ KIM
JORDIE BELLAIRE | DAVE SHARPE
#4
Faith®
DRE SIDE

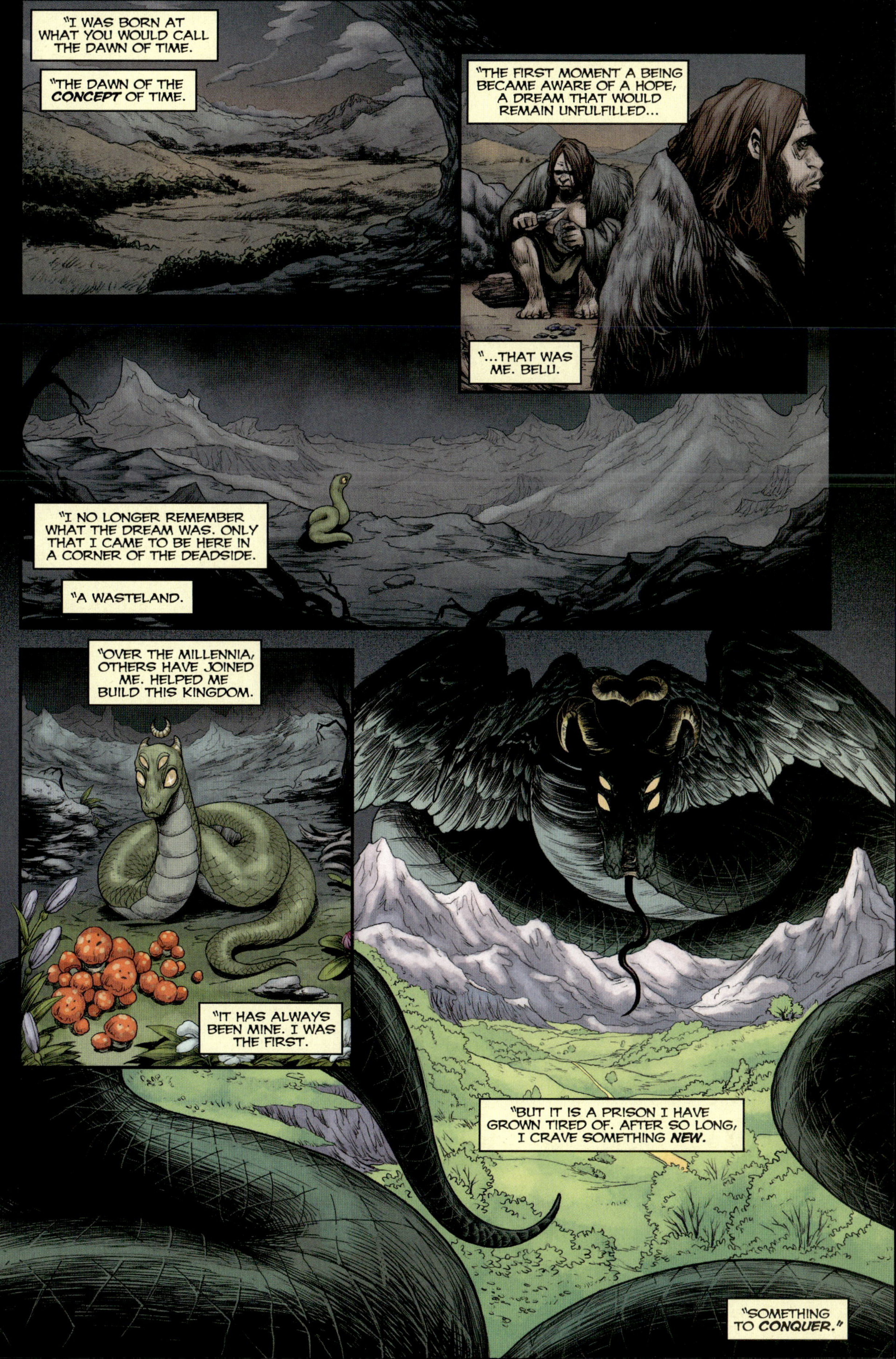
"I WAS BORN AT WHAT YOU WOULD CALL THE DAWN OF TIME.
"THE DAWN OF THE *CONCEPT* OF TIME.
"THE FIRST MOMENT A BEING BECAME AWARE OF A HOPE, A DREAM THAT WOULD REMAIN UNFULFILLED...
"...THAT WAS ME. BELU.
"I NO LONGER REMEMBER WHAT THE DREAM WAS. ONLY THAT I CAME TO BE HERE IN A CORNER OF THE DEADSIDE.
"A WASTELAND.
"OVER THE MILLENNIA, OTHERS HAVE JOINED ME. HELPED ME BUILD THIS KINGDOM.
"IT HAS ALWAYS BEEN MINE. I WAS THE FIRST.
"BUT IT IS A PRISON I HAVE GROWN TIRED OF. AFTER SO LONG, I CRAVE SOMETHING ***NEW***.
"SOMETHING TO ***CONQUER***."

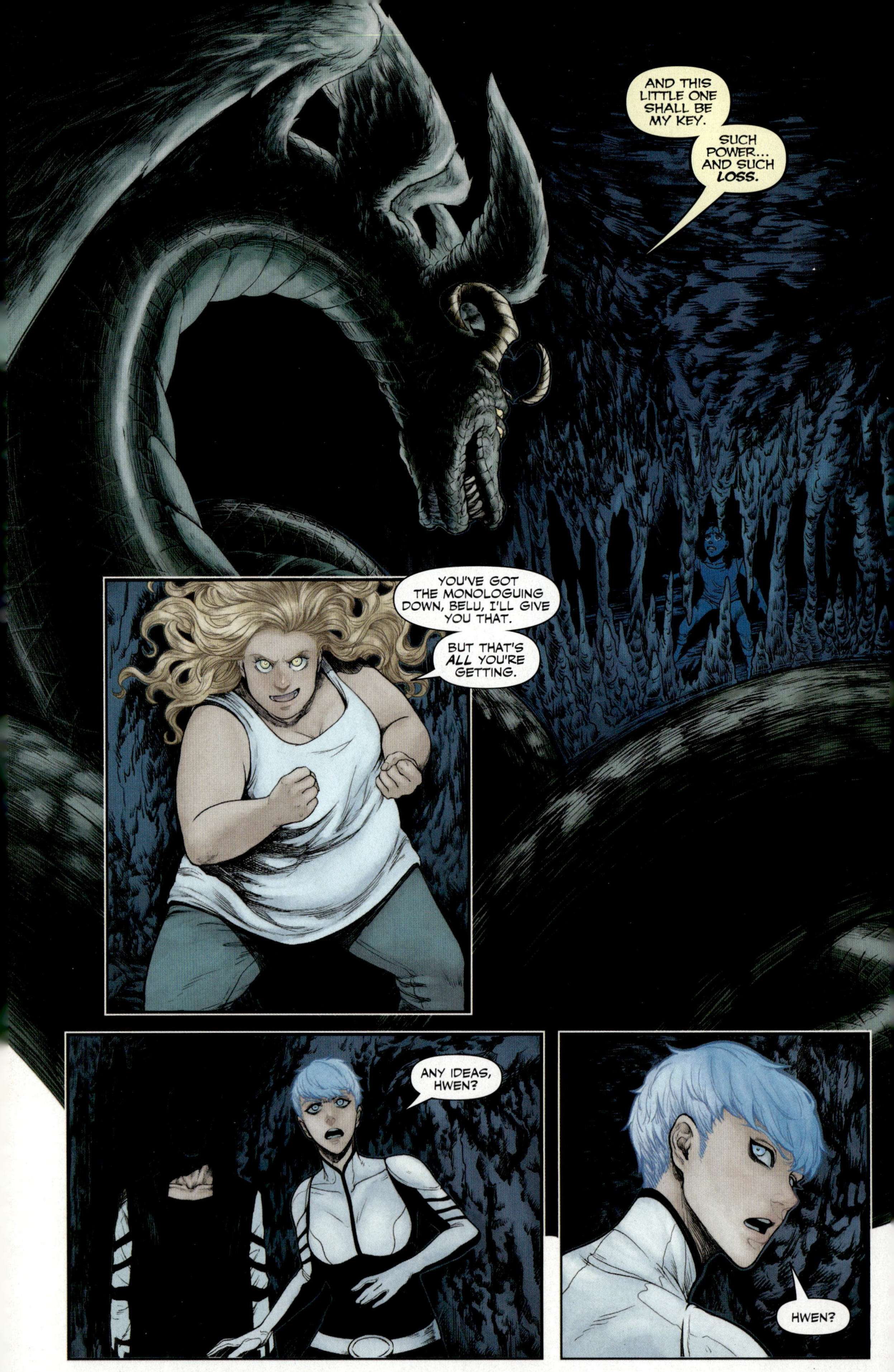
AND THIS LITTLE ONE SHALL BE MY KEY.
SUCH POWER... AND SUCH LOSS.
YOU'VE GOT THE MONOLOGUING DOWN, BELU, I'LL GIVE YOU THAT.
BUT THAT'S ALL YOU'RE GETTING.
ANY IDEAS, HWEN?
HWEN?

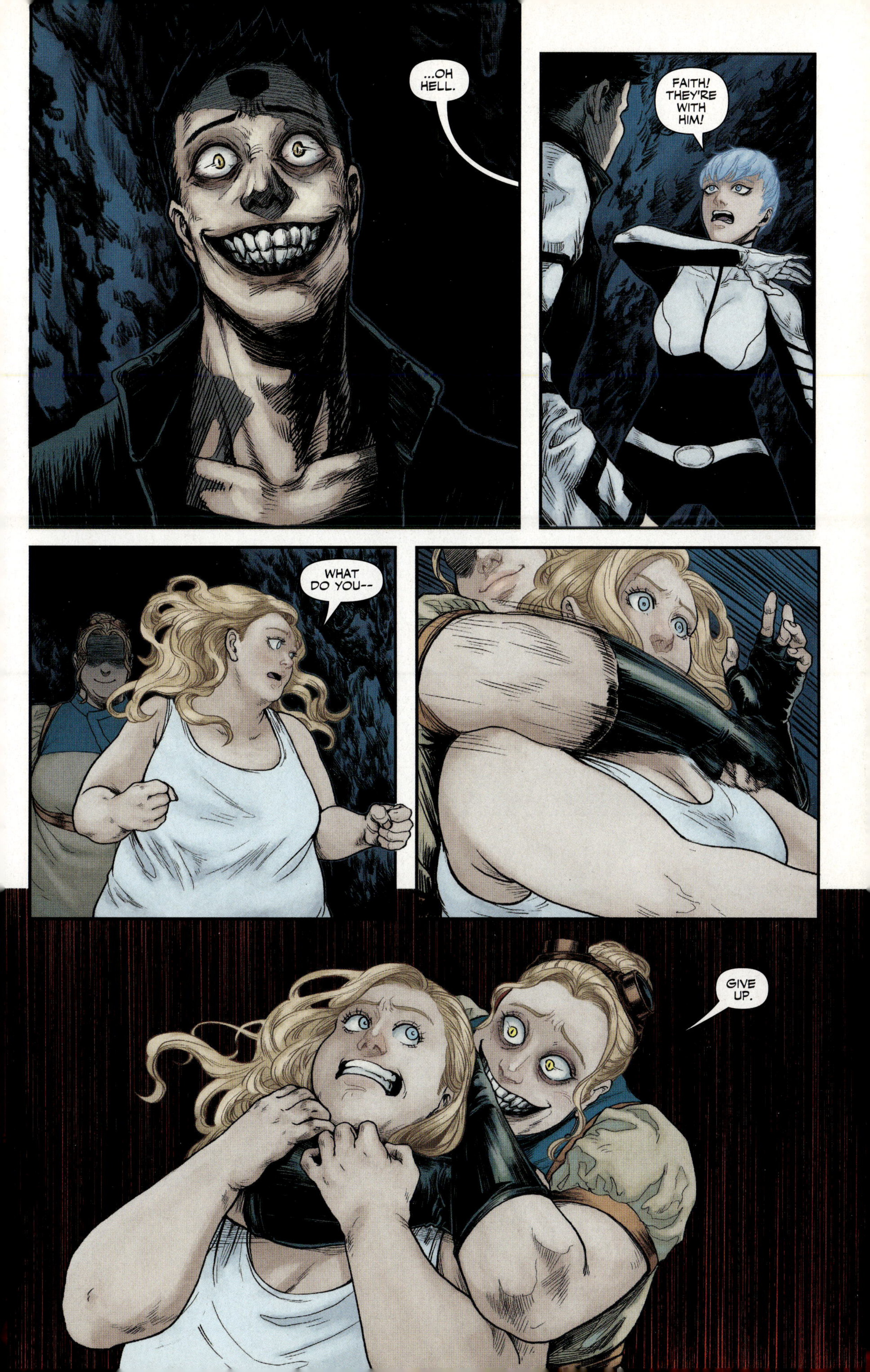
...OH HELL.
FAITH! THEY'RE WITH HIM!
WHAT DO YOU--
GIVE UP.

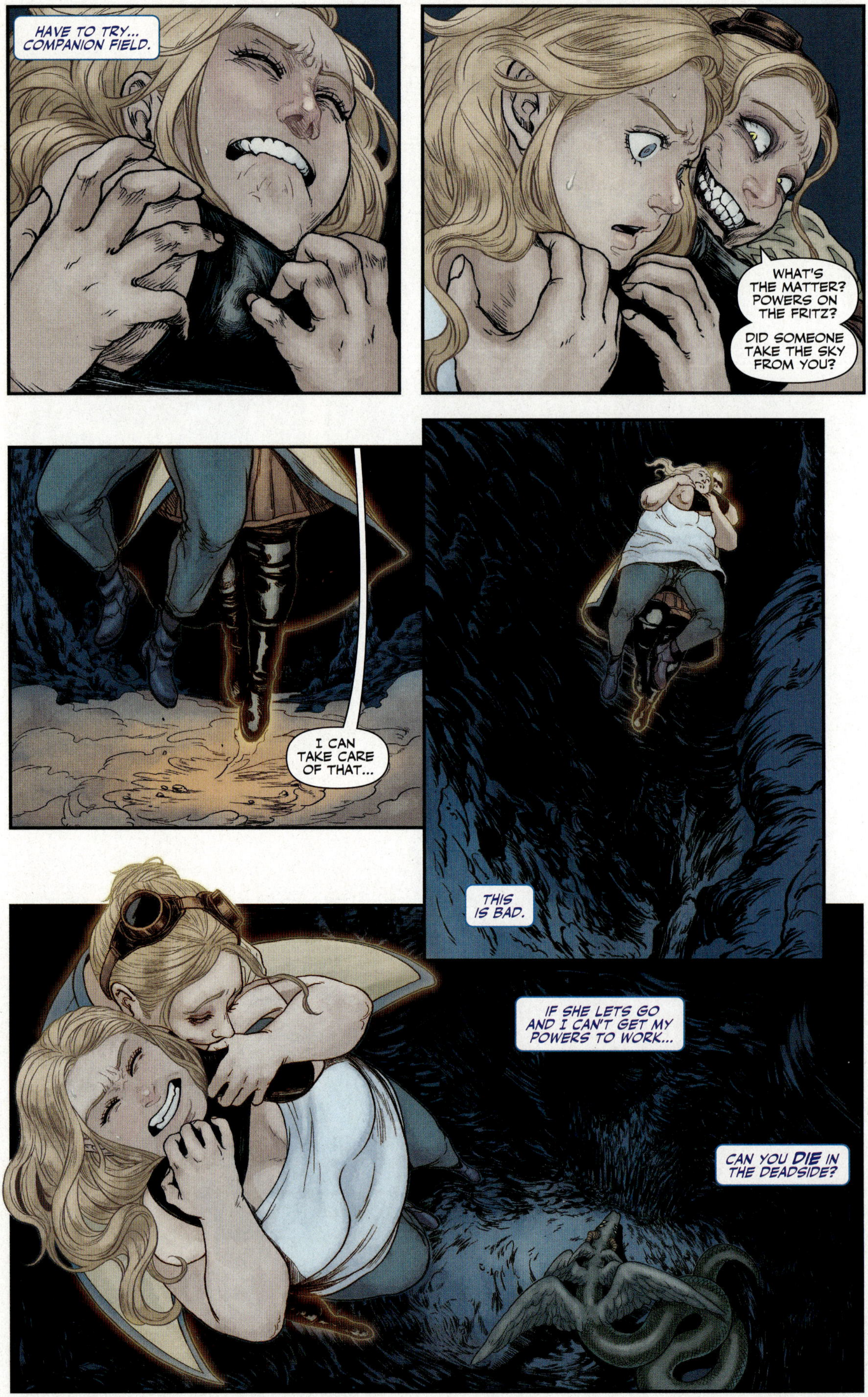
HAVE TO TRY... COMPANION FIELD.
WHAT'S THE MATTER? POWERS ON THE FRITZ?
DID SOMEONE TAKE THE SKY FROM YOU?
I CAN TAKE CARE OF THAT...
THIS IS BAD.
IF SHE LETS GO AND I CAN'T GET MY POWERS TO WORK...
CAN YOU DIE IN THE DEADSIDE?

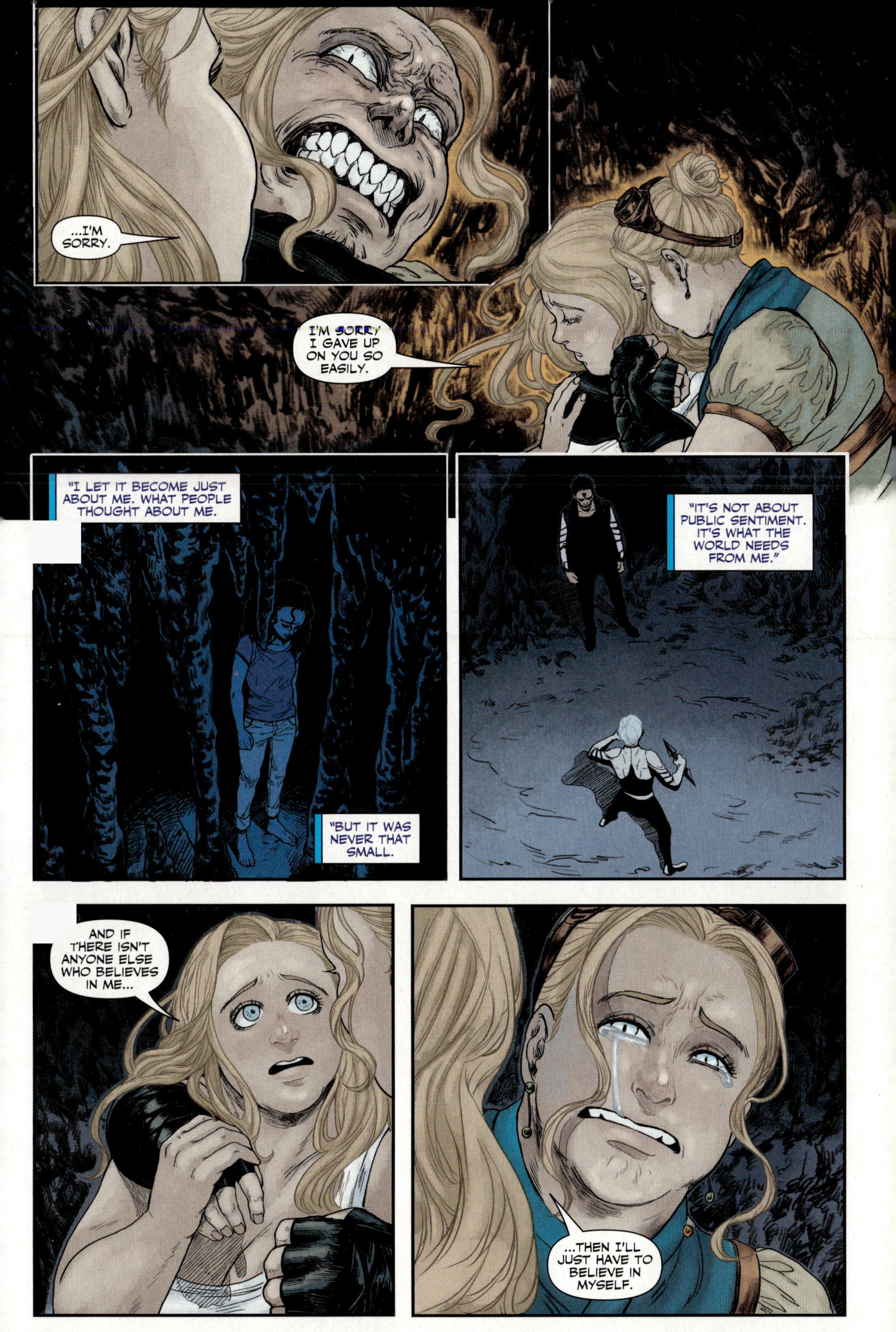
...I'M SORRY.
I'M SORRY I GAVE UP ON YOU SO EASILY.
"I LET IT BECOME JUST ABOUT ME. WHAT PEOPLE THOUGHT ABOUT ME.
"BUT IT WAS NEVER THAT SMALL.
"IT'S NOT ABOUT PUBLIC SENTIMENT. IT'S WHAT THE WORLD NEEDS FROM ME."
AND IF THERE ISN'T ANYONE ELSE WHO BELIEVES IN ME...
...THEN I'LL JUST HAVE TO BELIEVE IN MYSELF.

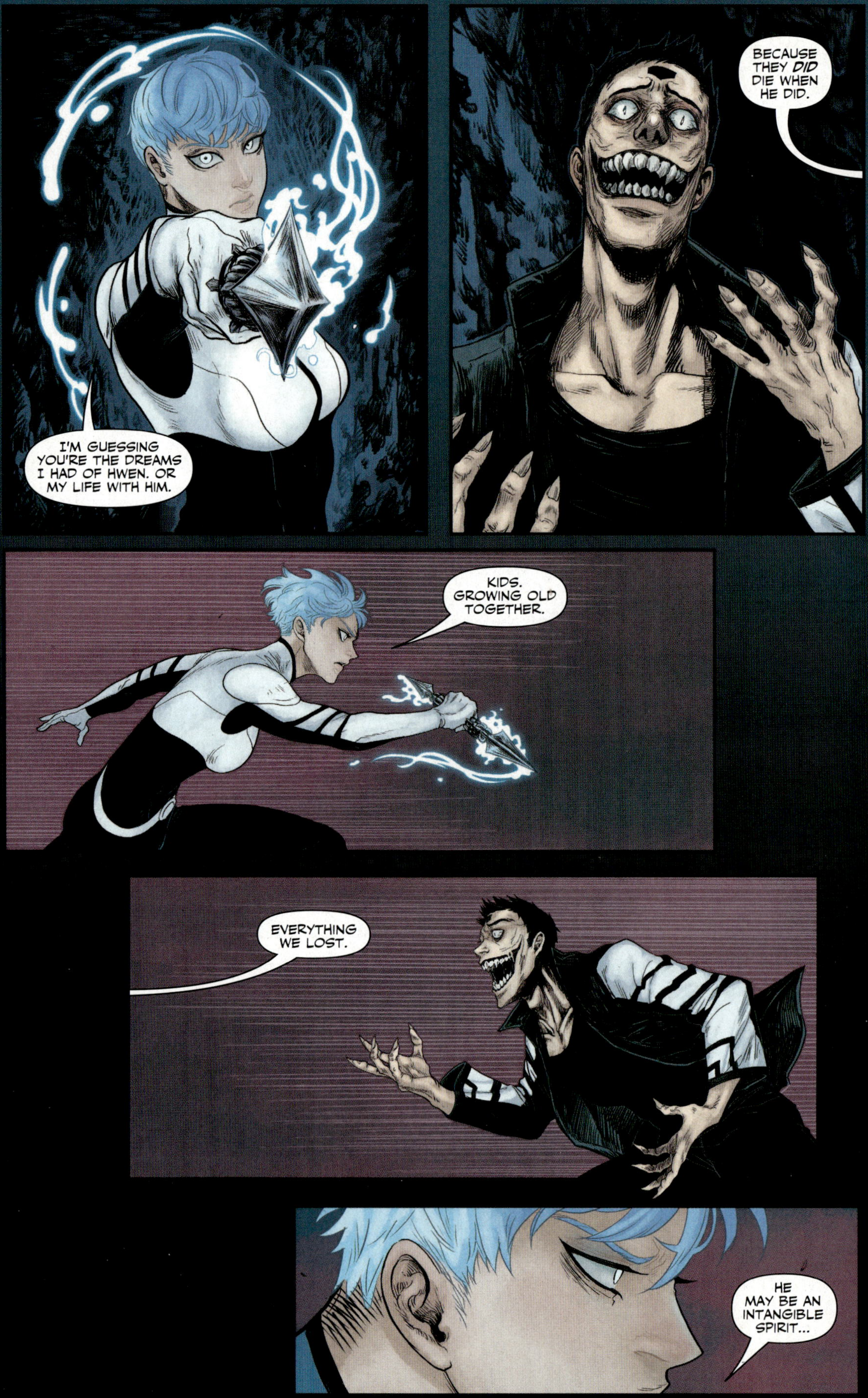
I'M GUESSING YOU'RE THE DREAMS I HAD OF HWEN. OR MY LIFE WITH HIM.
BECAUSE THEY *DID* DIE WHEN HE DID.
KIDS. GROWING OLD TOGETHER.
EVERYTHING WE LOST.
HE MAY BE AN INTANGIBLE SPIRIT...

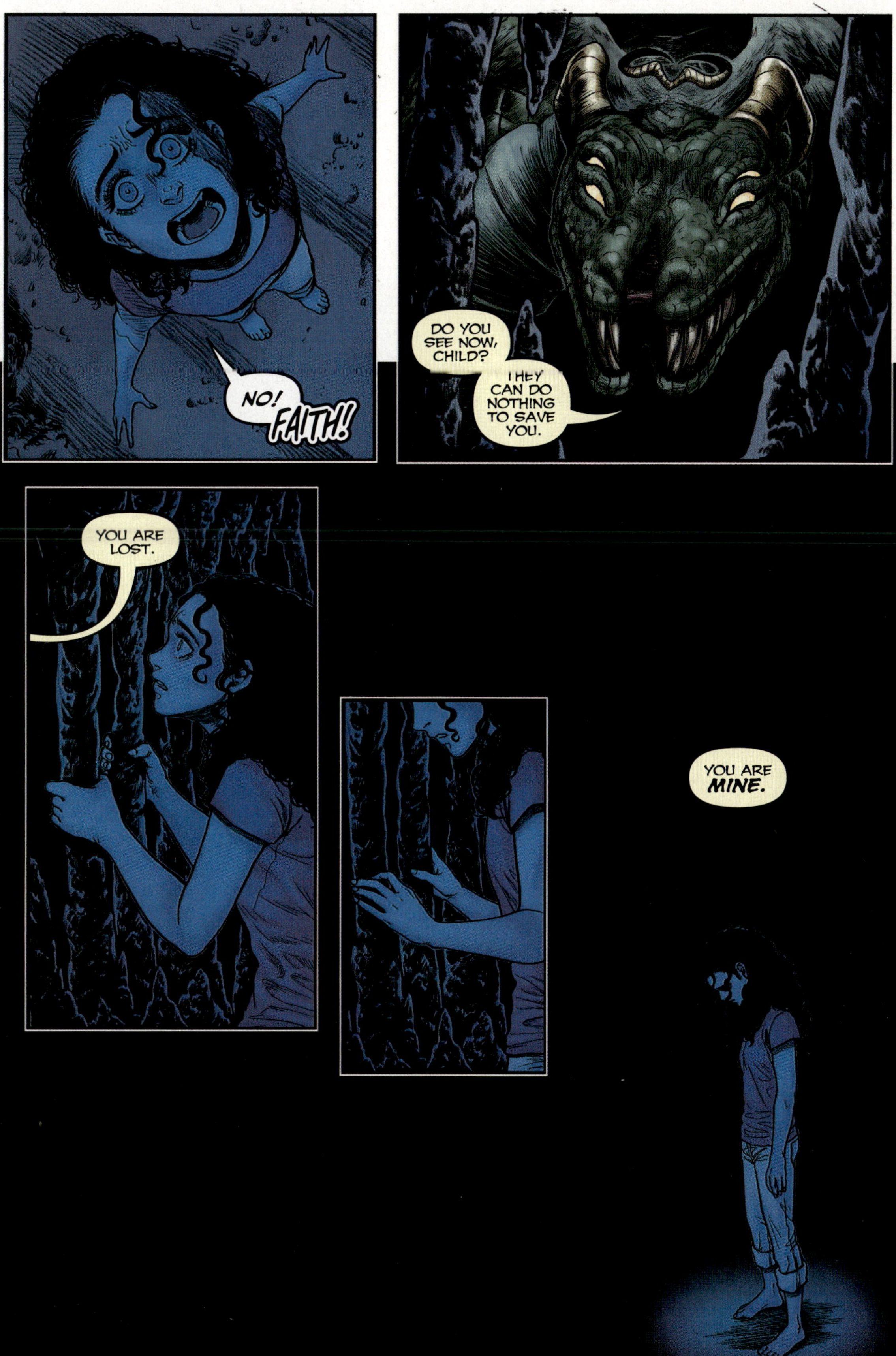
NO! FAITH!
DO YOU SEE NOW, CHILD?
THEY CAN DO NOTHING TO SAVE YOU.
YOU ARE LOST.
YOU ARE MINE.

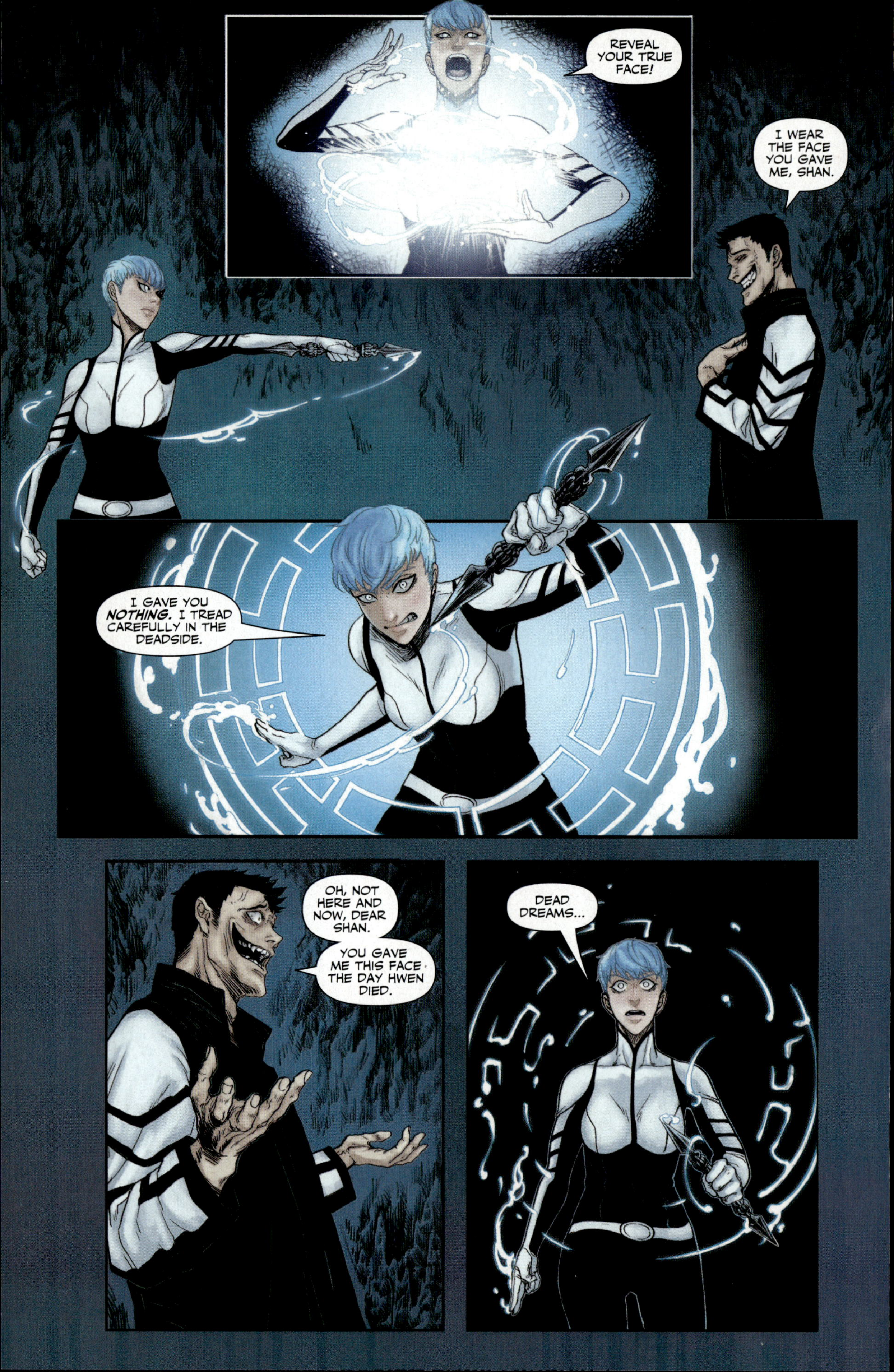
REVEAL YOUR TRUE FACE!
I WEAR THE FACE YOU GAVE ME, SHAN.
I GAVE YOU *NOTHING.* I TREAD CAREFULLY IN THE DEADSIDE.
OH, NOT HERE AND NOW, DEAR SHAN.
YOU GAVE ME THIS FACE THE DAY HWEN DIED.
DEAD DREAMS...

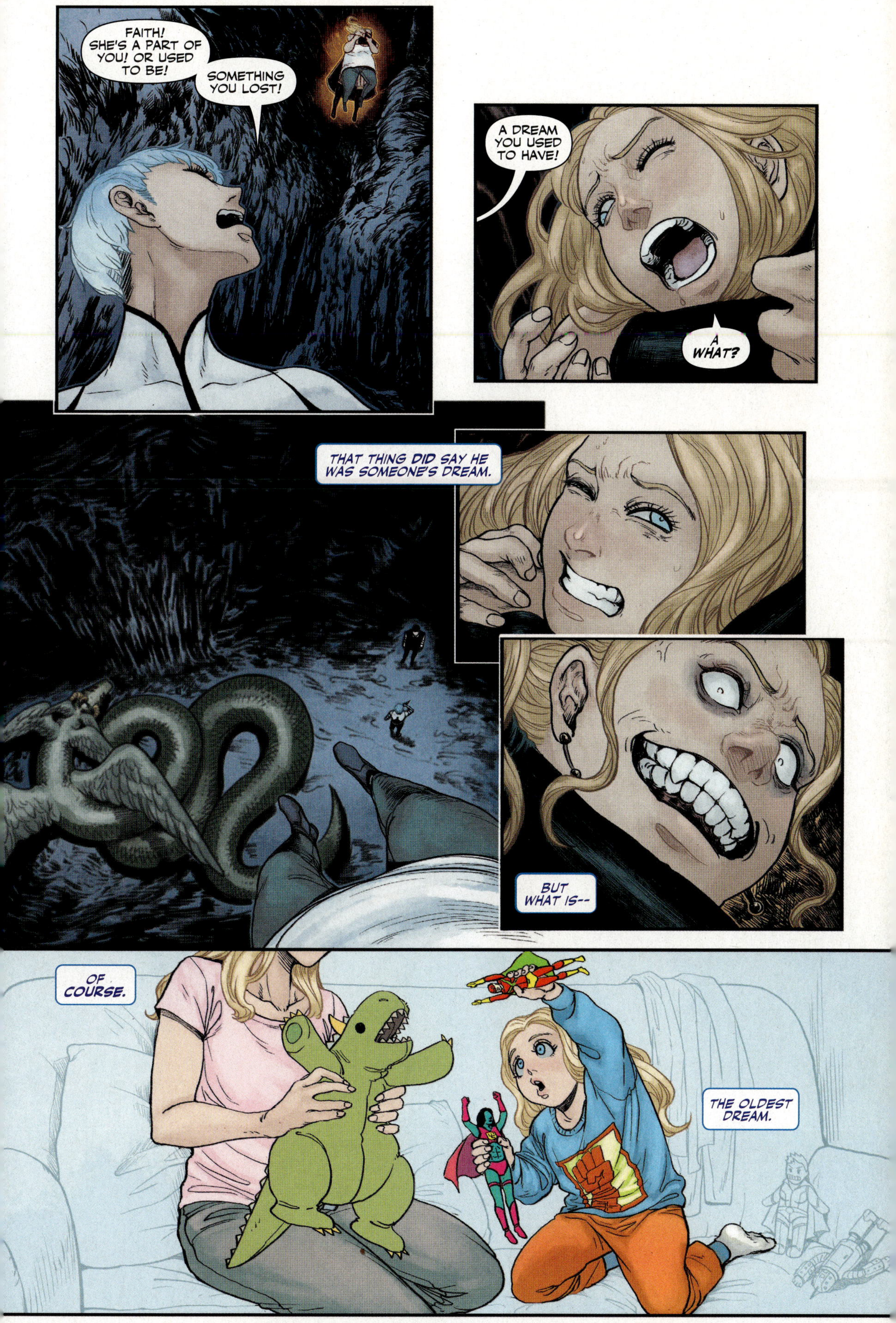
FAITH! SHE'S A PART OF YOU! OR USED TO BE!
SOMETHING YOU LOST!
A DREAM YOU USED TO HAVE!
A WHAT?
THAT THING DID SAY HE WAS SOMEONE'S DREAM.
BUT WHAT IS--
OF COURSE.
THE OLDEST DREAM.

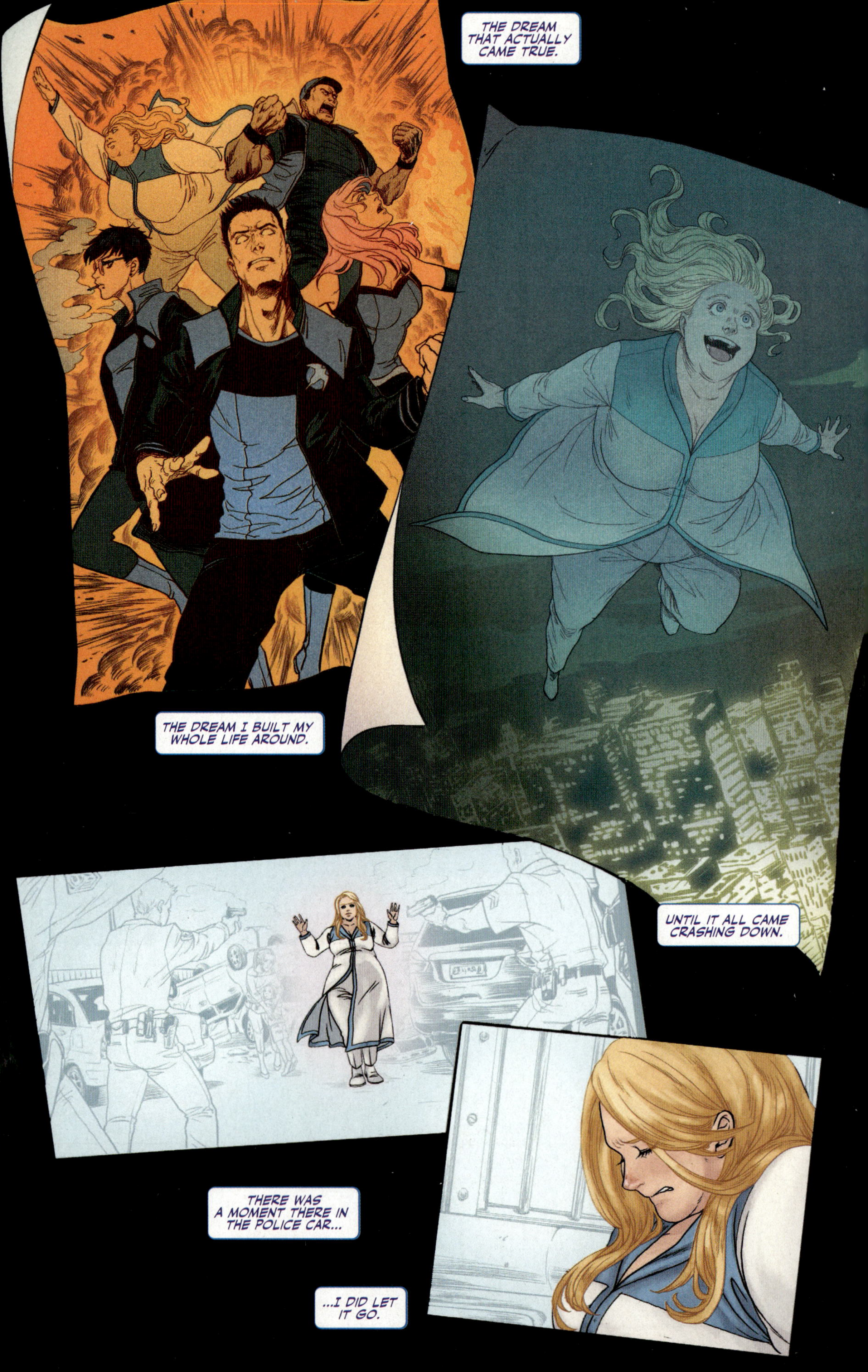
THE DREAM THAT ACTUALLY CAME TRUE.
THE DREAM I BUILT MY WHOLE LIFE AROUND.
UNTIL IT ALL CAME CRASHING DOWN.
THERE WAS A MOMENT THERE IN THE POLICE CAR...
...I DID LET IT GO.

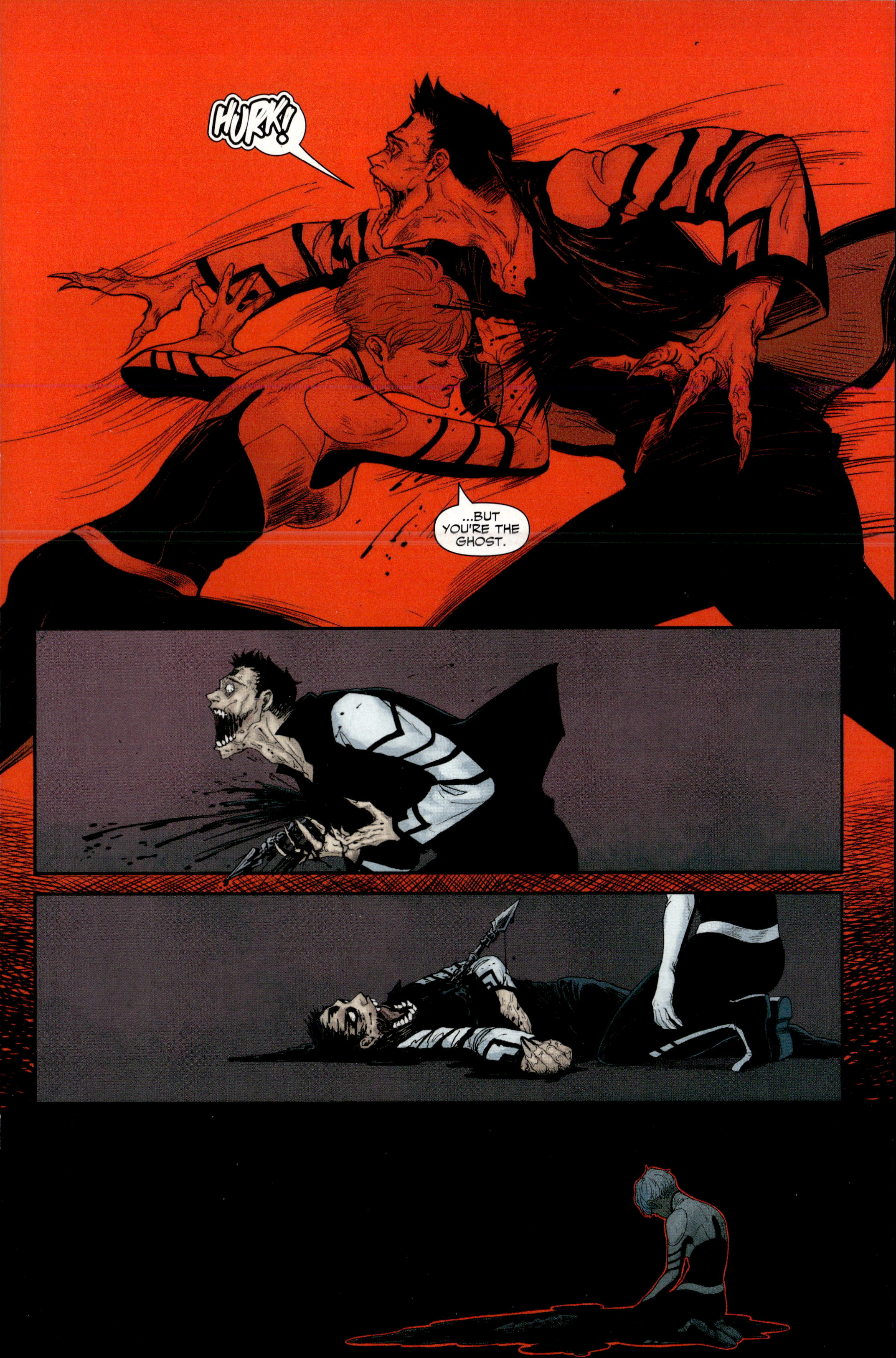
HURK!
...BUT YOU'RE THE GHOST.

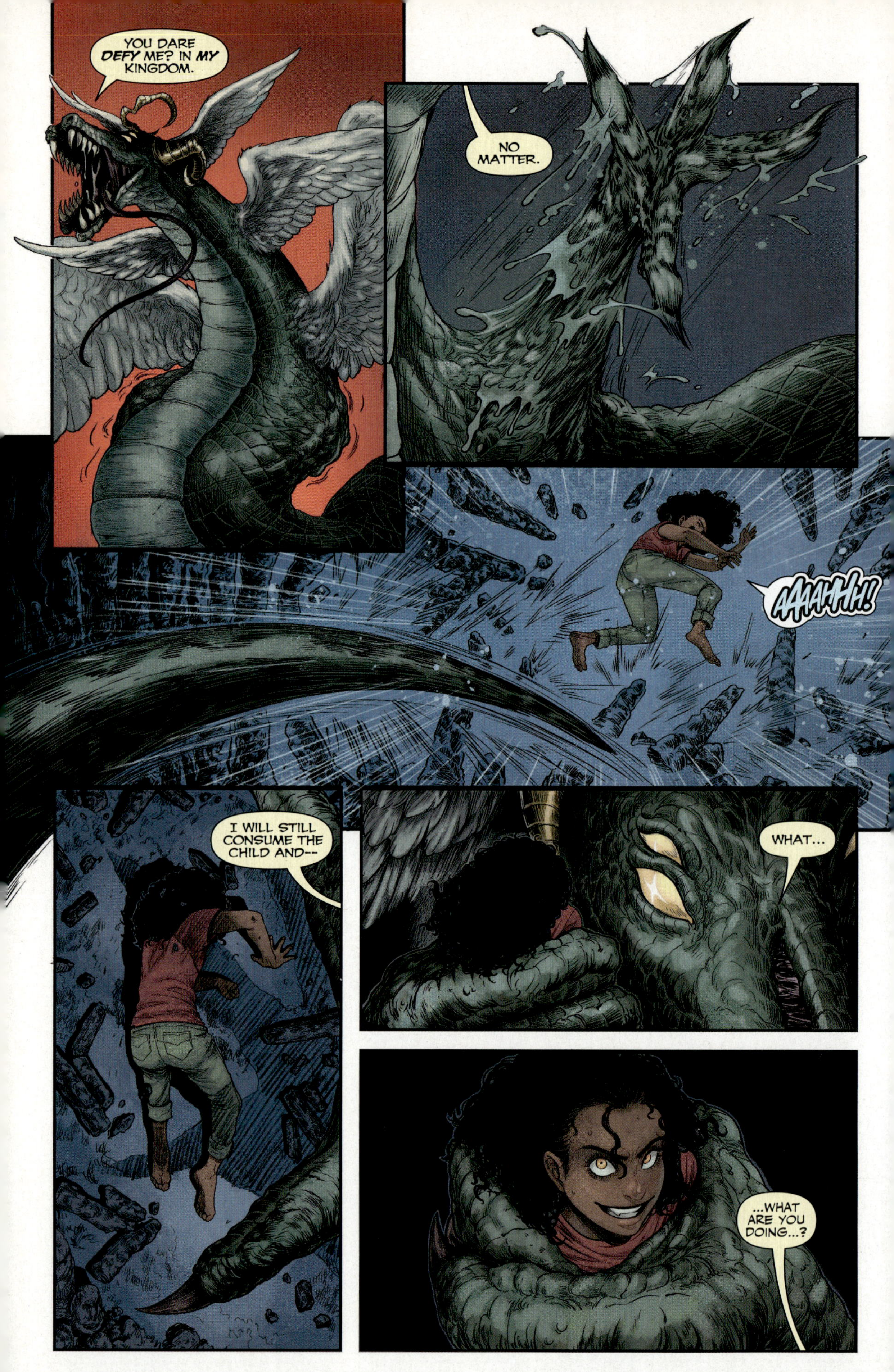
YOU DARE DEFY ME? IN MY KINGDOM.
NO MATTER.
AAAAHHH!
I WILL STILL CONSUME THE CHILD AND--
WHAT...
...WHAT ARE YOU DOING...?

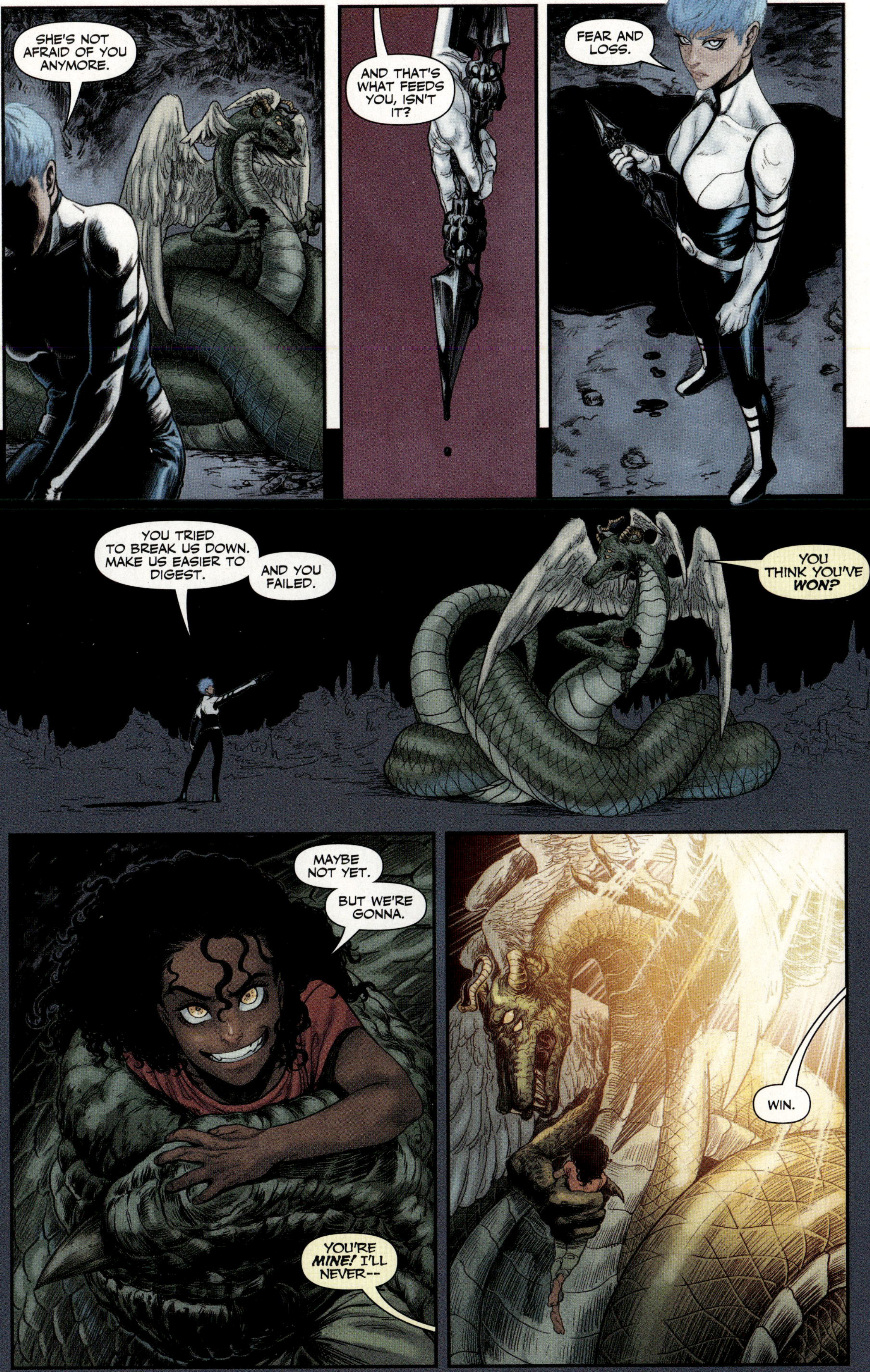
SHE'S NOT AFRAID OF YOU ANYMORE.
AND THAT'S WHAT FEEDS YOU, ISN'T IT?
FEAR AND LOSS.
YOU TRIED TO BREAK US DOWN. MAKE US EASIER TO DIGEST.
AND YOU FAILED.
YOU THINK YOU'VE WON?
MAYBE NOT YET.
BUT WE'RE GONNA.
YOU'RE MINE! I'LL NEVER--
WIN.

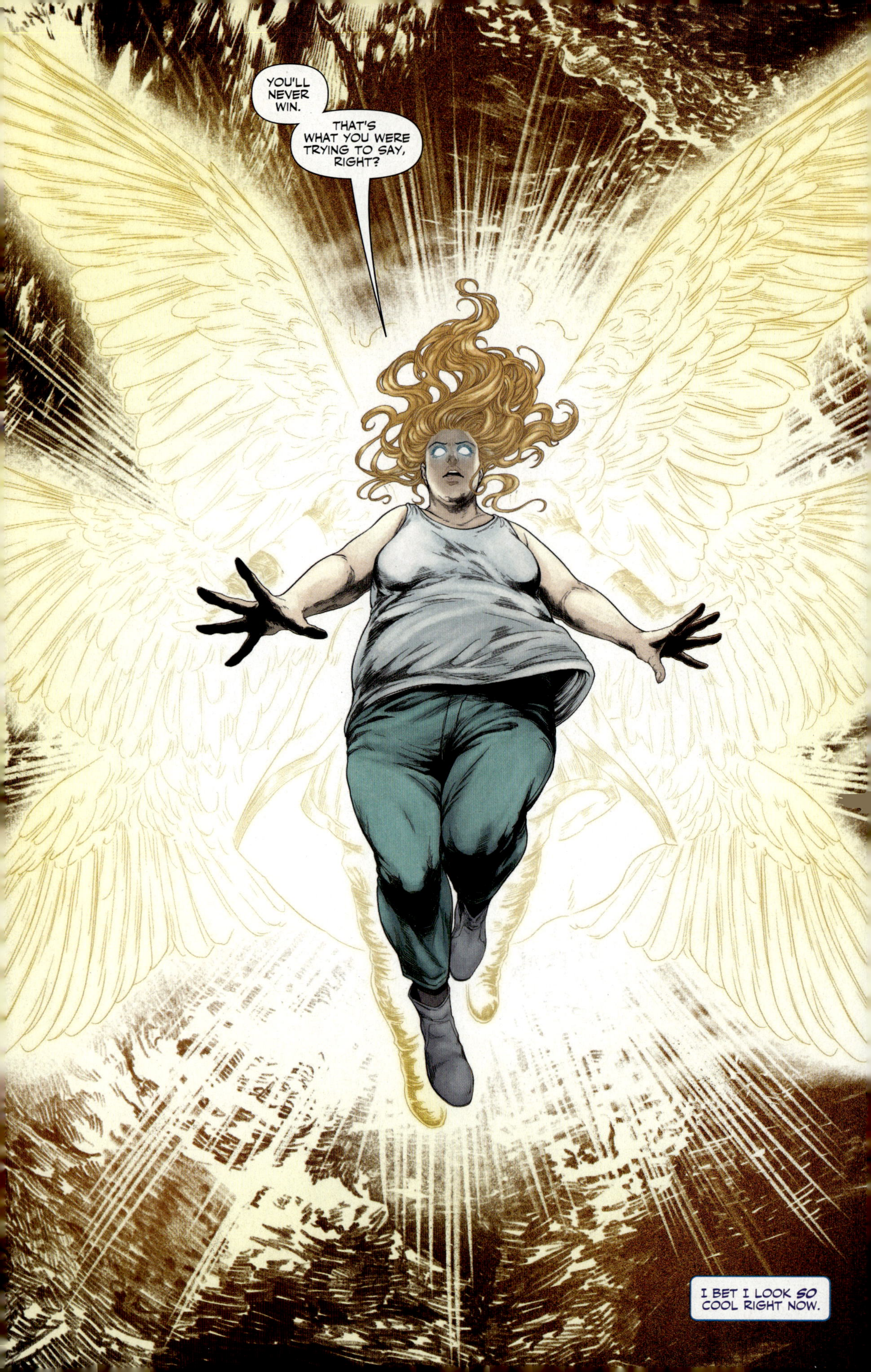
YOU'LL NEVER WIN.
THAT'S WHAT YOU WERE TRYING TO SAY, RIGHT?
I BET I LOOK *SO* COOL RIGHT NOW.

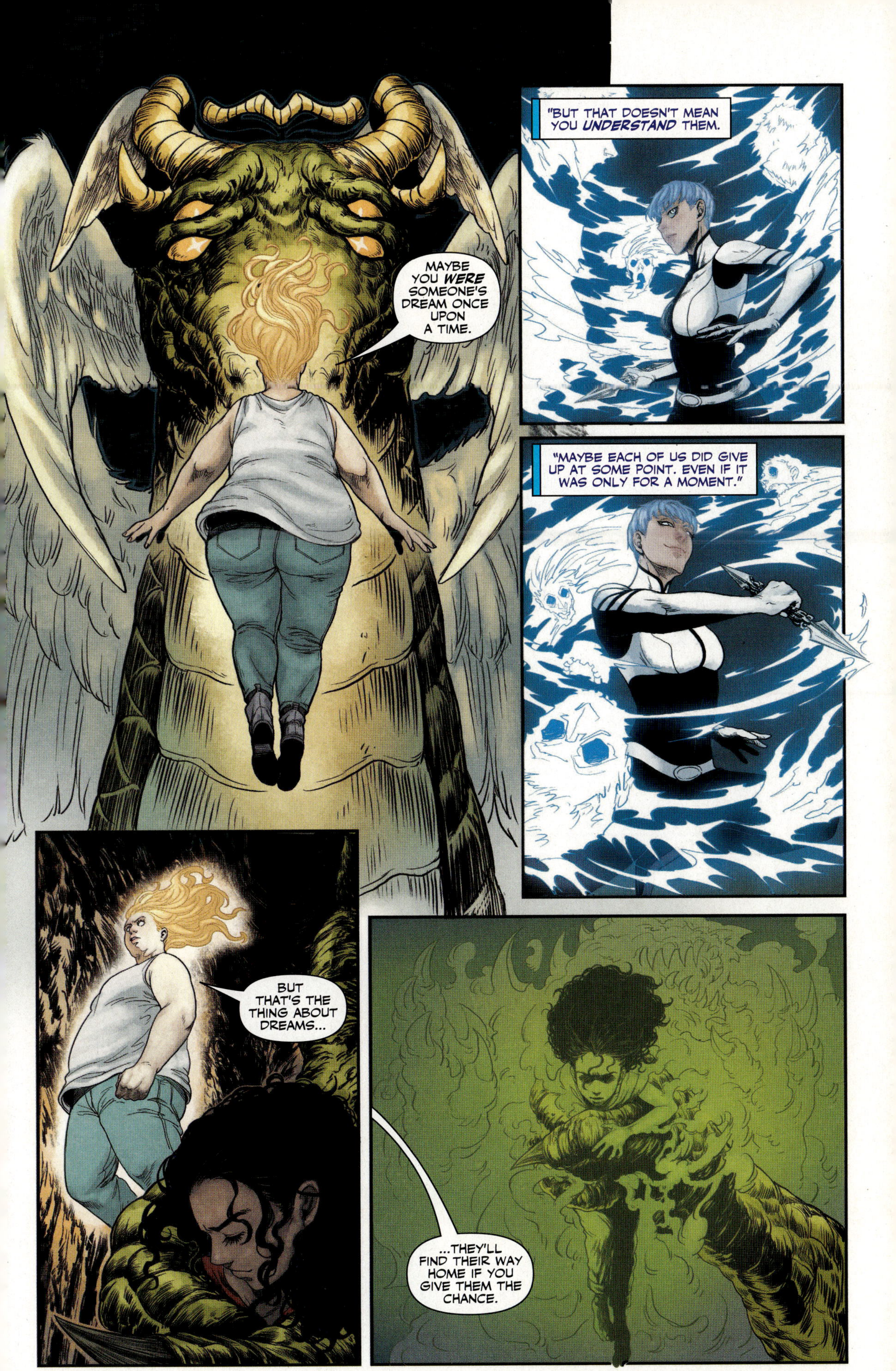
MAYBE YOU *WERE* SOMEONE'S DREAM ONCE UPON A TIME.
"BUT THAT DOESN'T MEAN YOU *UNDERSTAND* THEM.
"MAYBE EACH OF US DID GIVE UP AT SOME POINT. EVEN IF IT WAS ONLY FOR A MOMENT."
BUT THAT'S THE THING ABOUT DREAMS...
...THEY'LL FIND THEIR WAY HOME IF YOU GIVE THEM THE CHANCE.

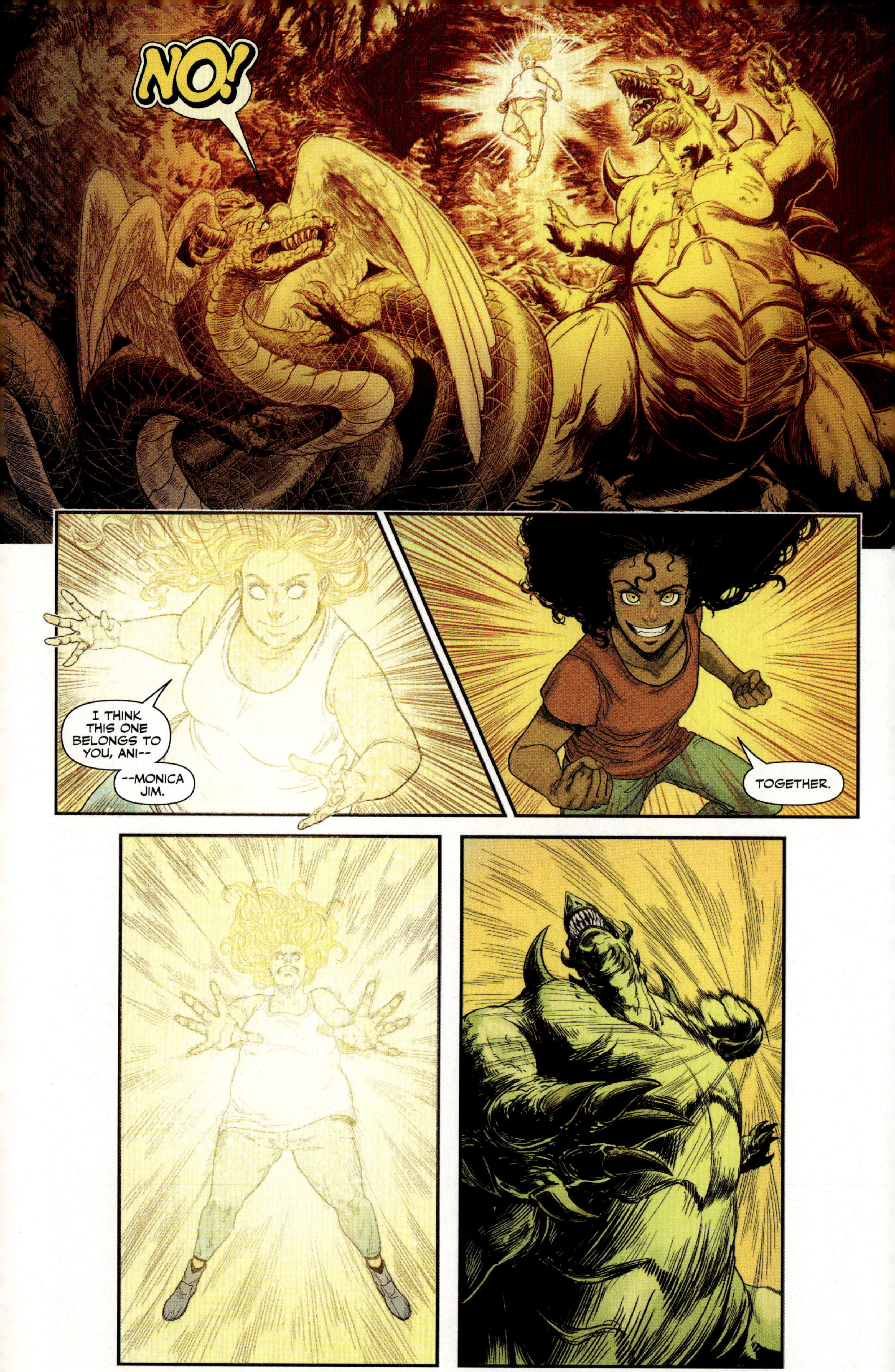
NO!
I THINK THIS ONE BELONGS TO YOU, ANI--
--MONICA JIM.
TOGETHER.

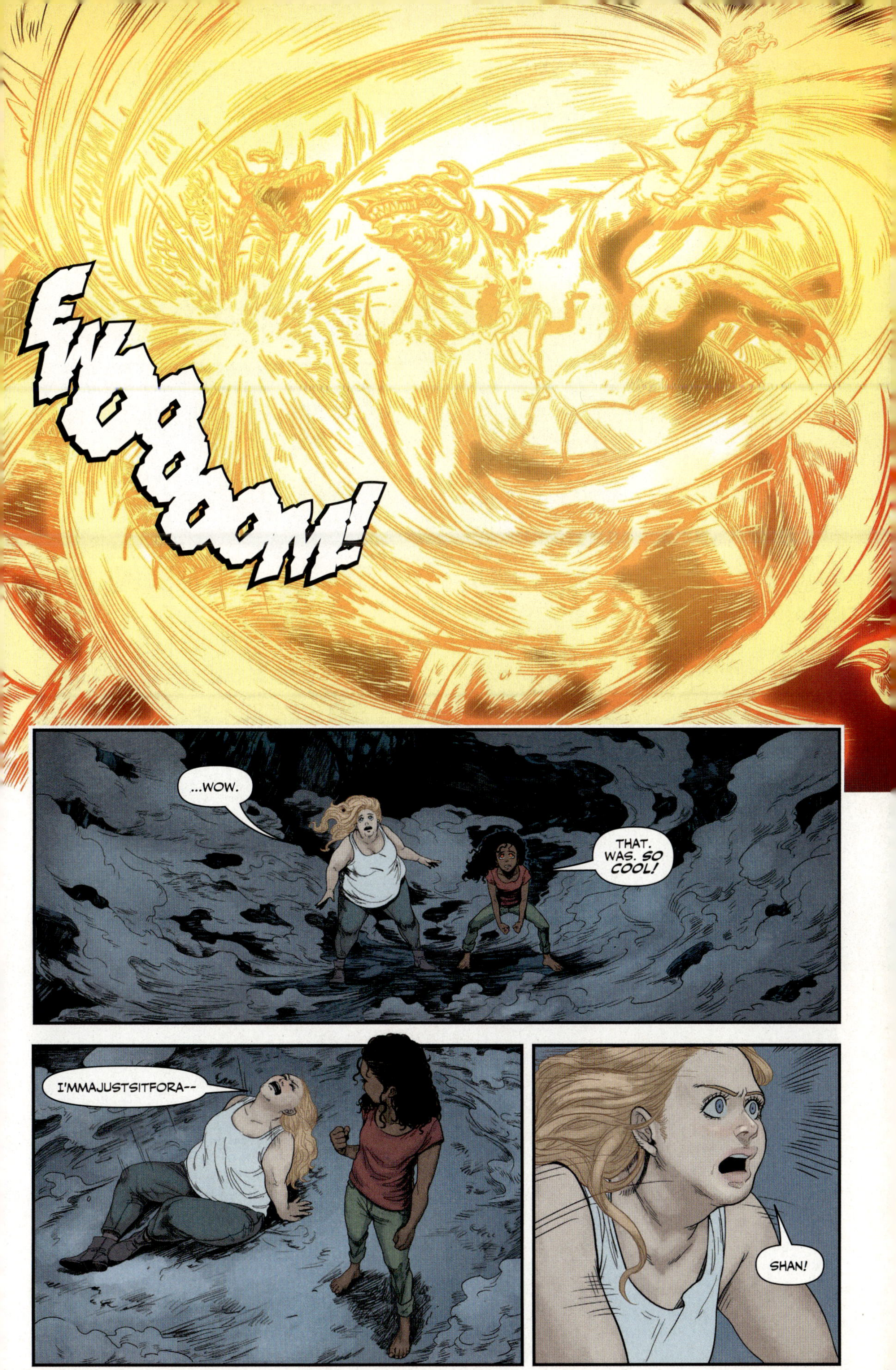

FWOOOOOM!
...WOW.
THAT. WAS. SO COOL!
I'MMAJUSTSITFORA--
SHAN!

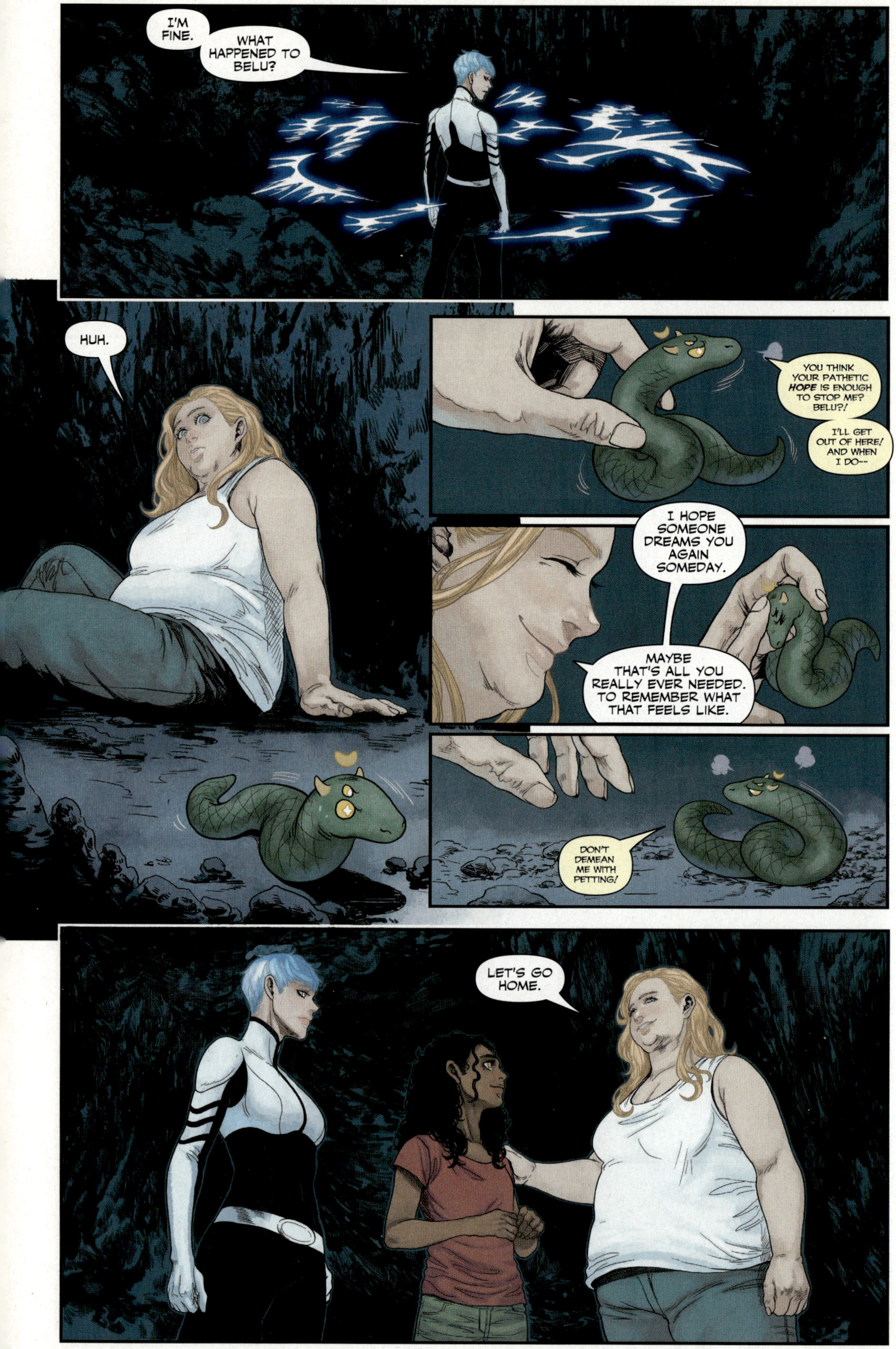
I'M FINE.
WHAT HAPPENED TO BELU?
HUH.
YOU THINK YOUR PATHETIC HOPE IS ENOUGH TO STOP ME? BELU?!
I'LL GET OUT OF HERE! AND WHEN I DO--
I HOPE SOMEONE DREAMS YOU AGAIN SOMEDAY.
MAYBE THAT'S ALL YOU REALLY EVER NEEDED. TO REMEMBER WHAT THAT FEELS LIKE.
DON'T DEMEAN ME WITH PETTING!
LET'S GO HOME.

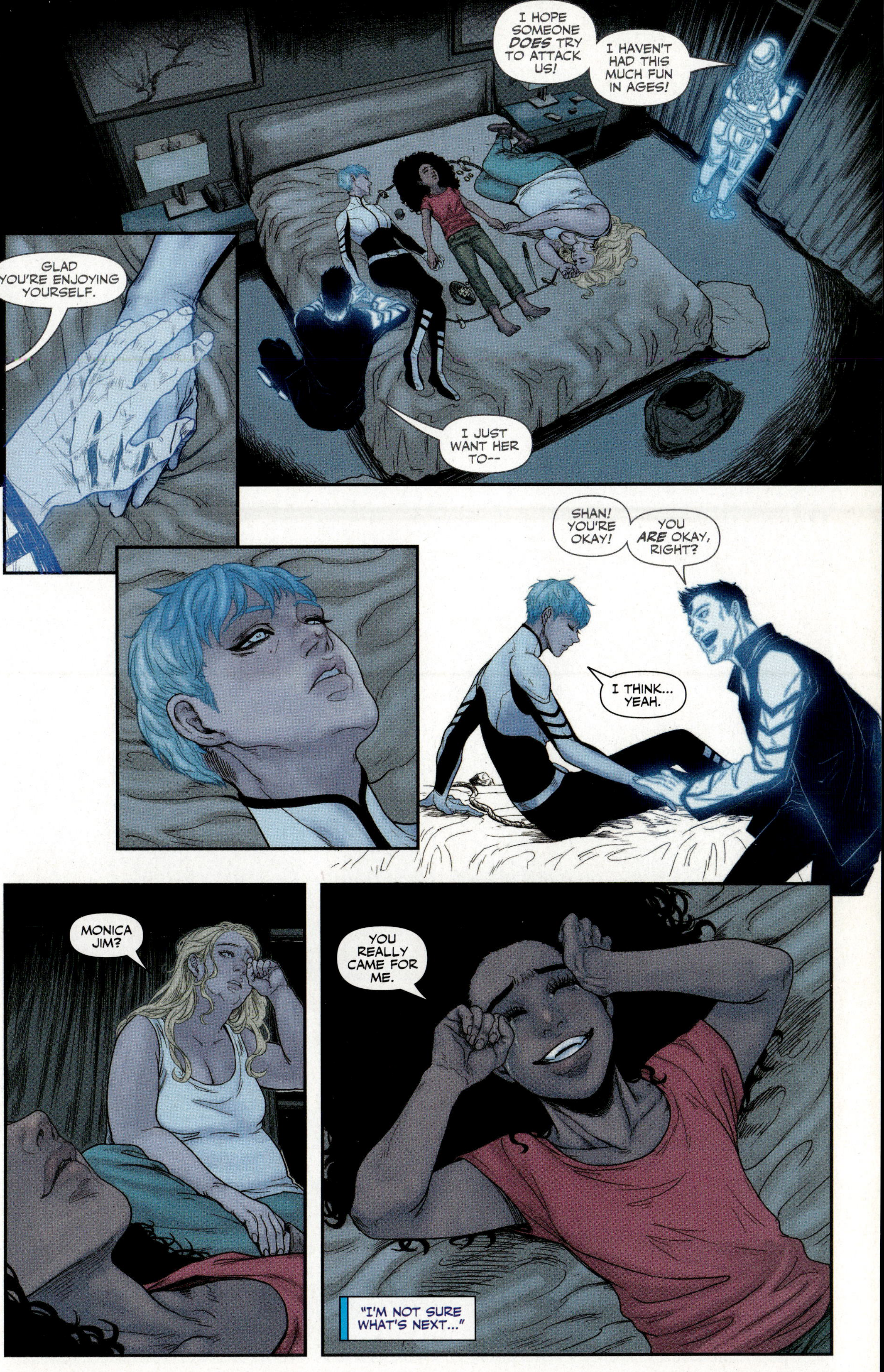
I HOPE SOMEONE *DOES* TRY TO ATTACK US!
I HAVEN'T HAD THIS MUCH FUN IN AGES!
GLAD YOU'RE ENJOYING YOURSELF.
I JUST WANT HER TO--
SHAN! YOU'RE OKAY!
YOU *ARE* OKAY, RIGHT?
I THINK... YEAH.
MONICA JIM?
YOU REALLY CAME FOR ME.
"I'M NOT SURE WHAT'S NEXT..."

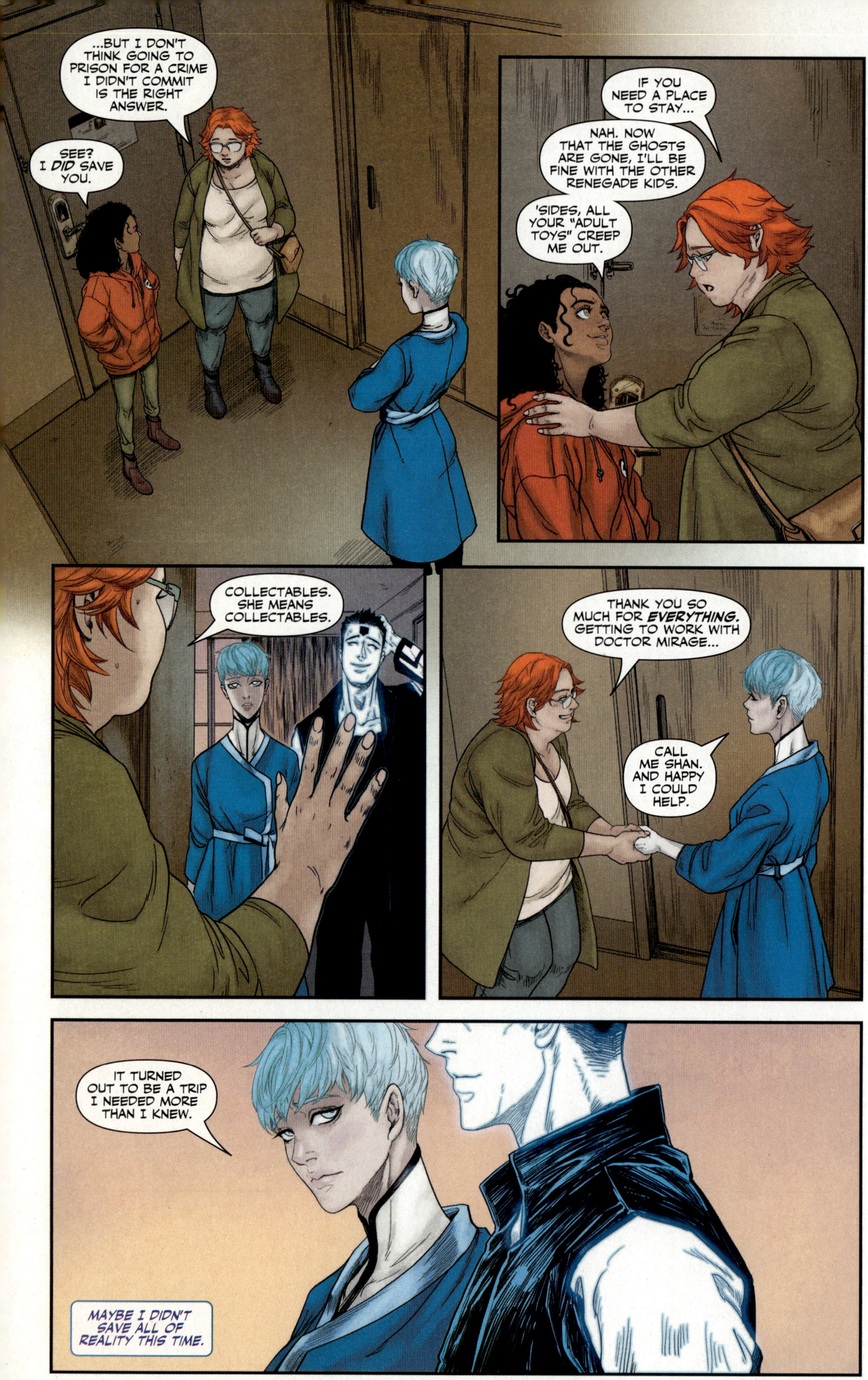
...BUT I DON'T THINK GOING TO PRISON FOR A CRIME I DIDN'T COMMIT IS THE RIGHT ANSWER.
SEE? I *DID* SAVE YOU.
IF YOU NEED A PLACE TO STAY...
NAH. NOW THAT THE GHOSTS ARE GONE, I'LL BE FINE WITH THE OTHER RENEGADE KIDS.
'SIDES, ALL YOUR "ADULT TOYS" CREEP ME OUT.
COLLECTABLES. SHE MEANS COLLECTABLES.
THANK YOU SO MUCH FOR *EVERYTHING.* GETTING TO WORK WITH DOCTOR MIRAGE...
CALL ME SHAN. AND HAPPY I COULD HELP.
IT TURNED OUT TO BE A TRIP I NEEDED MORE THAN I KNEW.
MAYBE I DIDN'T SAVE ALL OF REALITY THIS TIME.

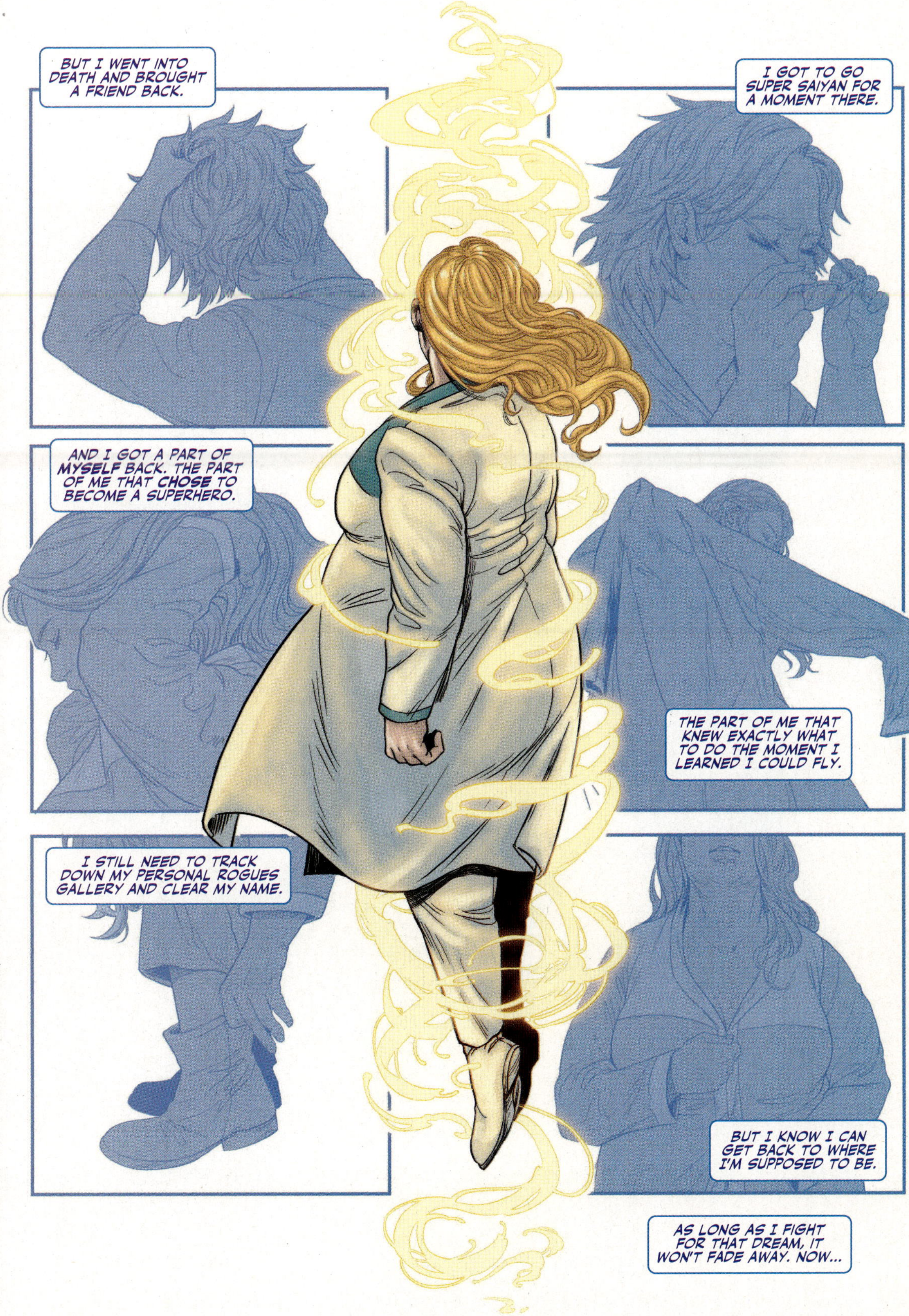
BUT I WENT INTO DEATH AND BROUGHT A FRIEND BACK.
I GOT TO GO SUPER SAIYAN FOR A MOMENT THERE.
AND I GOT A PART OF MYSELF BACK. THE PART OF ME THAT CHOSE TO BECOME A SUPERHERO.
THE PART OF ME THAT KNEW EXACTLY WHAT TO DO THE MOMENT I LEARNED I COULD FLY.
I STILL NEED TO TRACK DOWN MY PERSONAL ROGUES GALLERY AND CLEAR MY NAME.
BUT I KNOW I CAN GET BACK TO WHERE I'M SUPPOSED TO BE.
AS LONG AS I FIGHT FOR THAT DREAM, IT WON'T FADE AWAY. NOW...

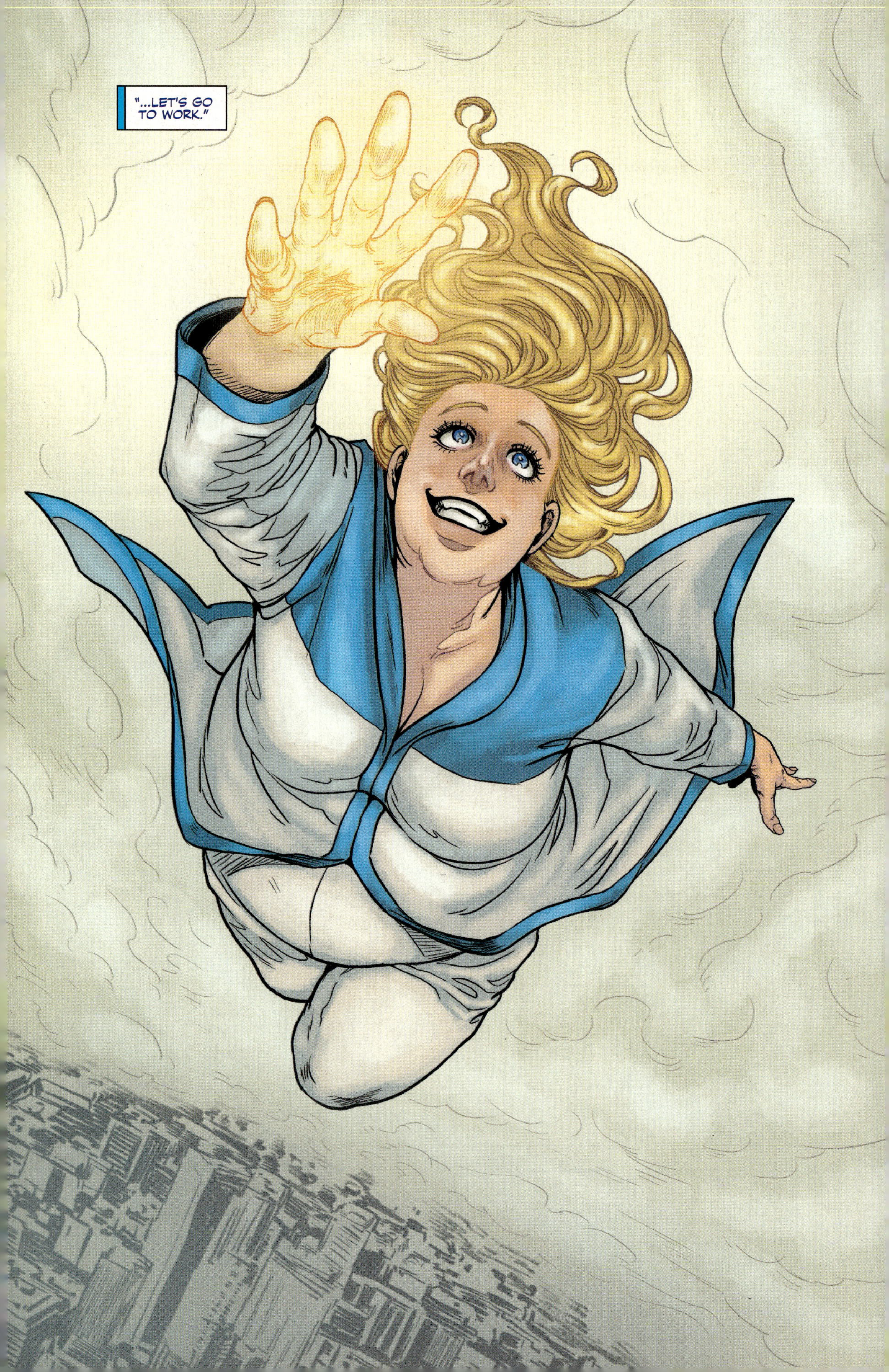
"...LET'S GO TO WORK."

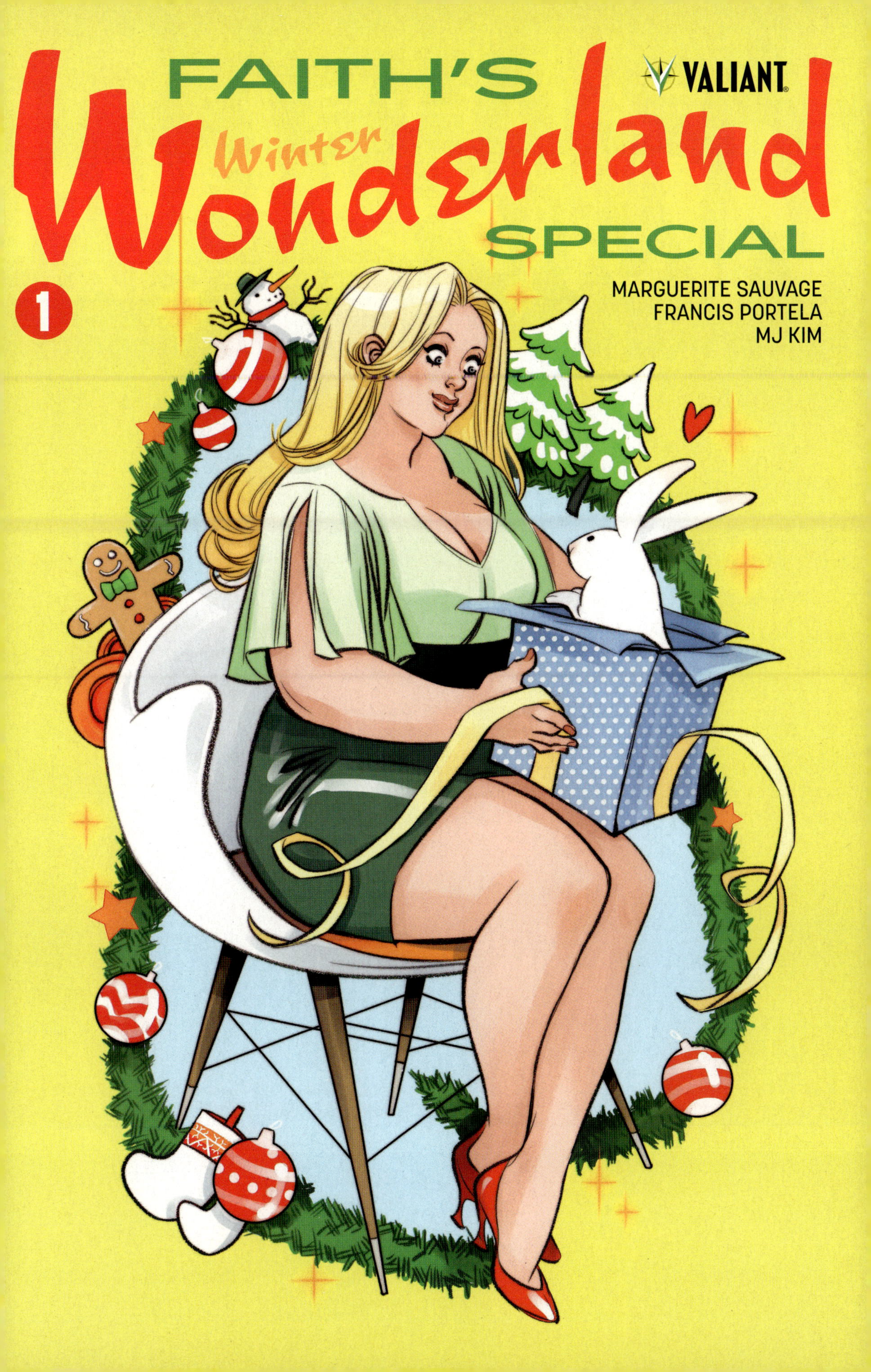
FAITH'S
Winter
Wonderland
SPECIAL
VALIANT
1
MARGUERITE SAUVAGE
FRANCIS PORTELA
MJ KIM

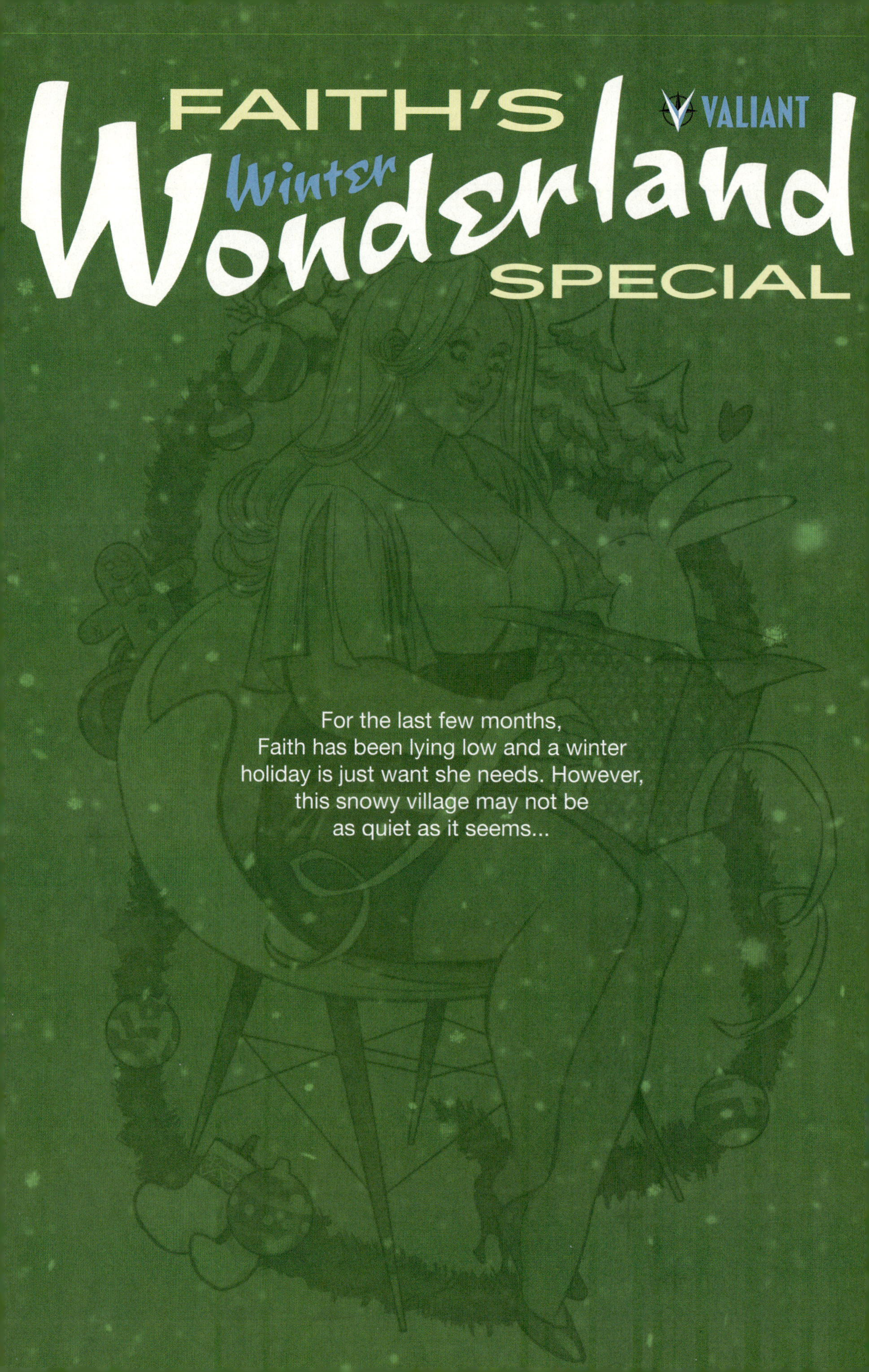
FAITH'S
VALIANT
Winter
Wonderland
SPECIAL
For the last few months,
Faith has been lying low and a winter
holiday is just want she needs. However,
this snowy village may not be
as quiet as it seems...

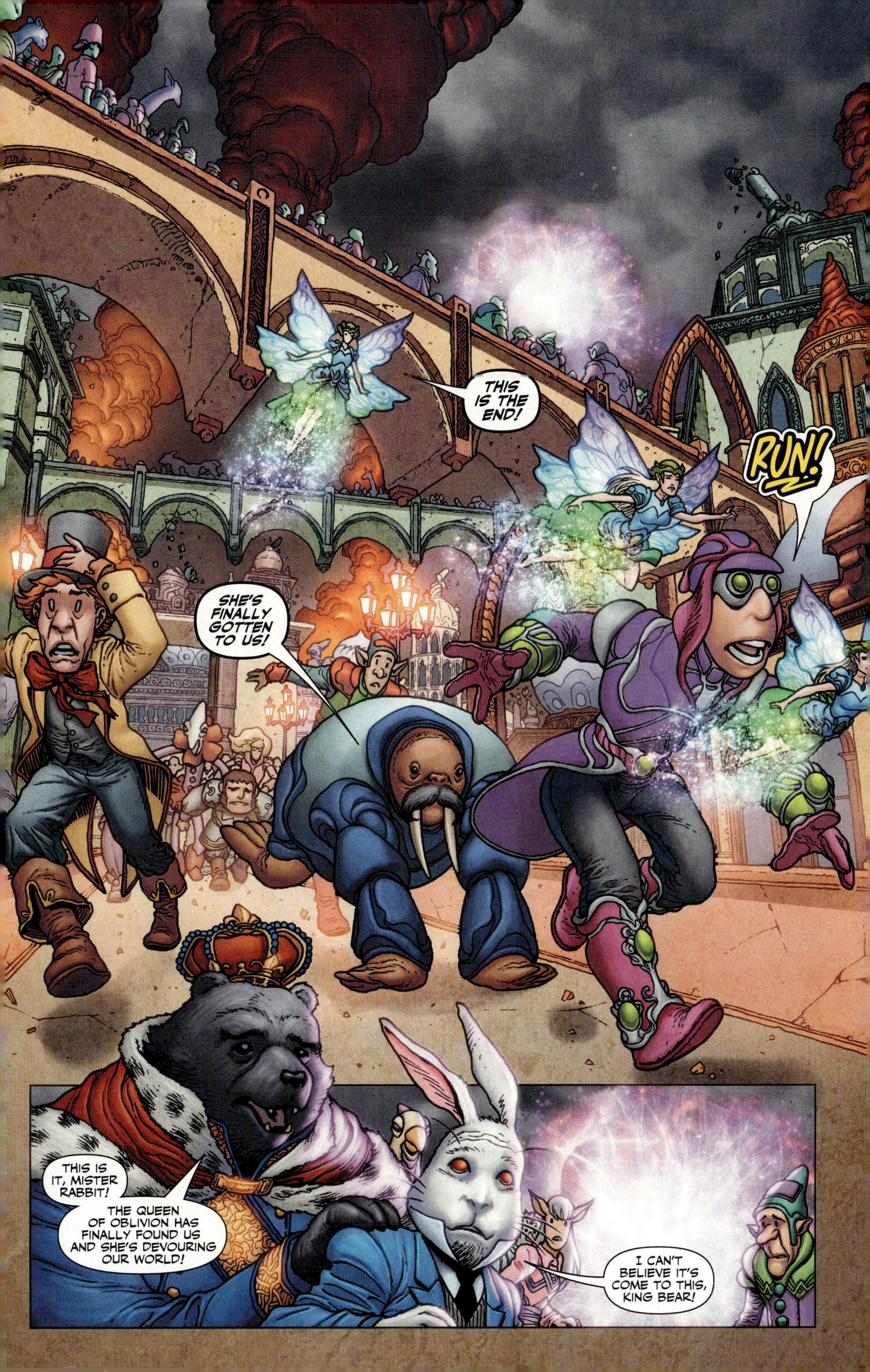
THIS IS THE END!
RUN!
SHE'S FINALLY GOTTEN TO US!
THIS IS IT, MISTER RABBIT!
THE QUEEN OF OBLIVION HAS FINALLY FOUND US AND SHE'S DEVOURING OUR WORLD!
I CAN'T BELIEVE IT'S COME TO THIS, KING BEAR!

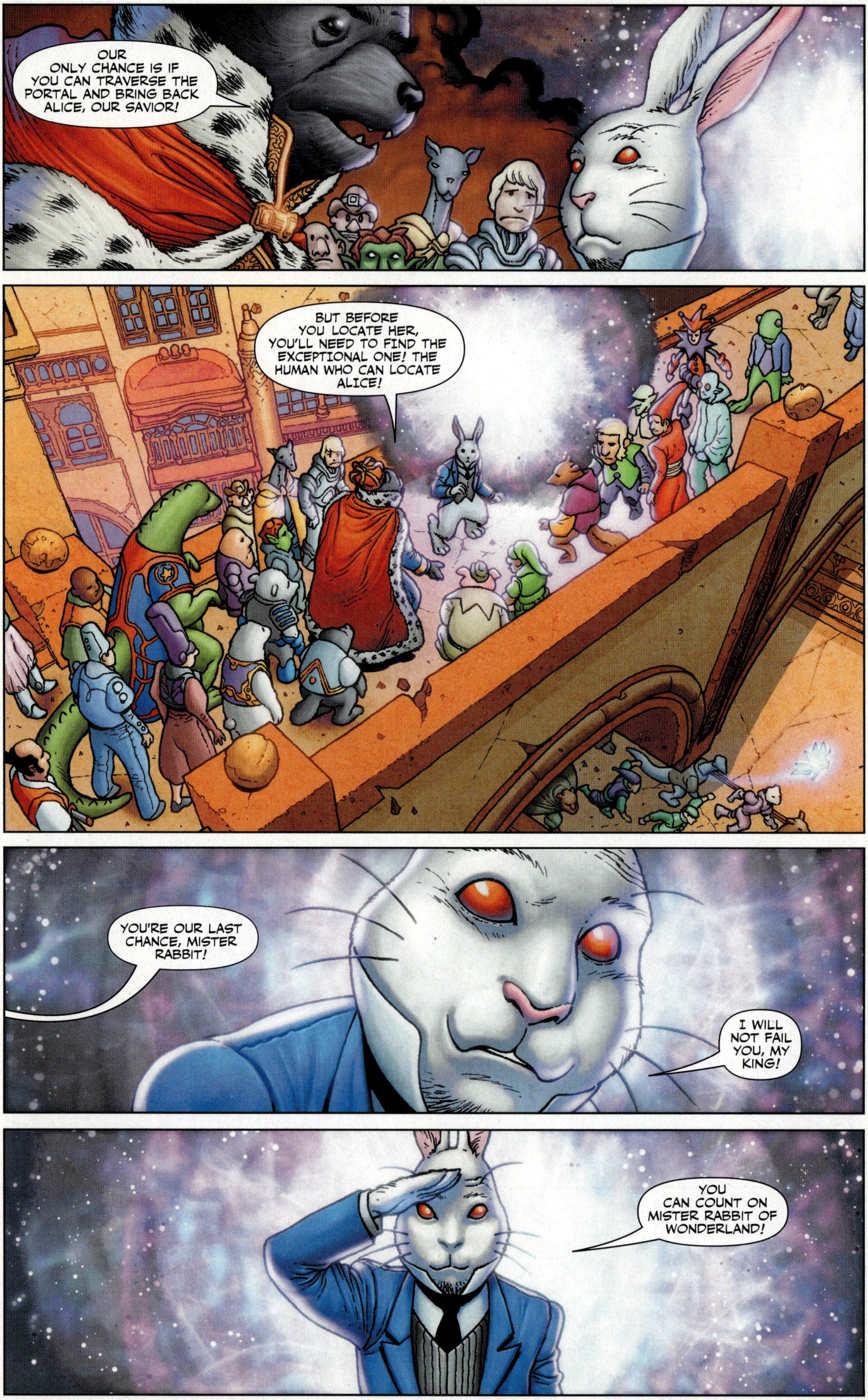
OUR ONLY CHANCE IS IF YOU CAN TRAVERSE THE PORTAL AND BRING BACK ALICE, OUR SAVIOR!
BUT BEFORE YOU LOCATE HER, YOU'LL NEED TO FIND THE EXCEPTIONAL ONE! THE HUMAN WHO CAN LOCATE ALICE!
YOU'RE OUR LAST CHANCE, MISTER RABBIT!
I WILL NOT FAIL YOU, MY KING!
YOU CAN COUNT ON MISTER RABBIT OF WONDERLAND!

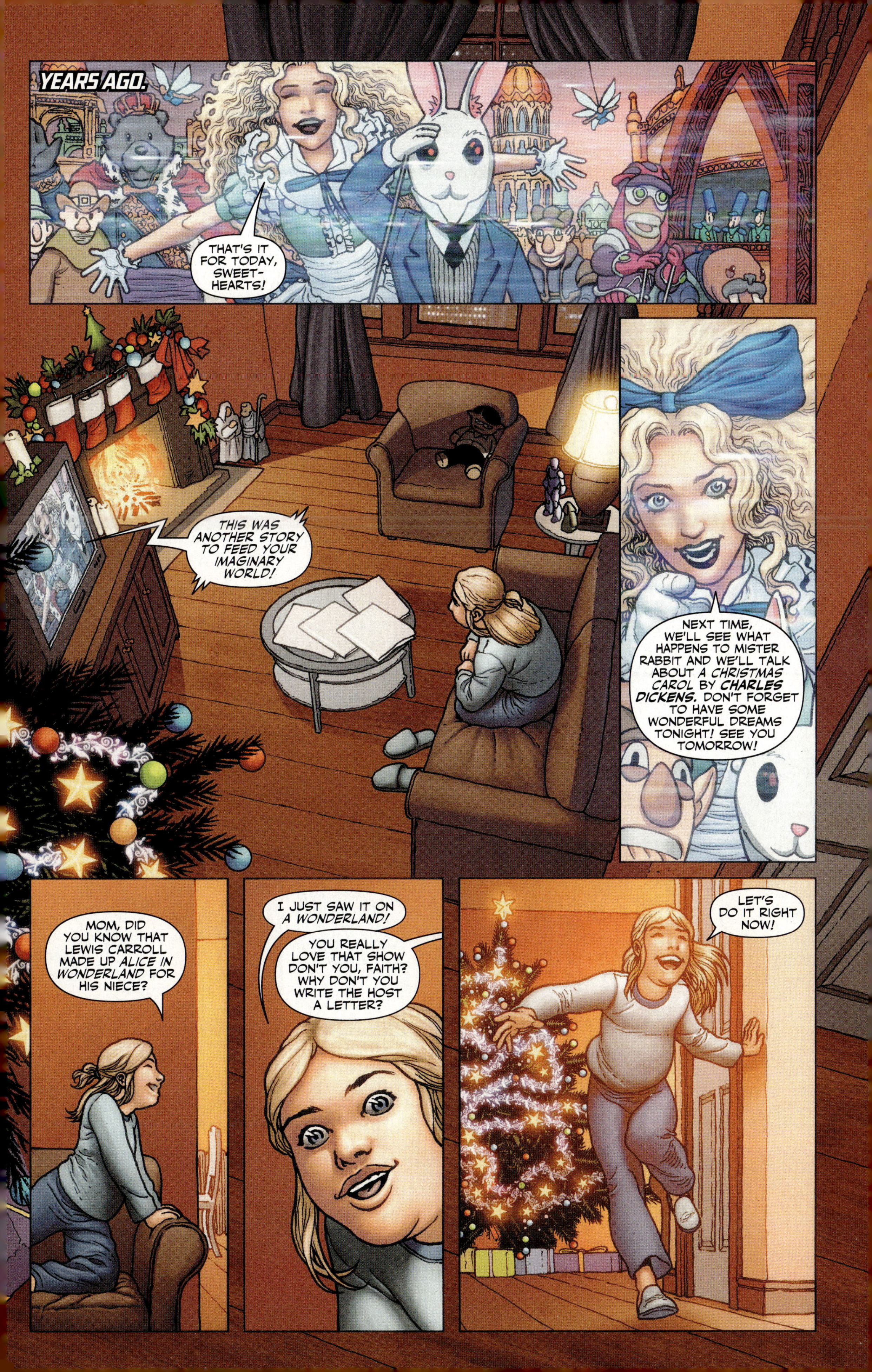
YEARS AGO.
THAT'S IT FOR TODAY, SWEET-HEARTS!
THIS WAS ANOTHER STORY TO FEED YOUR IMAGINARY WORLD!
NEXT TIME, WE'LL SEE WHAT HAPPENS TO MISTER RABBIT AND WE'LL TALK ABOUT *A CHRISTMAS CAROL* BY **CHARLES DICKENS.** DON'T FORGET TO HAVE SOME WONDERFUL DREAMS TONIGHT! SEE YOU TOMORROW!
MOM, DID YOU KNOW THAT LEWIS CARROLL MADE UP *ALICE IN WONDERLAND* FOR HIS NIECE?
I JUST SAW IT ON *A WONDERLAND!*
YOU REALLY LOVE THAT SHOW DON'T YOU, FAITH? WHY DON'T YOU WRITE THE HOST A LETTER?
LET'S DO IT RIGHT NOW!

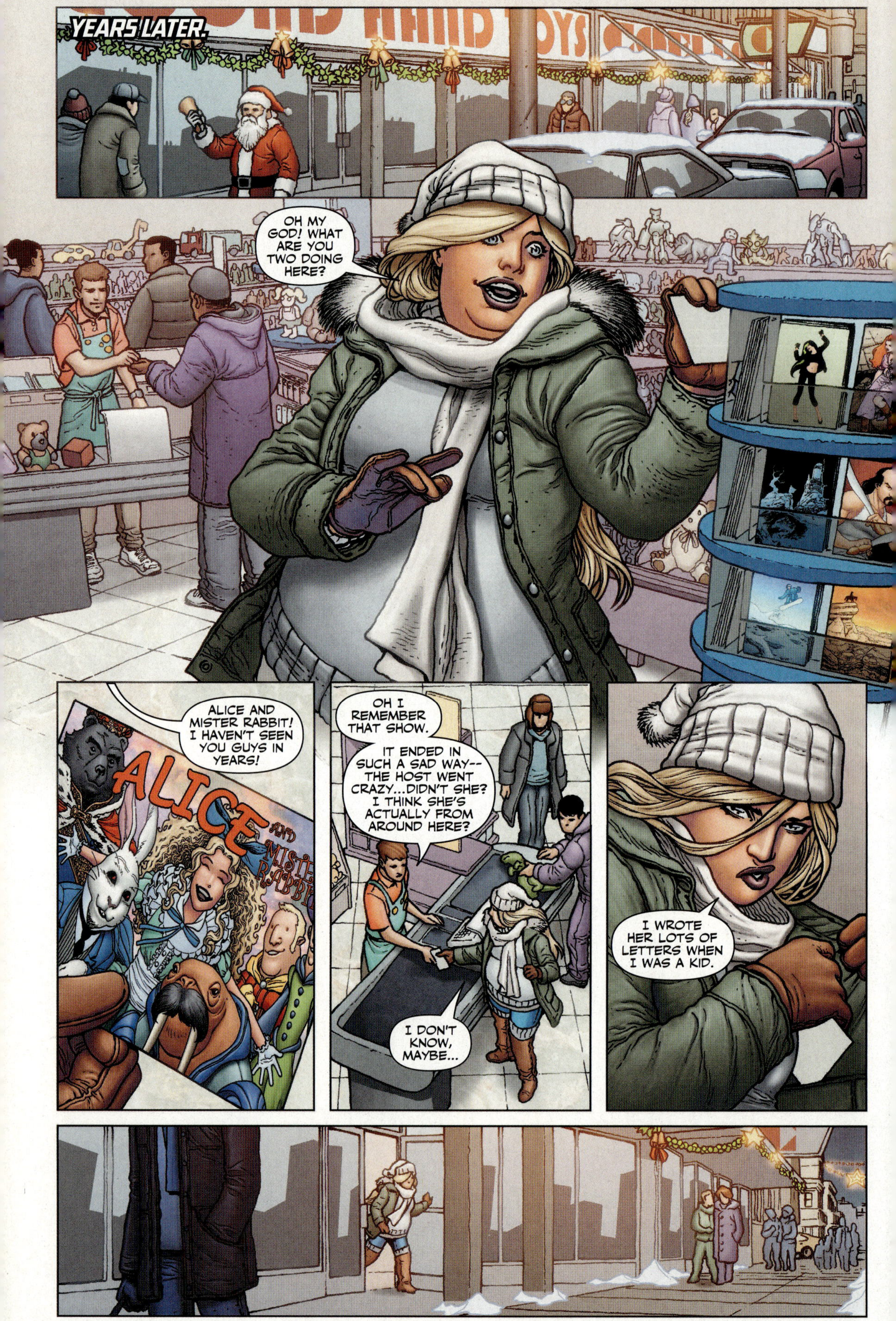
YEARS LATER.
OH MY GOD! WHAT ARE YOU TWO DOING HERE?
ALICE AND MISTER RABBIT! I HAVEN'T SEEN YOU GUYS IN YEARS!
ALICE AND MISTER RABBIT
OH I REMEMBER THAT SHOW.
IT ENDED IN SUCH A SAD WAY-- THE HOST WENT CRAZY...DIDN'T SHE? I THINK SHE'S ACTUALLY FROM AROUND HERE?
I DON'T KNOW, MAYBE...
I WROTE HER LOTS OF LETTERS WHEN I WAS A KID.

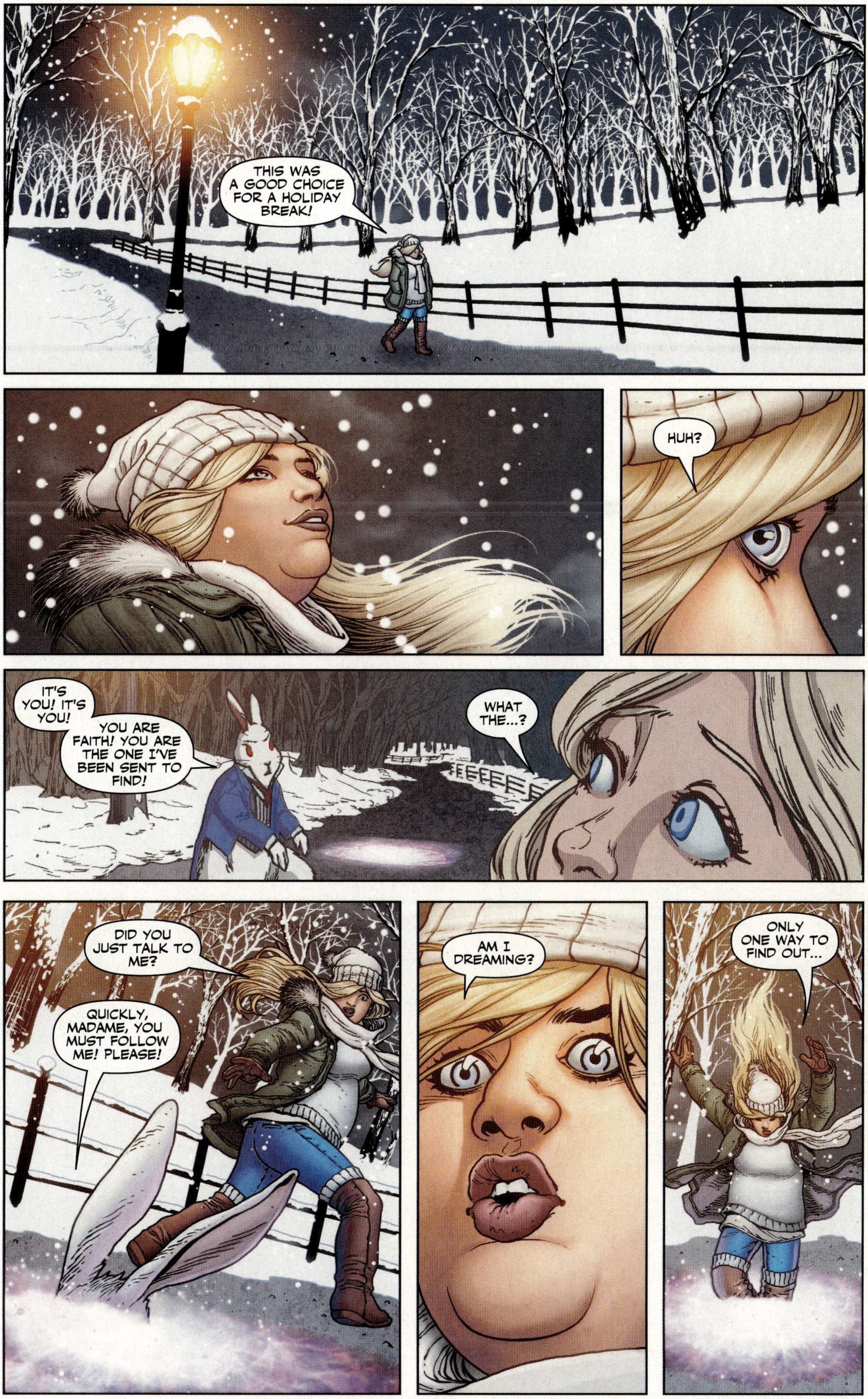
THIS WAS A GOOD CHOICE FOR A HOLIDAY BREAK!
HUH?
IT'S YOU! IT'S YOU!
YOU ARE FAITH! YOU ARE THE ONE I'VE BEEN SENT TO FIND!
WHAT THE...?
DID YOU JUST TALK TO ME?
QUICKLY, MADAME, YOU MUST FOLLOW ME! PLEASE!
AM I DREAMING?
ONLY ONE WAY TO FIND OUT...

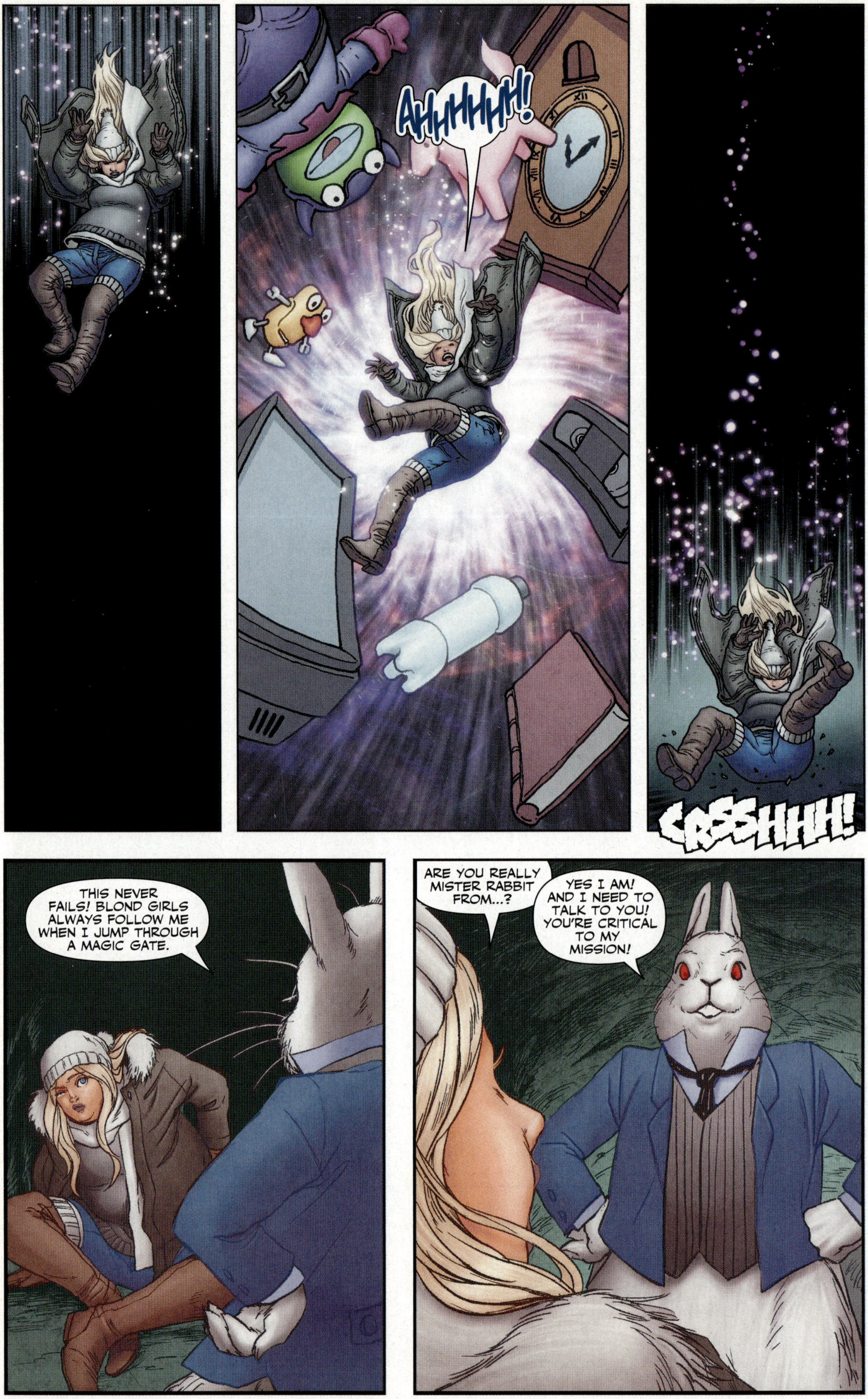
AHHHHHH!
CRSSHHH!
THIS NEVER FAILS! BLOND GIRLS ALWAYS FOLLOW ME WHEN I JUMP THROUGH A MAGIC GATE.
ARE YOU REALLY MISTER RABBIT FROM...?
YES I AM! AND I NEED TO TALK TO YOU! YOU'RE CRITICAL TO MY MISSION!

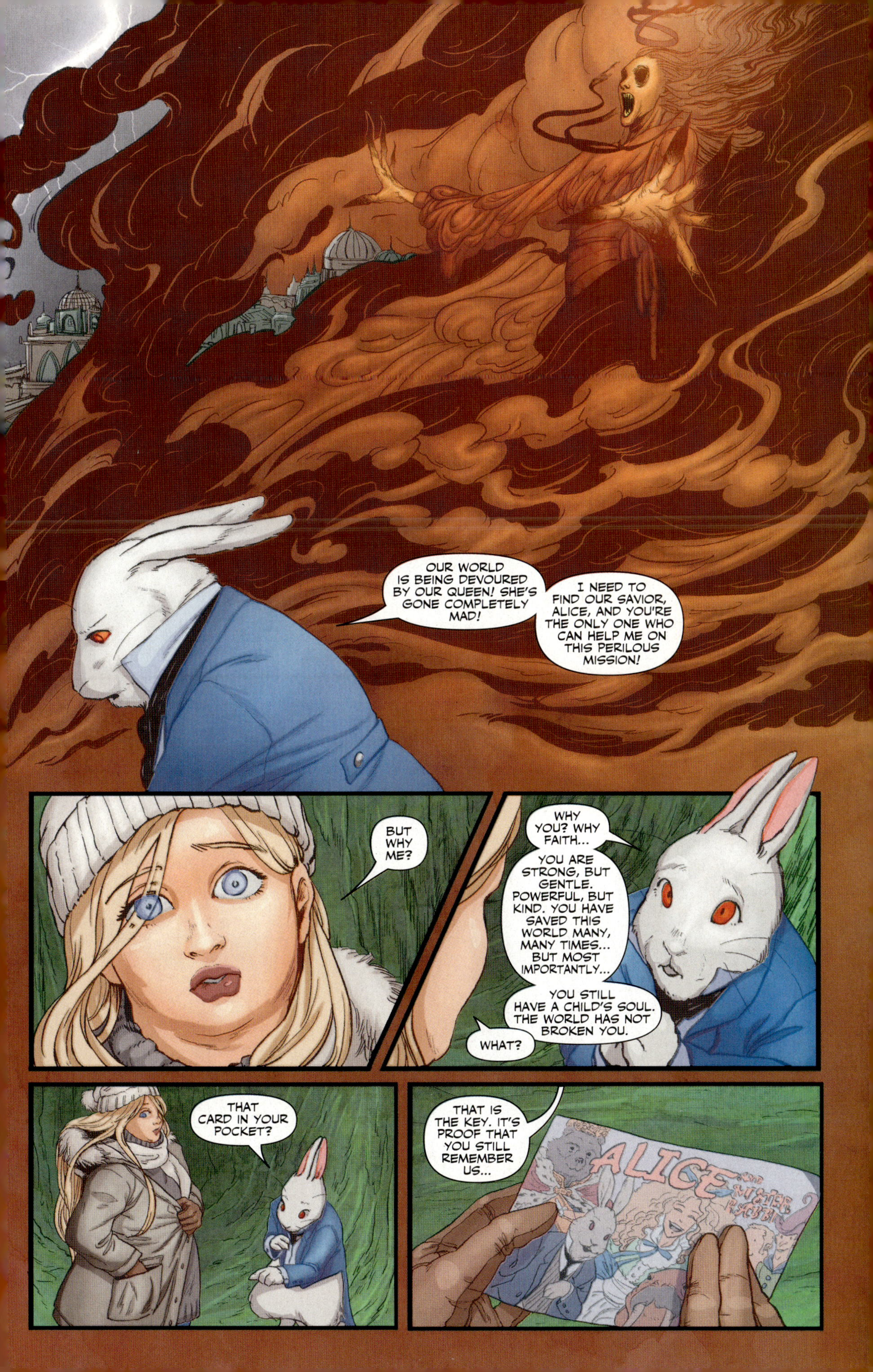

OUR WORLD IS BEING DEVOURED BY OUR QUEEN! SHE'S GONE COMPLETELY MAD!
I NEED TO FIND OUR SAVIOR, ALICE, AND YOU'RE THE ONLY ONE WHO CAN HELP ME ON THIS PERILOUS MISSION!
BUT WHY ME?
WHY YOU? WHY FAITH...
YOU ARE STRONG, BUT GENTLE. POWERFUL, BUT KIND. YOU HAVE SAVED THIS WORLD MANY, MANY TIMES... BUT MOST IMPORTANTLY...
YOU STILL HAVE A CHILD'S SOUL. THE WORLD HAS NOT BROKEN YOU.
WHAT?
THAT CARD IN YOUR POCKET?
THAT IS THE KEY. IT'S PROOF THAT YOU STILL REMEMBER US...
ALICE

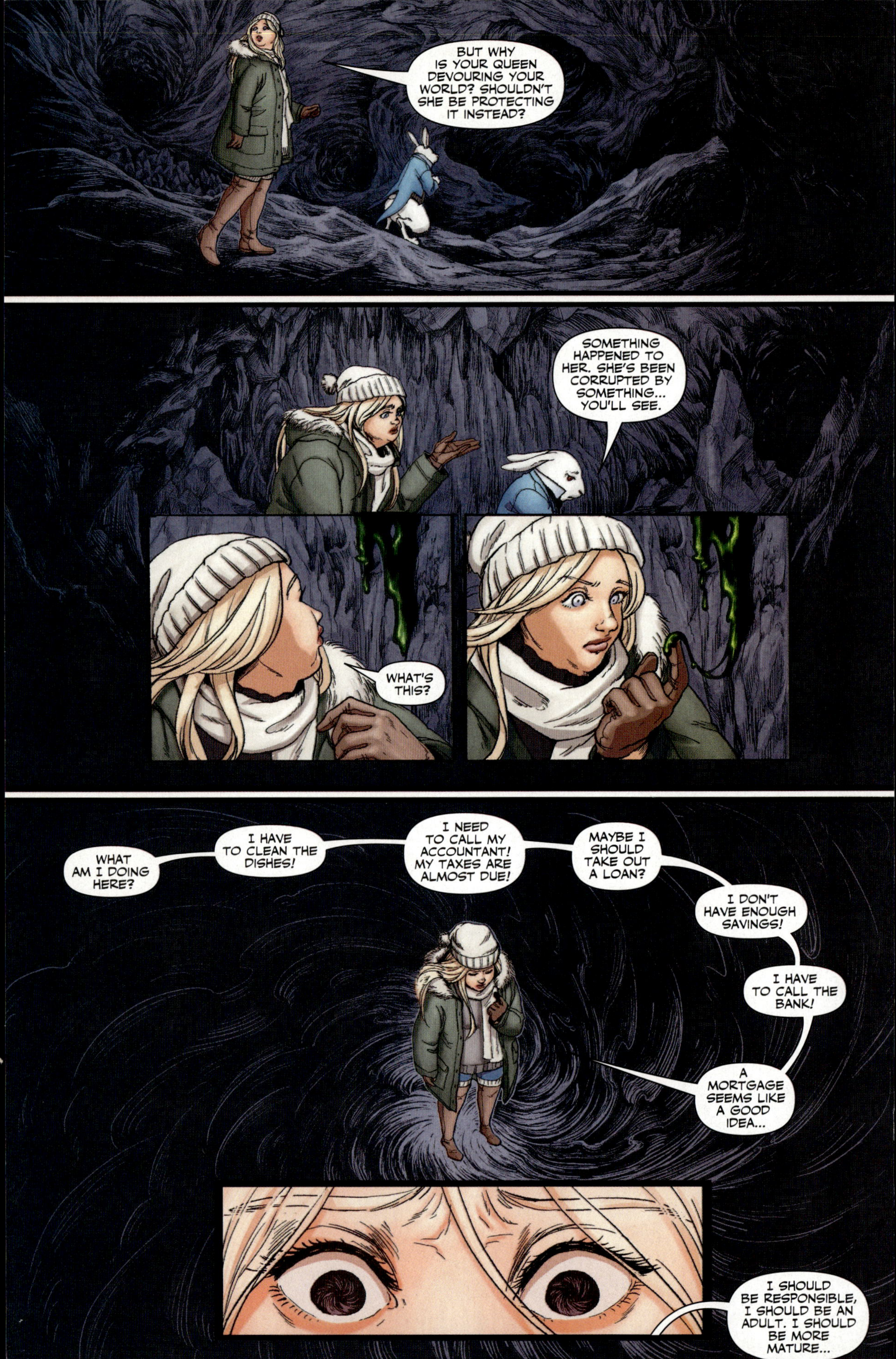
BUT WHY IS YOUR QUEEN DEVOURING YOUR WORLD? SHOULDN'T SHE BE PROTECTING IT INSTEAD?
SOMETHING HAPPENED TO HER. SHE'S BEEN CORRUPTED BY SOMETHING... YOU'LL SEE.
WHAT'S THIS?
WHAT AM I DOING HERE?
I HAVE TO CLEAN THE DISHES!
I NEED TO CALL MY ACCOUNTANT! MY TAXES ARE ALMOST DUE!
MAYBE I SHOULD TAKE OUT A LOAN?
I DON'T HAVE ENOUGH SAVINGS!
I HAVE TO CALL THE BANK!
A MORTGAGE SEEMS LIKE A GOOD IDEA...
I SHOULD BE RESPONSIBLE, I SHOULD BE AN ADULT. I SHOULD BE MORE MATURE...

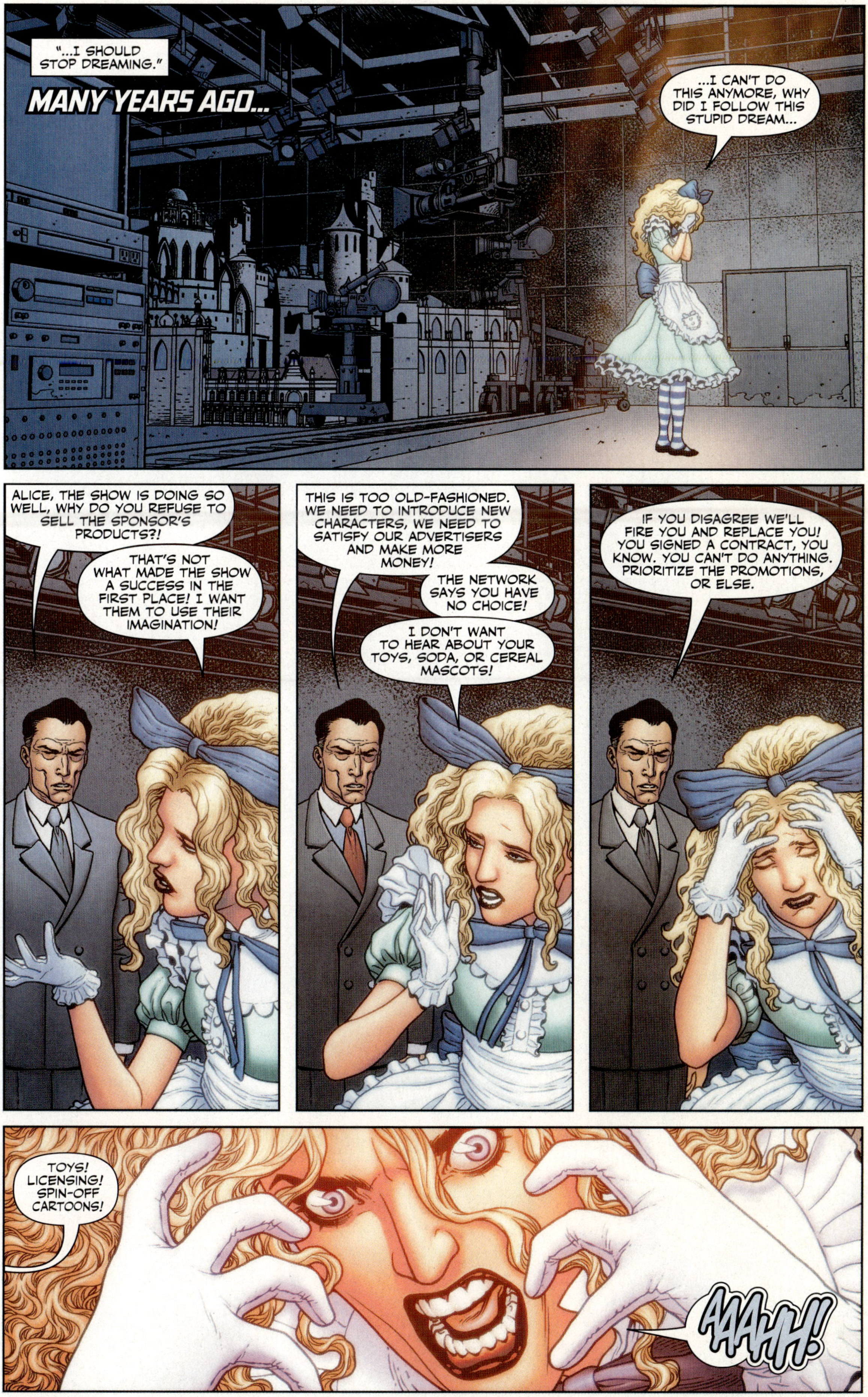
"...I SHOULD STOP DREAMING."
MANY YEARS AGO...
...I CAN'T DO THIS ANYMORE, WHY DID I FOLLOW THIS STUPID DREAM...
ALICE, THE SHOW IS DOING SO WELL, WHY DO YOU REFUSE TO SELL THE SPONSOR'S PRODUCTS?!
THAT'S NOT WHAT MADE THE SHOW A SUCCESS IN THE FIRST PLACE! I WANT THEM TO USE THEIR IMAGINATION!
THIS IS TOO OLD-FASHIONED. WE NEED TO INTRODUCE NEW CHARACTERS, WE NEED TO SATISFY OUR ADVERTISERS AND MAKE MORE MONEY!
THE NETWORK SAYS YOU HAVE NO CHOICE!
I DON'T WANT TO HEAR ABOUT YOUR TOYS, SODA, OR CEREAL MASCOTS!
IF YOU DISAGREE WE'LL FIRE YOU AND REPLACE YOU! YOU SIGNED A CONTRACT, YOU KNOW. YOU CAN'T DO ANYTHING. PRIORITIZE THE PROMOTIONS, OR ELSE.
TOYS! LICENSING! SPIN-OFF CARTOONS!
AAAHH!

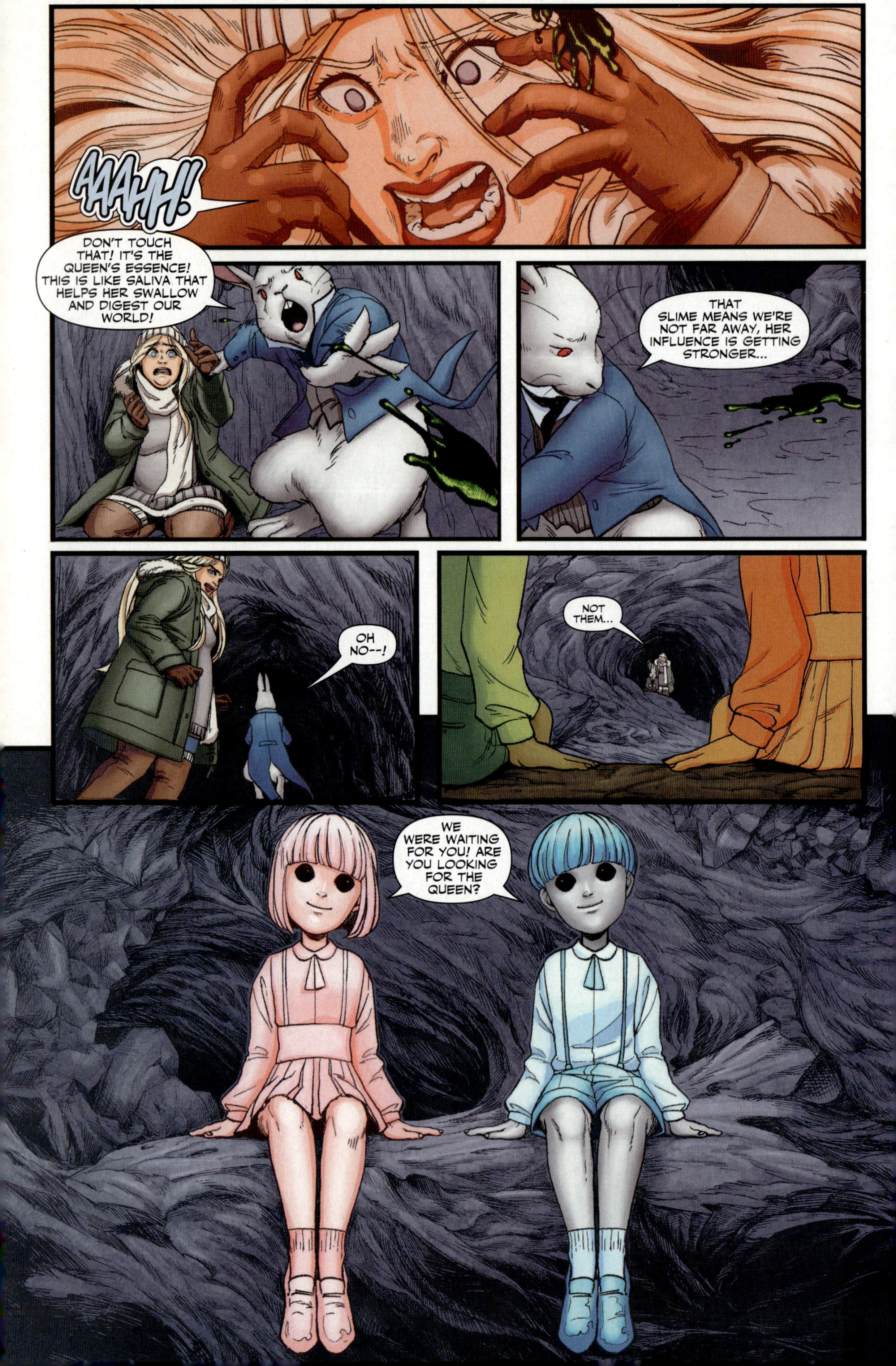
AAAHH!
DON'T TOUCH THAT! IT'S THE QUEEN'S ESSENCE! THIS IS LIKE SALIVA THAT HELPS HER SWALLOW AND DIGEST OUR WORLD!
THAT SLIME MEANS WE'RE NOT FAR AWAY, HER INFLUENCE IS GETTING STRONGER...
OH NO--!
NOT THEM...
WE WERE WAITING FOR YOU! ARE YOU LOOKING FOR THE QUEEN?

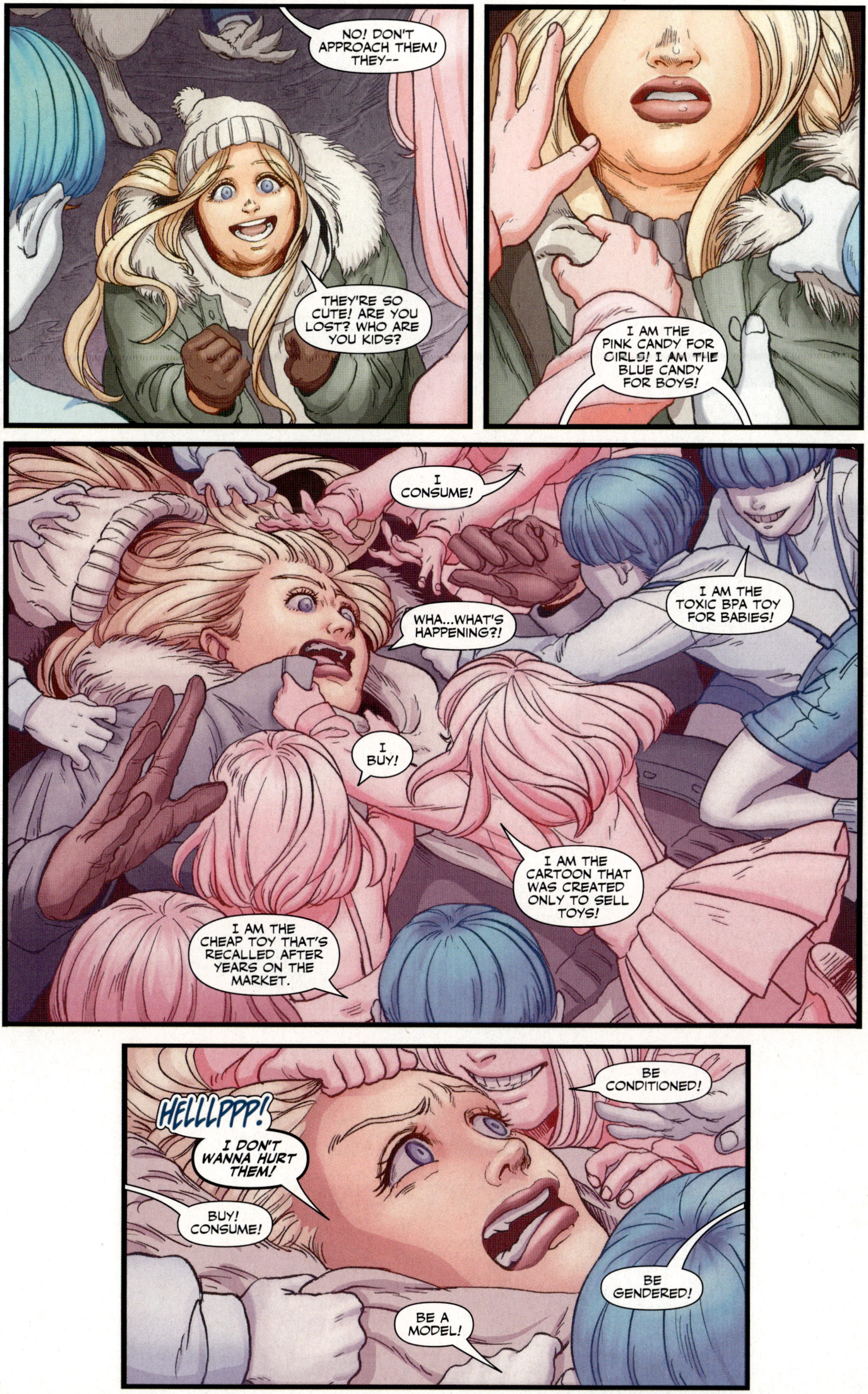
NO! DON'T APPROACH THEM! THEY--
THEY'RE SO CUTE! ARE YOU LOST? WHO ARE YOU KIDS?
I AM THE PINK CANDY FOR GIRLS! I AM THE BLUE CANDY FOR BOYS!
I CONSUME!
I AM THE TOXIC BPA TOY FOR BABIES!
WHA...WHAT'S HAPPENING?!
I BUY!
I AM THE CARTOON THAT WAS CREATED ONLY TO SELL TOYS!
I AM THE CHEAP TOY THAT'S RECALLED AFTER YEARS ON THE MARKET.
BE CONDITIONED!
HELLLPPP!
I DON'T WANNA HURT THEM!
BUY! CONSUME!
BE GENDERED!
BE A MODEL!

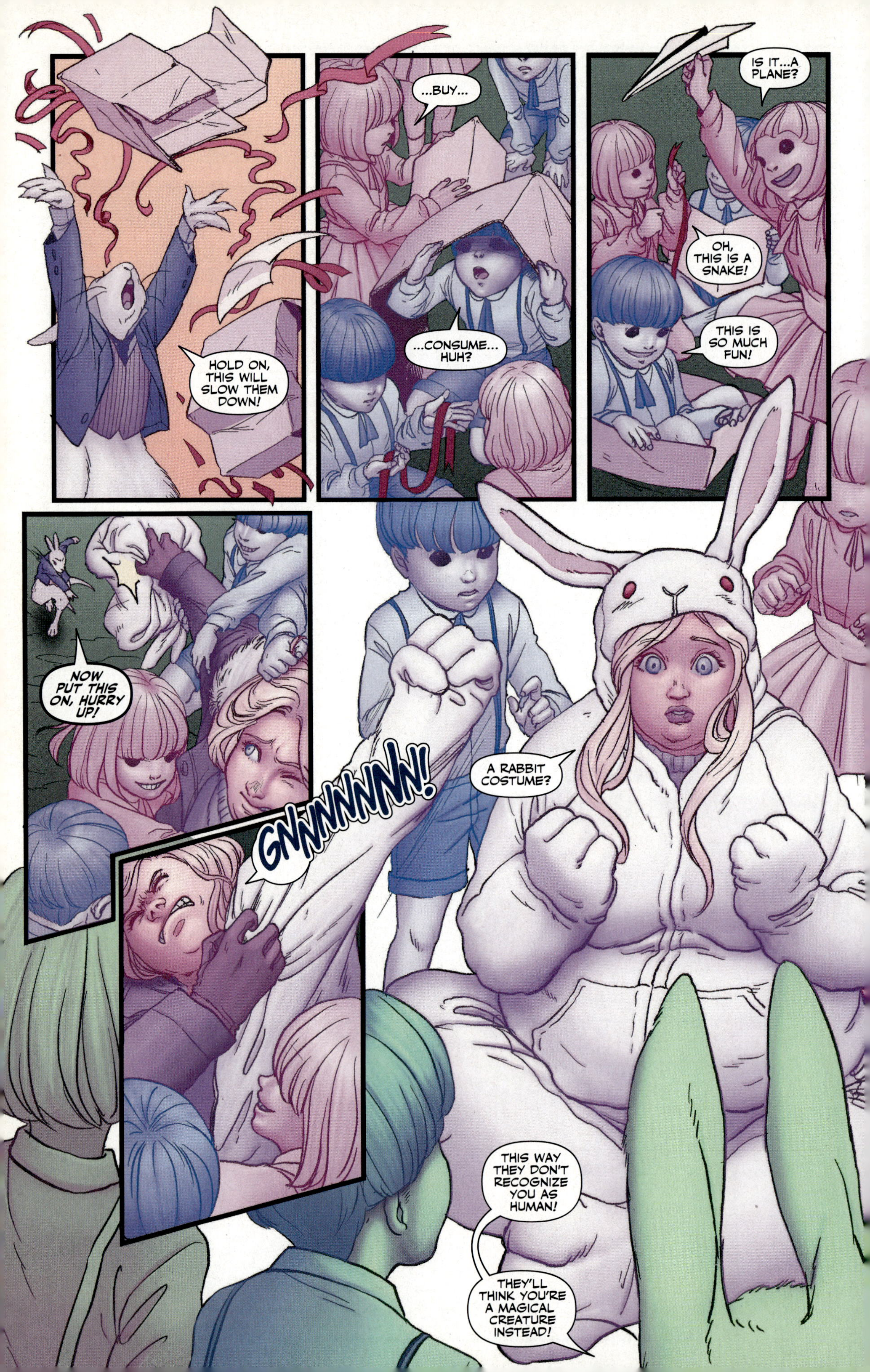
HOLD ON, THIS WILL SLOW THEM DOWN!
...BUY...
...CONSUME... HUH?
IS IT...A PLANE?
OH, THIS IS A SNAKE!
THIS IS SO MUCH FUN!
NOW PUT THIS ON, HURRY UP!
A RABBIT COSTUME?
GNNNNNNN!
THIS WAY THEY DON'T RECOGNIZE YOU AS HUMAN!
THEY'LL THINK YOU'RE A MAGICAL CREATURE INSTEAD!

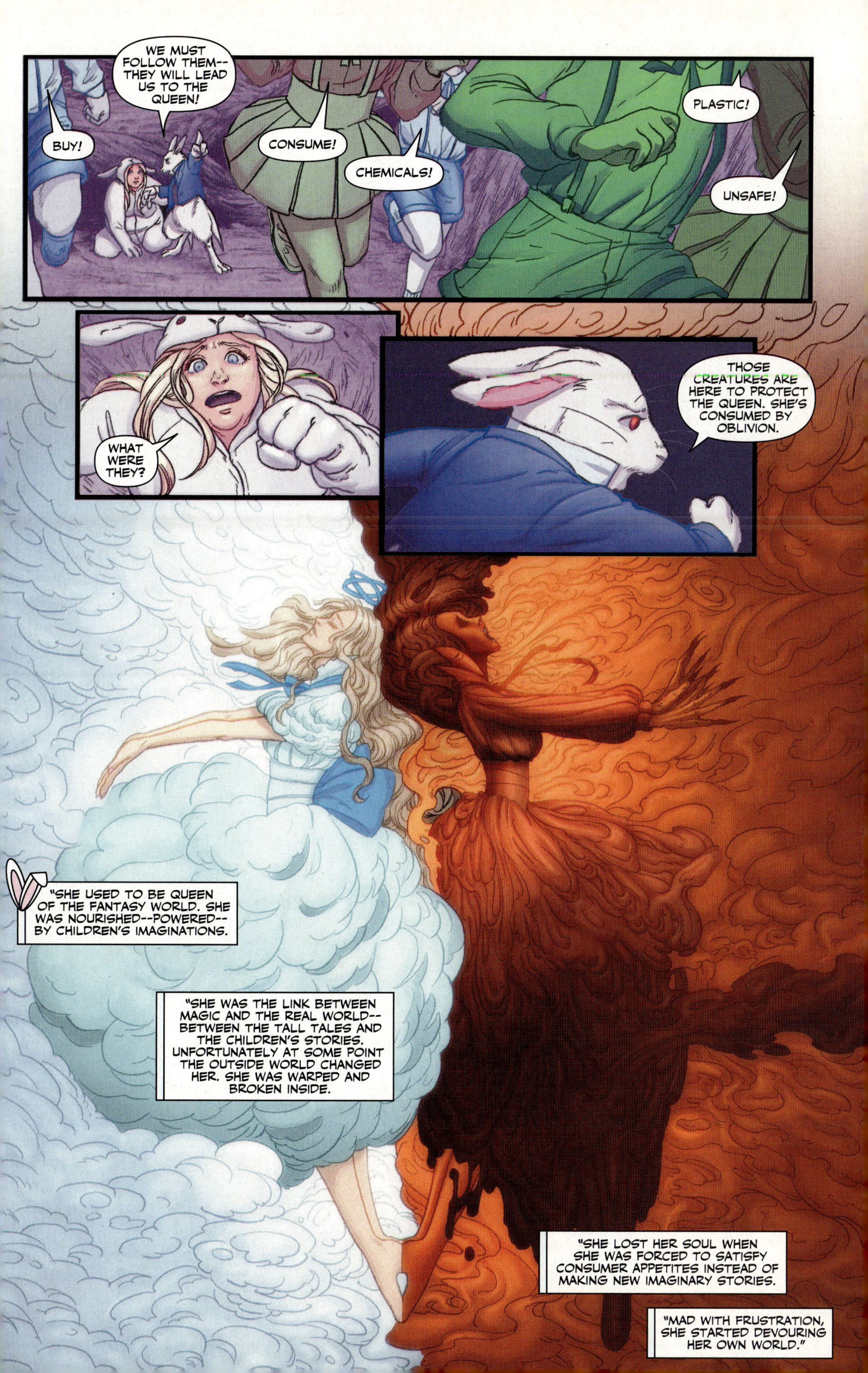

WE MUST FOLLOW THEM-- THEY WILL LEAD US TO THE QUEEN!
BUY!
CONSUME!
CHEMICALS!
PLASTIC!
UNSAFE!
WHAT WERE THEY?
THOSE CREATURES ARE HERE TO PROTECT THE QUEEN. SHE'S CONSUMED BY OBLIVION.
"SHE USED TO BE QUEEN OF THE FANTASY WORLD. SHE WAS NOURISHED--POWERED-- BY CHILDREN'S IMAGINATIONS.
"SHE WAS THE LINK BETWEEN MAGIC AND THE REAL WORLD-- BETWEEN THE TALL TALES AND THE CHILDREN'S STORIES. UNFORTUNATELY AT SOME POINT THE OUTSIDE WORLD CHANGED HER. SHE WAS WARPED AND BROKEN INSIDE.
"SHE LOST HER SOUL WHEN SHE WAS FORCED TO SATISFY CONSUMER APPETITES INSTEAD OF MAKING NEW IMAGINARY STORIES.
"MAD WITH FRUSTRATION, SHE STARTED DEVOURING HER OWN WORLD."

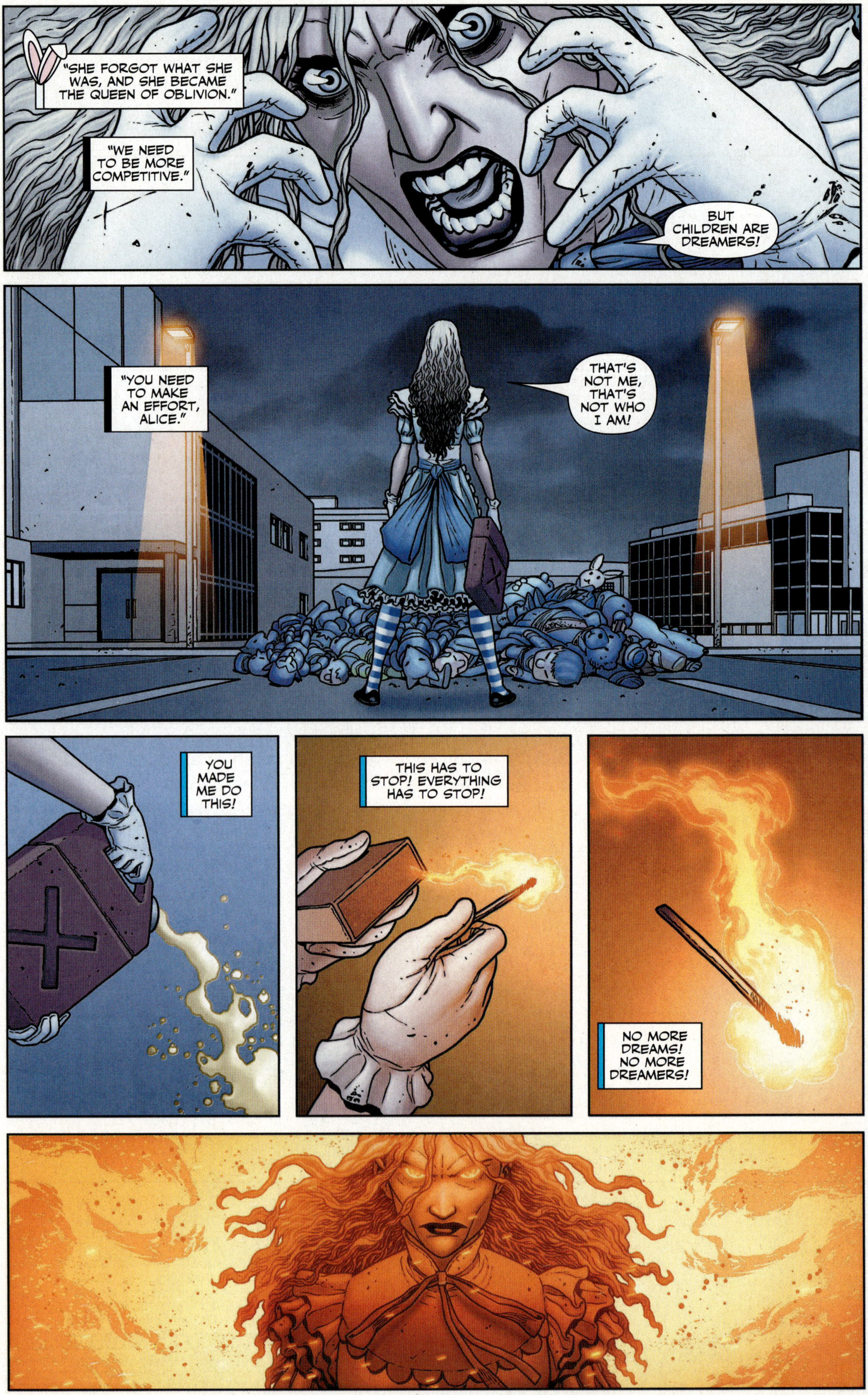
"SHE FORGOT WHAT SHE WAS, AND SHE BECAME THE QUEEN OF OBLIVION."
"WE NEED TO BE MORE COMPETITIVE."
BUT CHILDREN ARE DREAMERS!
"YOU NEED TO MAKE AN EFFORT, ALICE."
THAT'S NOT ME, THAT'S NOT WHO I AM!
YOU MADE ME DO THIS!
THIS HAS TO STOP! EVERYTHING HAS TO STOP!
NO MORE DREAMS! NO MORE DREAMERS!

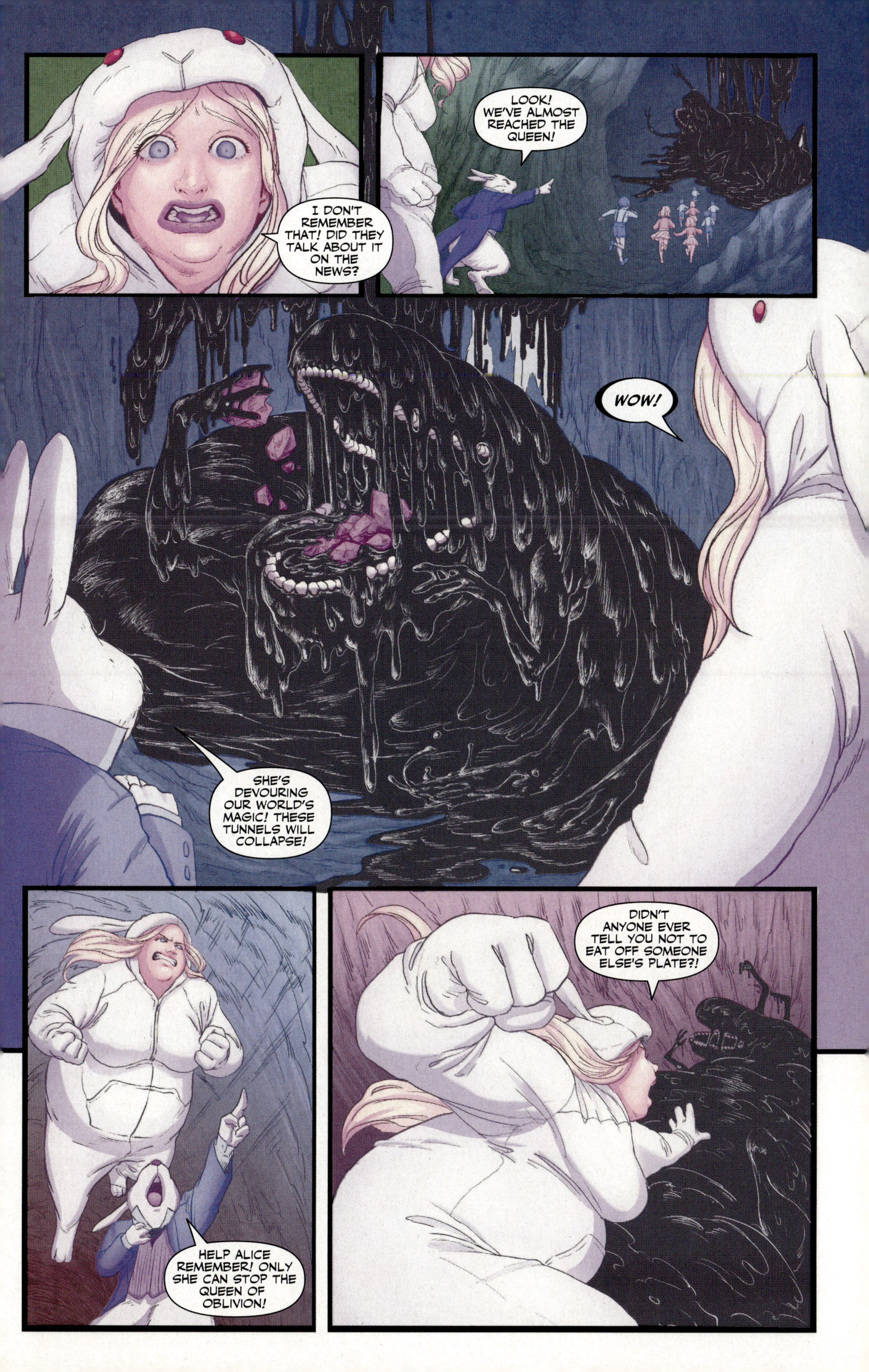
I DON'T REMEMBER THAT! DID THEY TALK ABOUT IT ON THE NEWS?
LOOK! WE'VE ALMOST REACHED THE QUEEN!
WOW!
SHE'S DEVOURING OUR WORLD'S MAGIC! THESE TUNNELS WILL COLLAPSE!
HELP ALICE REMEMBER! ONLY SHE CAN STOP THE QUEEN OF OBLIVION!
DIDN'T ANYONE EVER TELL YOU NOT TO EAT OFF SOMEONE ELSE'S PLATE?!

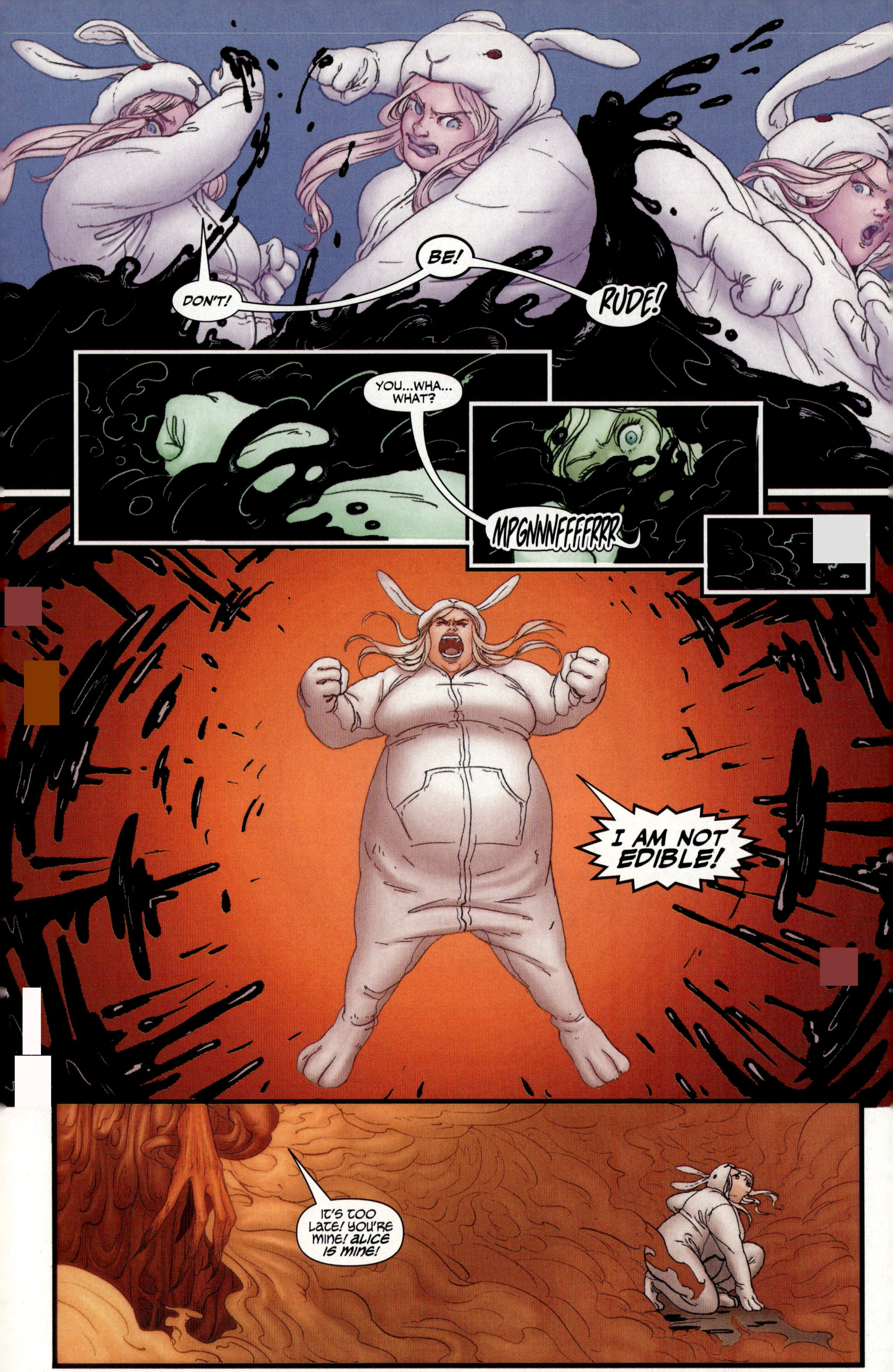
DON'T!
BE!
RUDE!
YOU...WHA... WHAT?
MPGNNNFFFFRRR
I AM NOT EDIBLE!
IT'S TOO LATE! YOU'RE MINE! ALICE IS MINE!

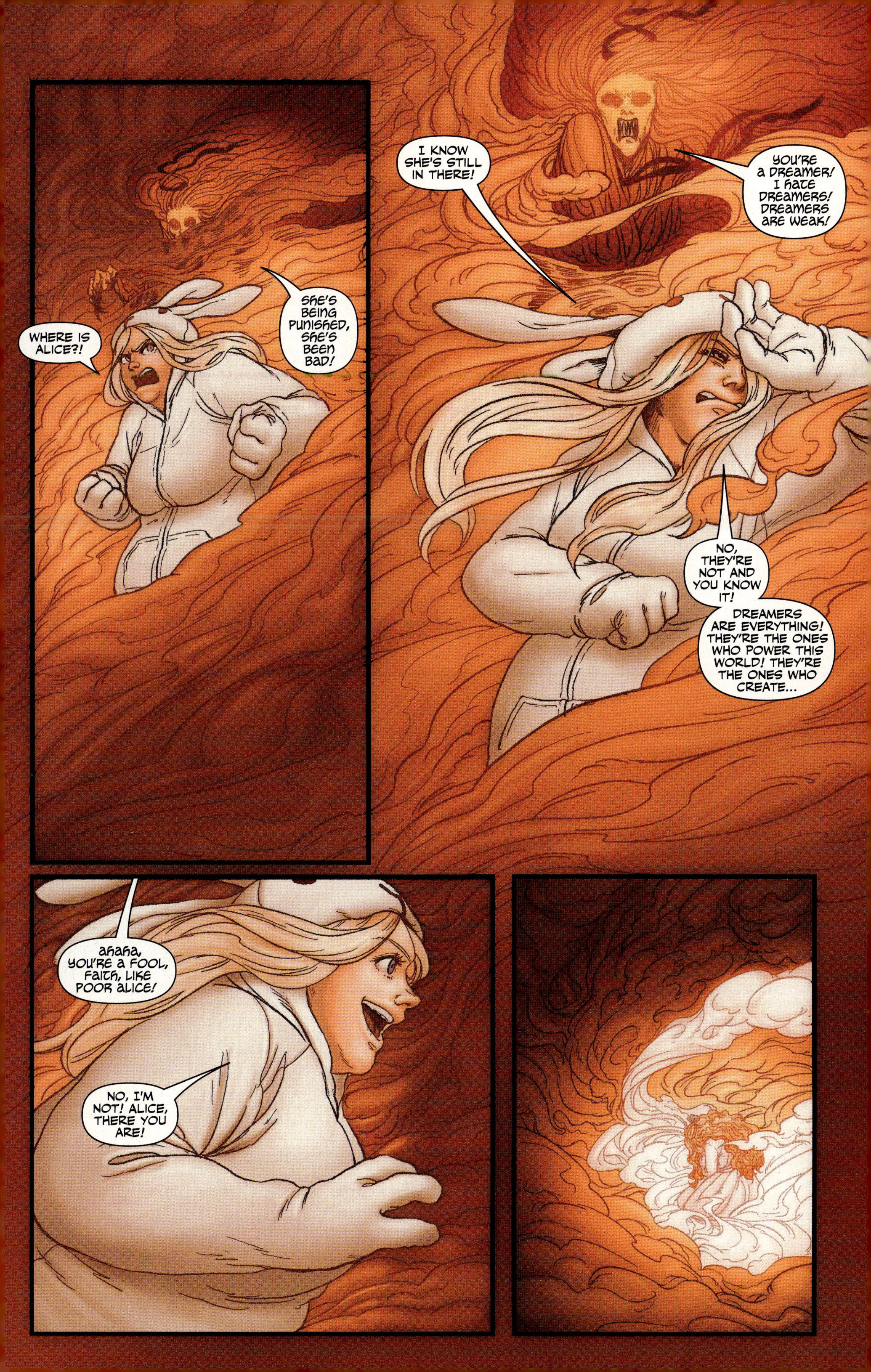

WHERE IS ALICE?!
SHE'S BEING PUNISHED, SHE'S BEEN BAD!
I KNOW SHE'S STILL IN THERE!
YOU'RE A DREAMER! I HATE DREAMERS! DREAMERS ARE WEAK!
NO, THEY'RE NOT AND YOU KNOW IT!
DREAMERS ARE EVERYTHING! THEY'RE THE ONES WHO POWER THIS WORLD! THEY'RE THE ONES WHO CREATE...
AHAHA, YOU'RE A FOOL, FAITH, LIKE POOR ALICE!
NO, I'M NOT! ALICE, THERE YOU ARE!

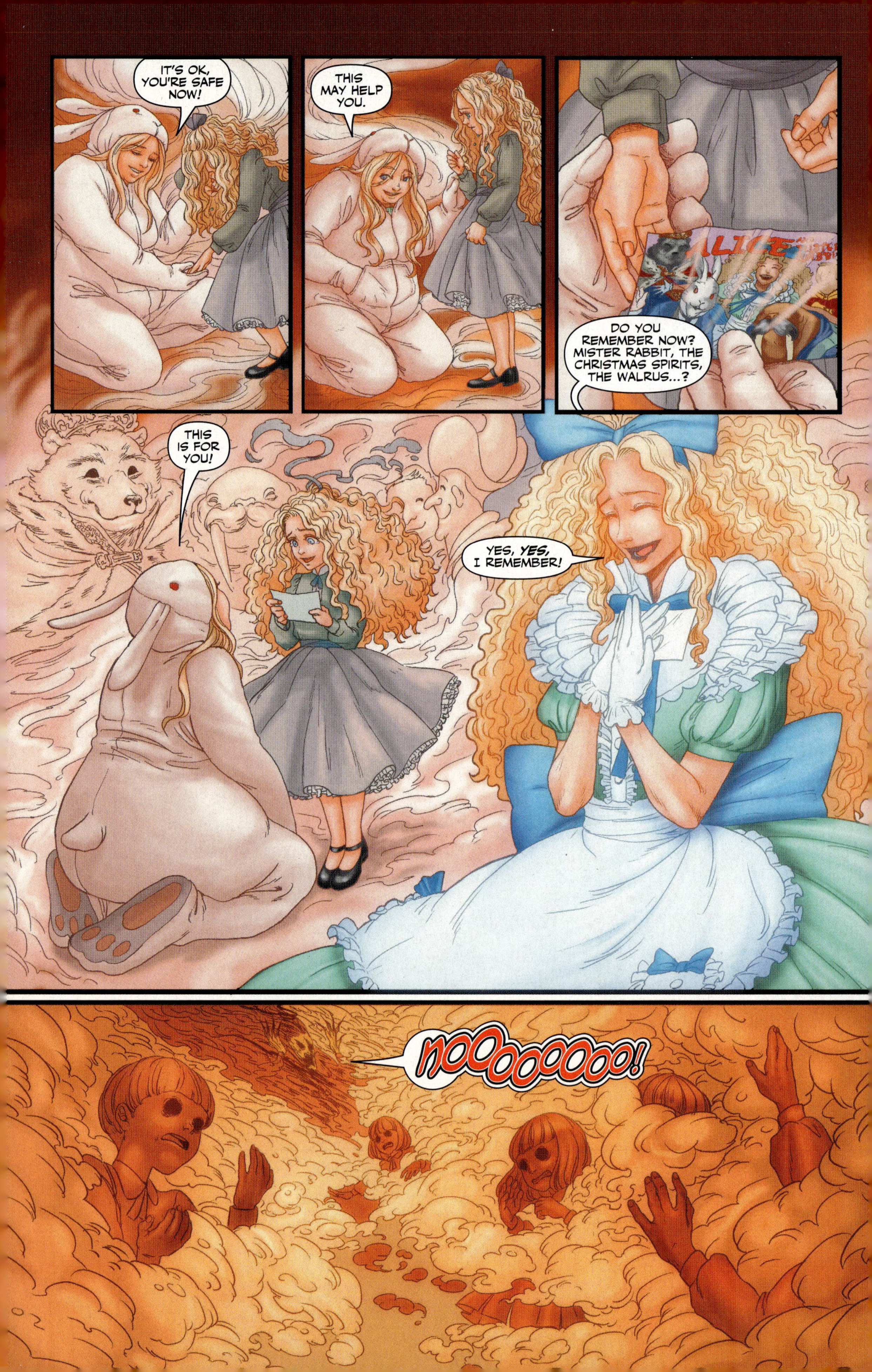
IT'S OK, YOU'RE SAFE NOW!
THIS MAY HELP YOU.
DO YOU REMEMBER NOW? MISTER RABBIT, THE CHRISTMAS SPIRITS, THE WALRUS...?
THIS IS FOR YOU!
YES, *YES*, I REMEMBER!
NOOOOOOOO!

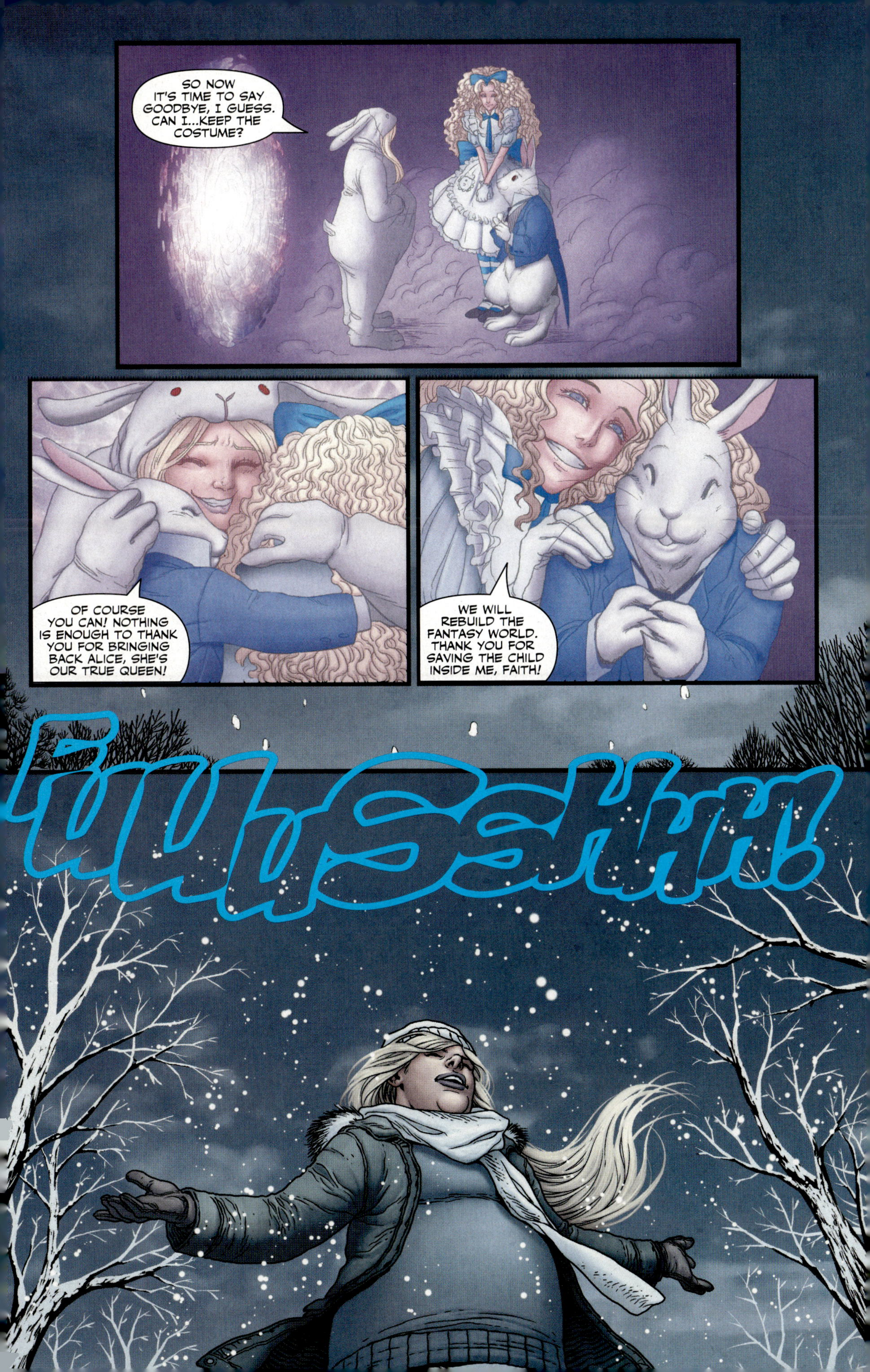
SO NOW IT'S TIME TO SAY GOODBYE, I GUESS. CAN I...KEEP THE COSTUME?
OF COURSE YOU CAN! NOTHING IS ENOUGH TO THANK YOU FOR BRINGING BACK ALICE, SHE'S OUR TRUE QUEEN!
WE WILL REBUILD THE FANTASY WORLD. THANK YOU FOR SAVING THE CHILD INSIDE ME, FAITH!

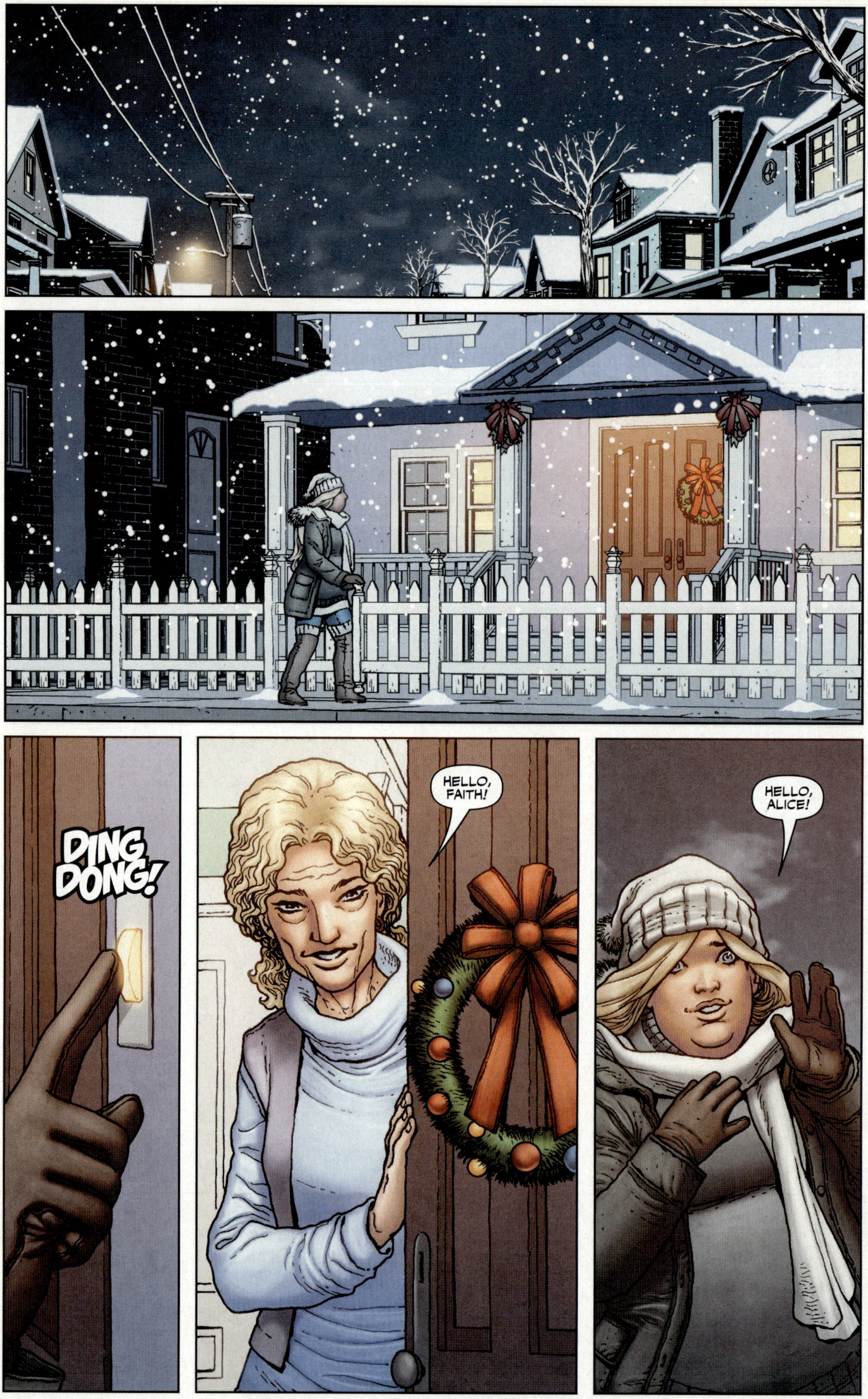
DING DONG!
HELLO, FAITH!
HELLO, ALICE!

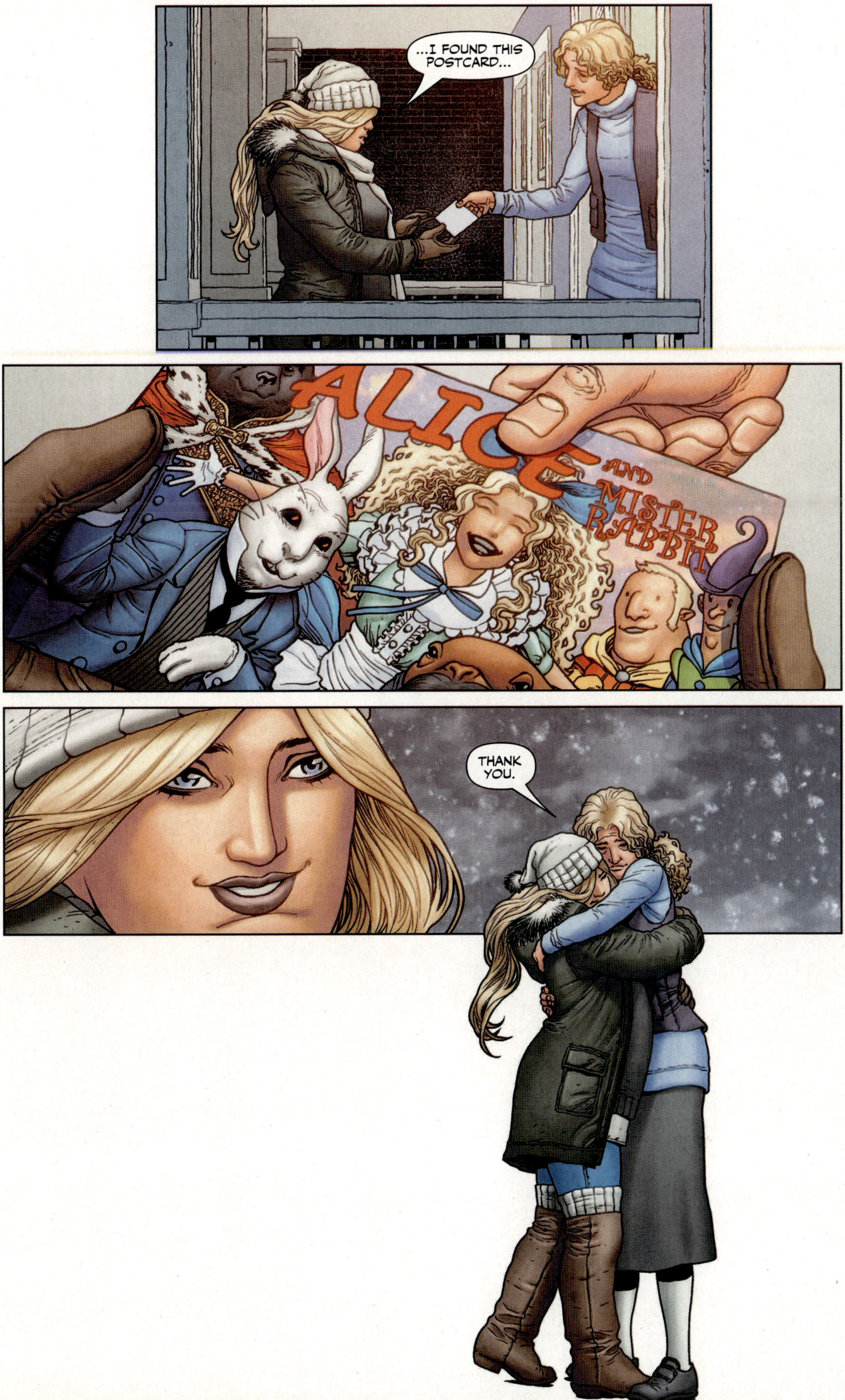
...I FOUND THIS POSTCARD...
ALICE AND MISTER RABBIT
THANK YOU.

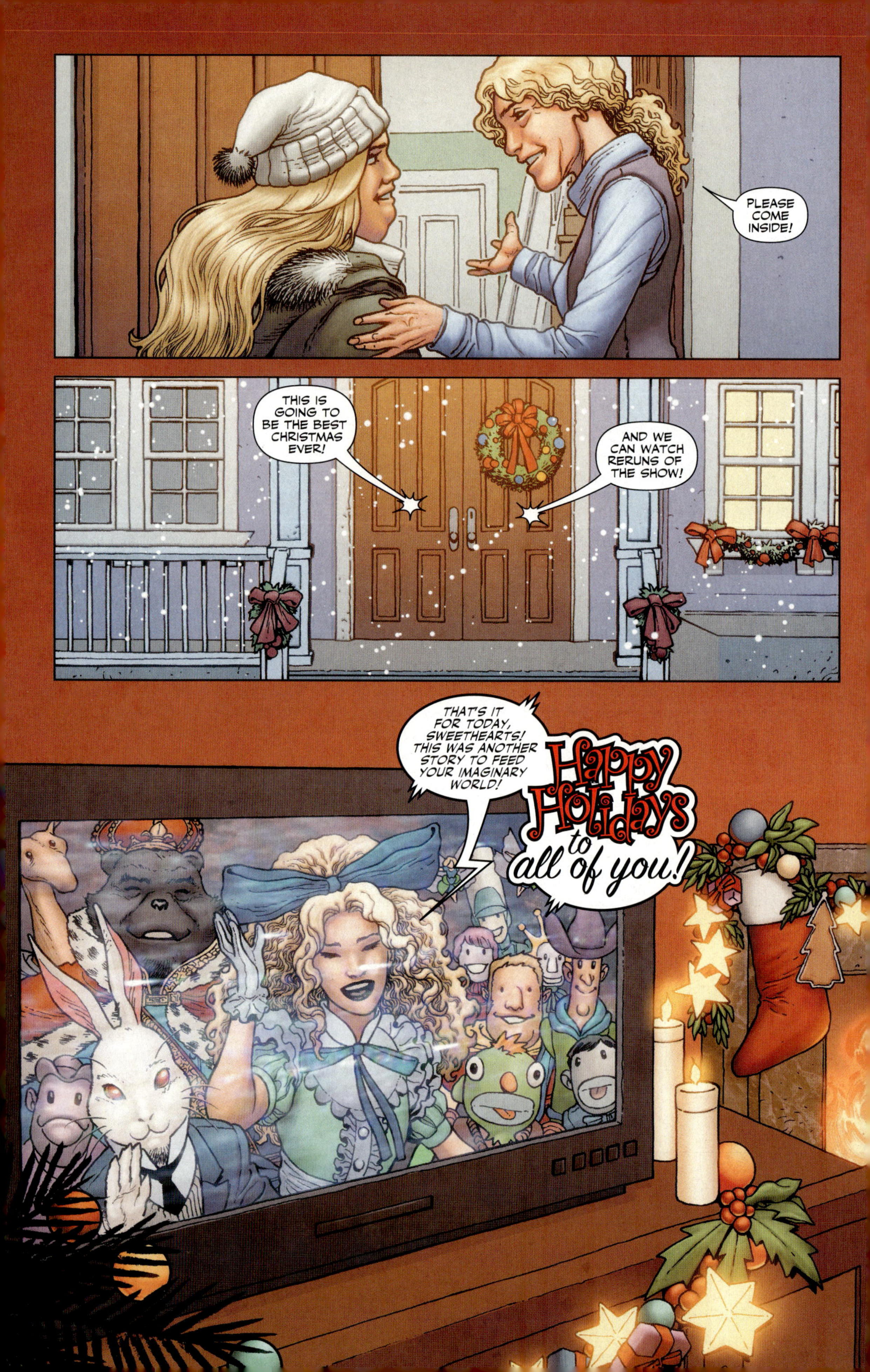
PLEASE COME INSIDE!
THIS IS GOING TO BE THE BEST CHRISTMAS EVER!
AND WE CAN WATCH RERUNS OF THE SHOW!
THAT'S IT FOR TODAY, SWEETHEARTS! THIS WAS ANOTHER STORY TO FEED YOUR IMAGINARY WORLD!
Happy Holidays to all of you!

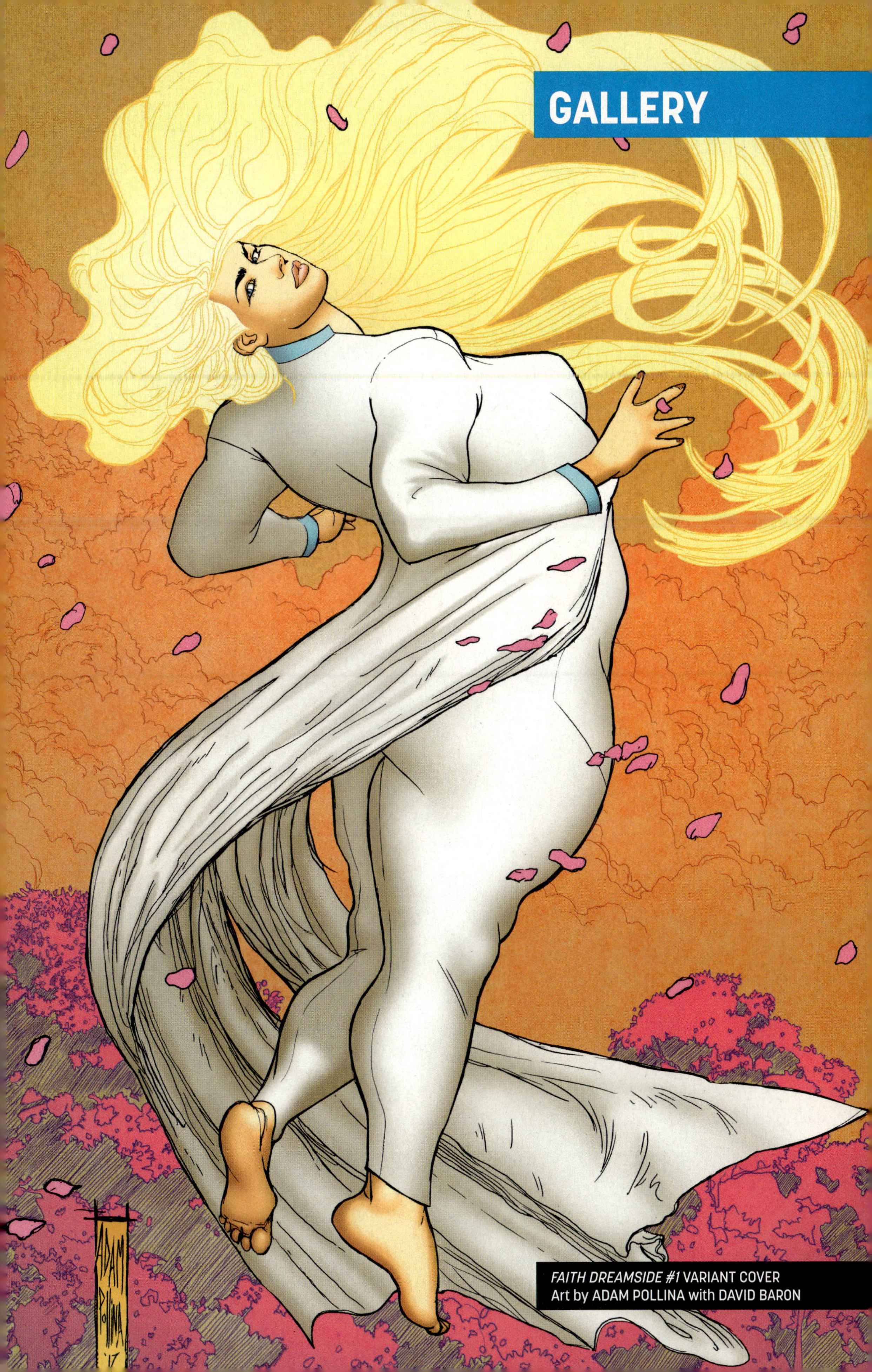

FAITH DREAMSIDE #1 VARIANT COVER
Art by ADAM POLLINA with DAVID BARON

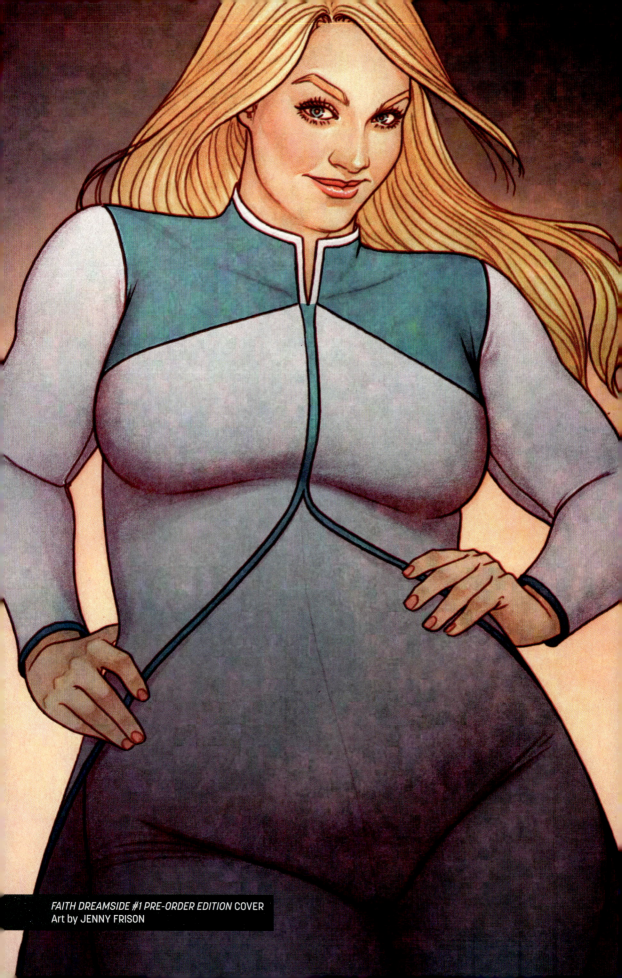

FAITH DREAMSIDE #1 PRE-ORDER EDITION COVER
Art by JENNY FRISON

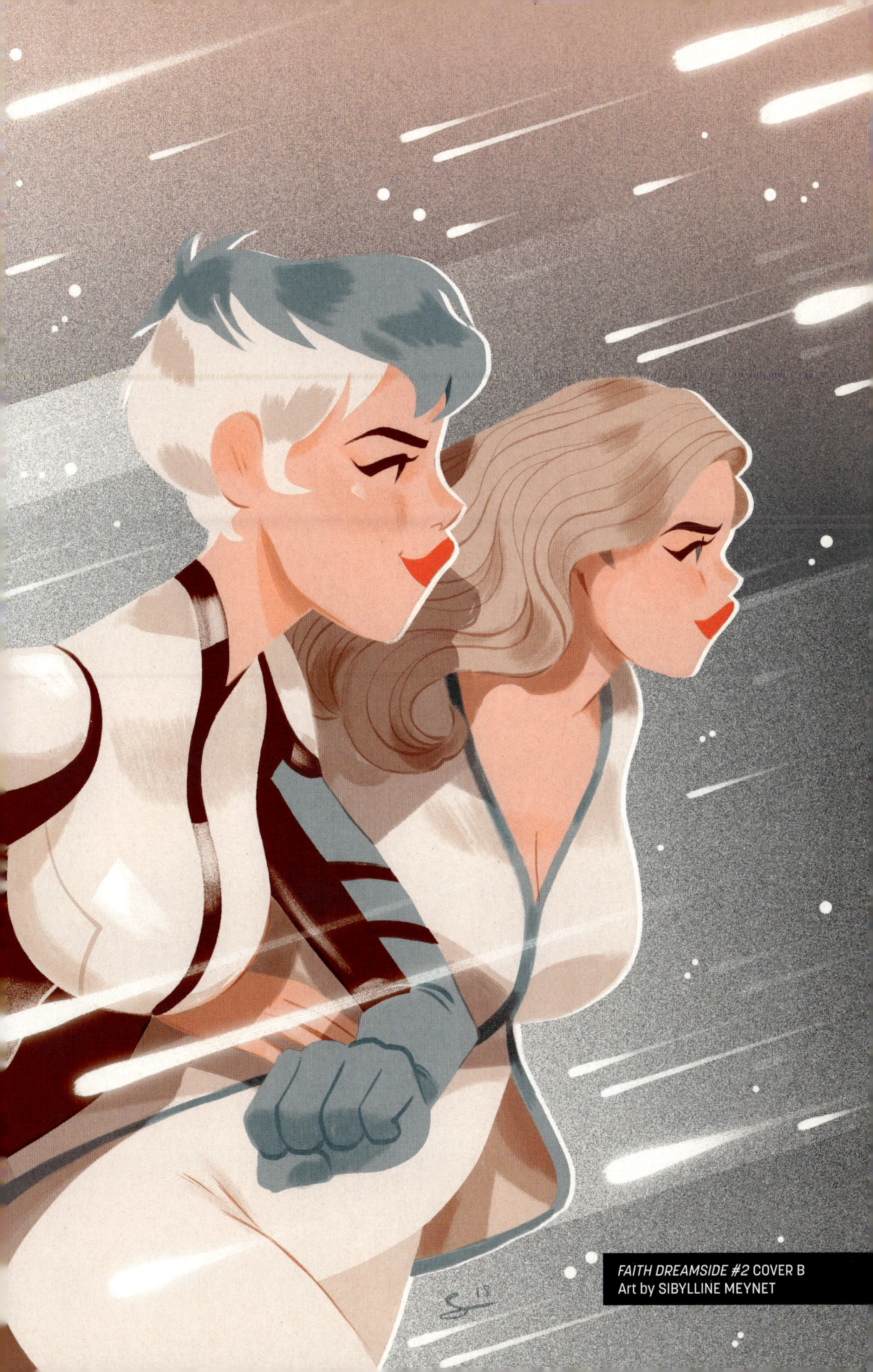

FAITH DREAMSIDE #2 COVER B
Art by SIBYLLINE MEYNET

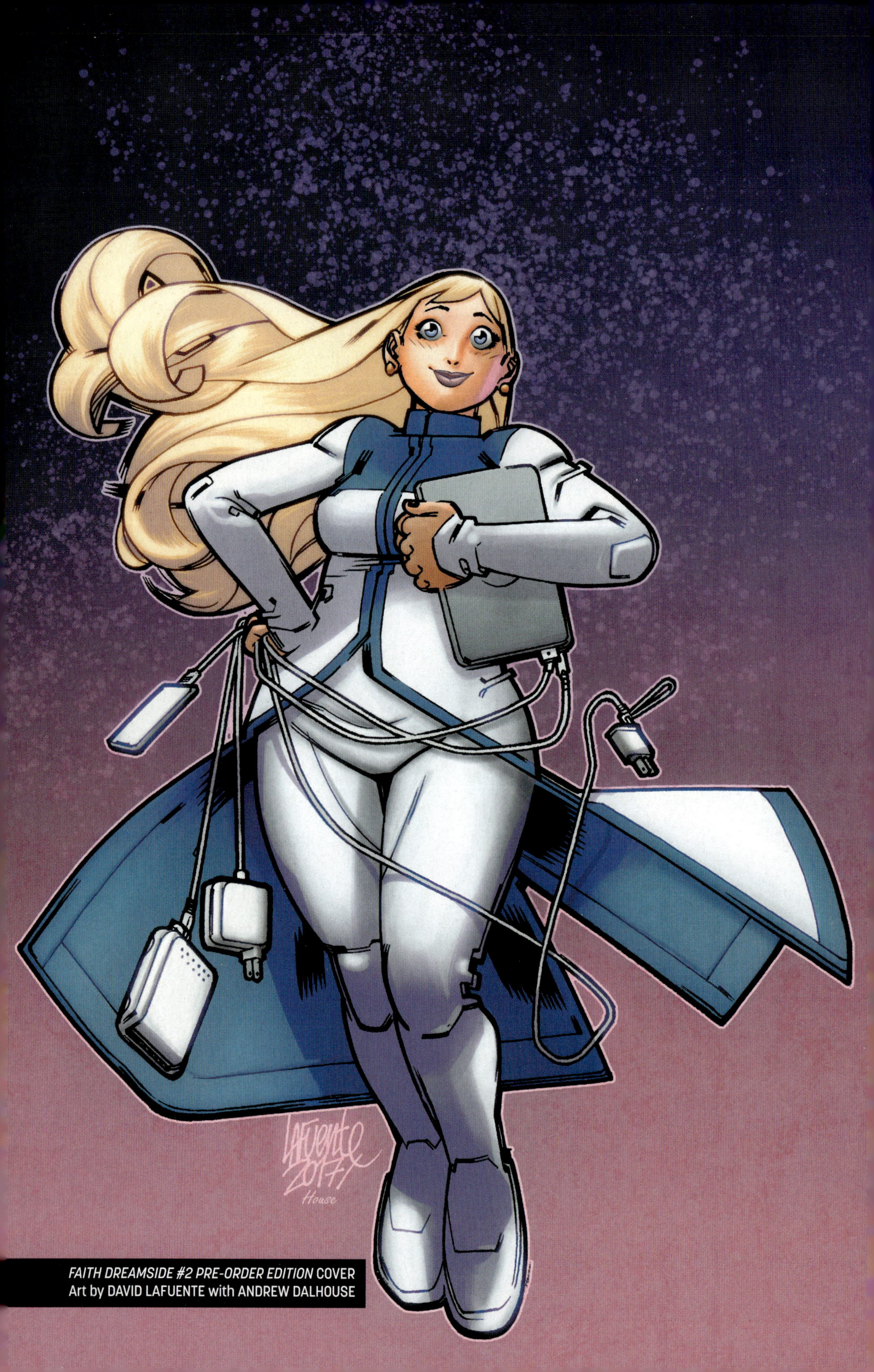

FAITH DREAMSIDE #2 PRE-ORDER EDITION COVER
Art by DAVID LAFUENTE with ANDREW DALHOUSE

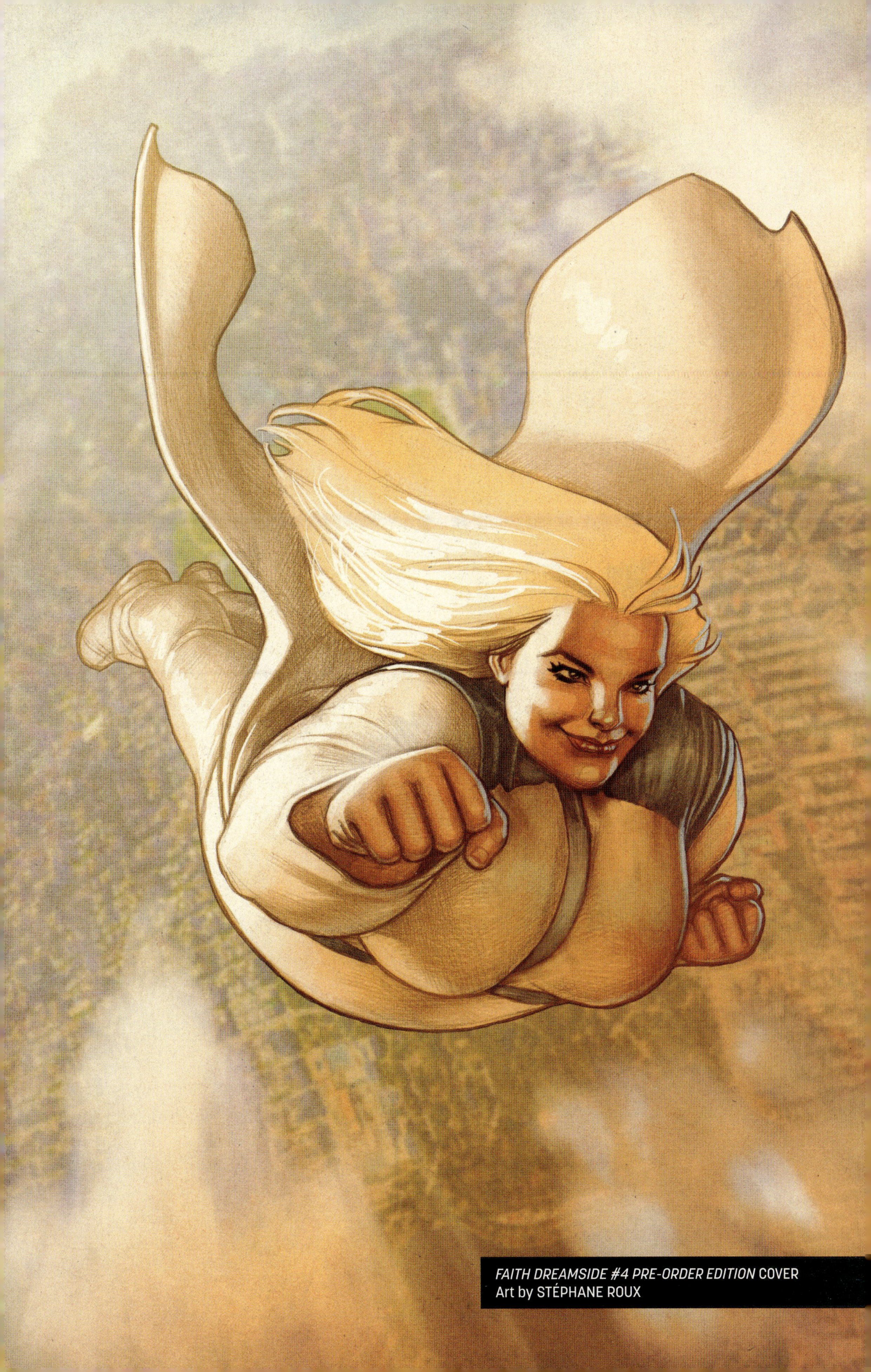

FAITH DREAMSIDE #4 PRE-ORDER EDITION COVER
Art by STÉPHANE ROUX

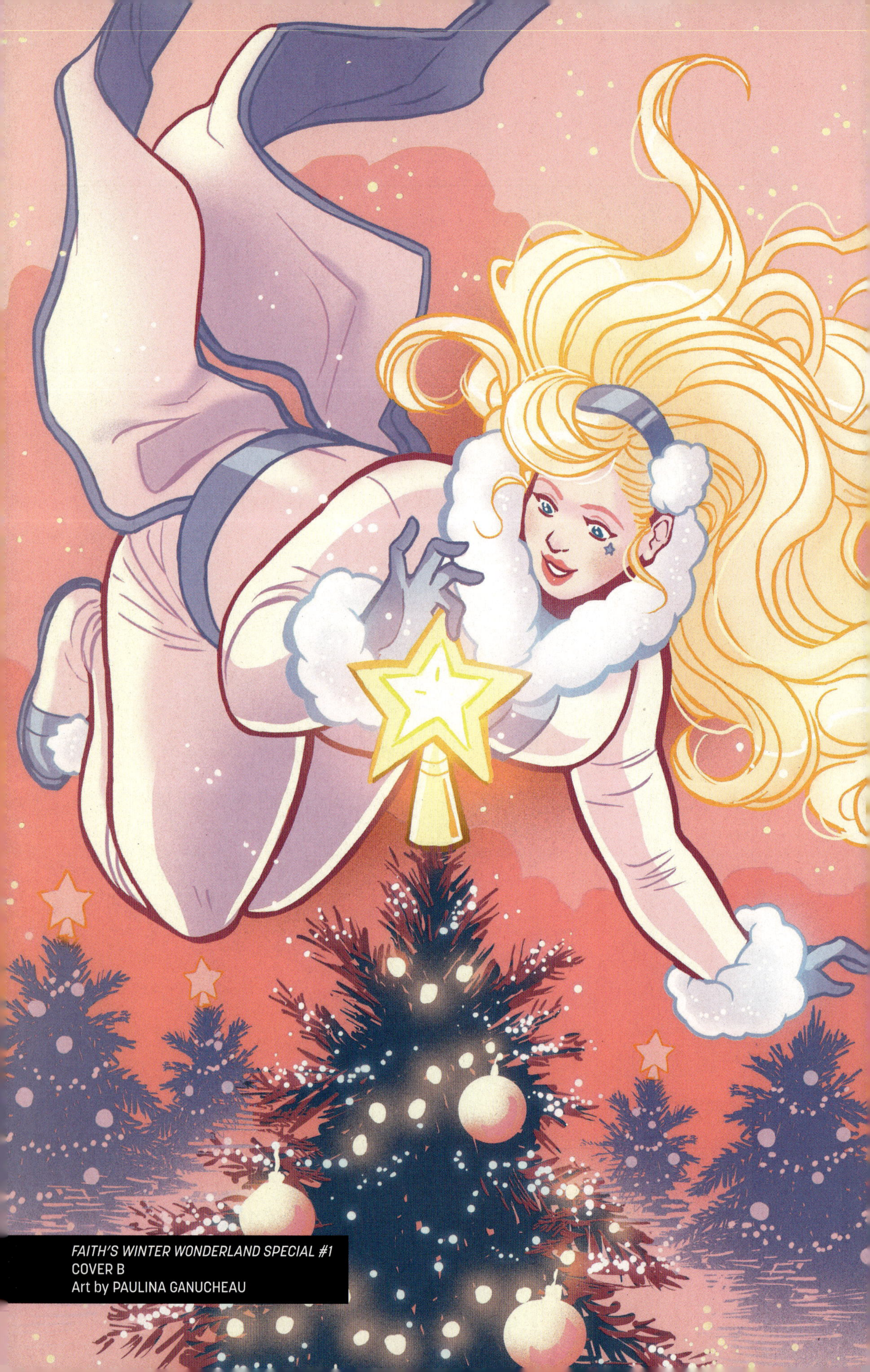

FAITH'S WINTER WONDERLAND SPECIAL #1
COVER B
Art by PAULINA GANUCHEAU

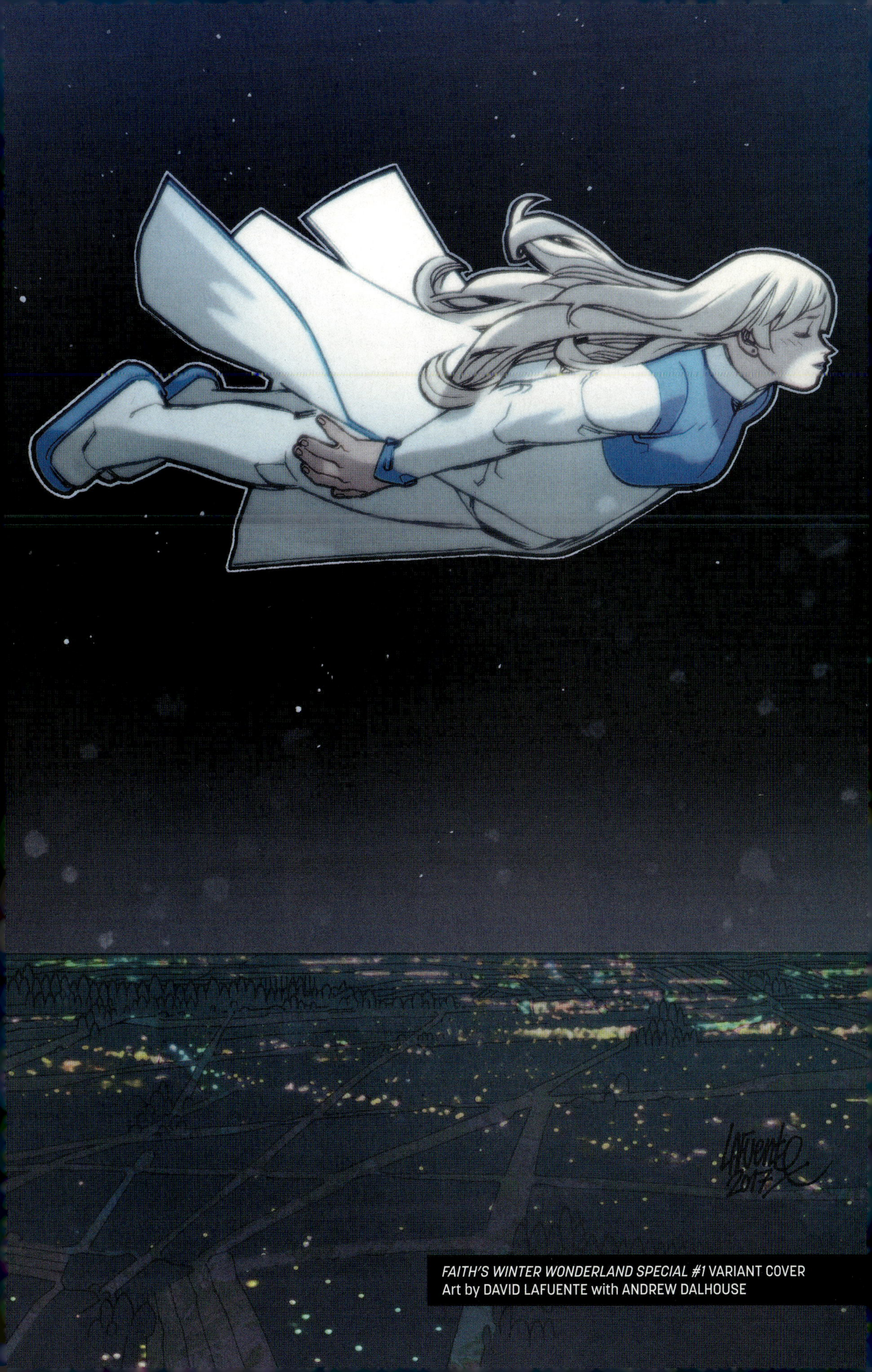

FAITH'S WINTER WONDERLAND SPECIAL #1 VARIANT COVER
Art by DAVID LAFUENTE with ANDREW DALHOUSE

FAITH DREAMSIDE #1, p. 5, 6, and (facing) 10
Art by MJ KIM

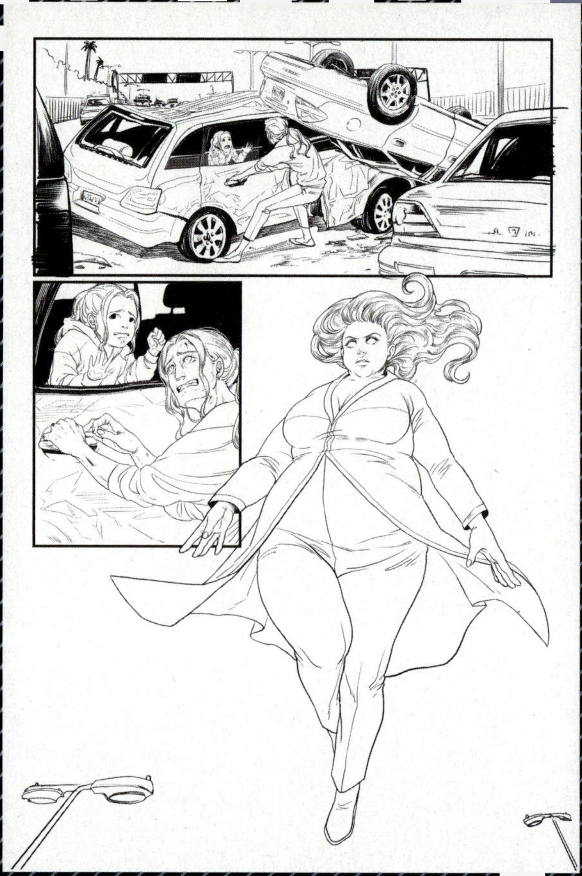

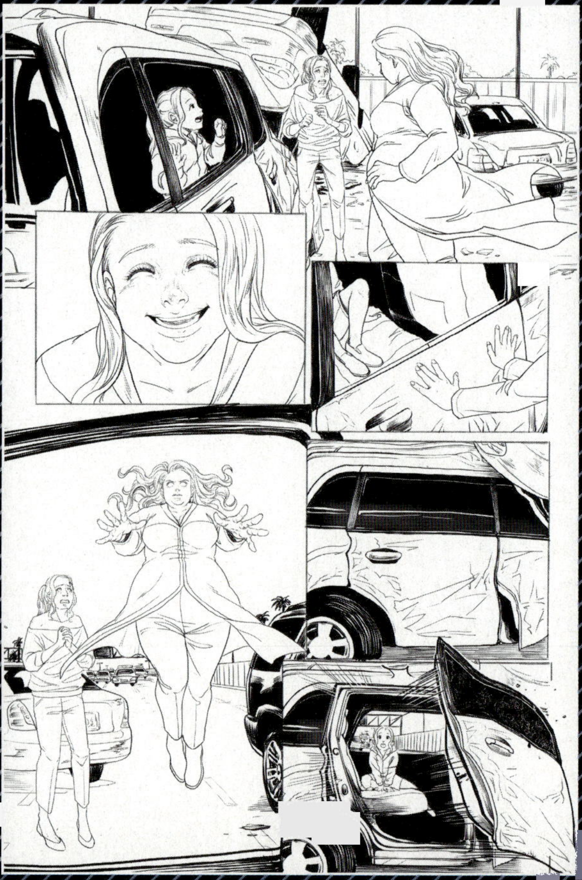

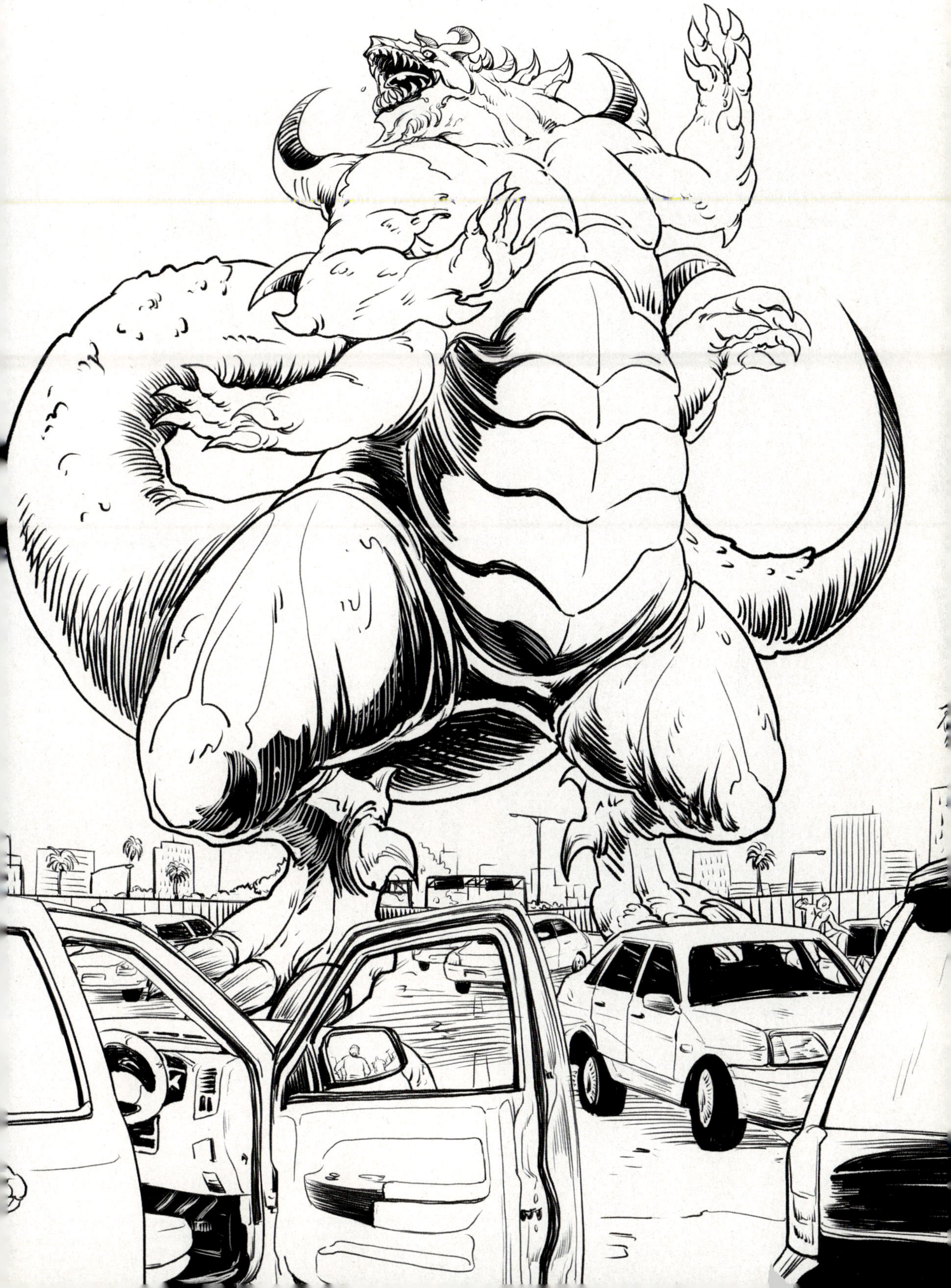

FAITH DREAMSIDE #2, p. 16, 17, and (facing) 18
Art by MJ KIM

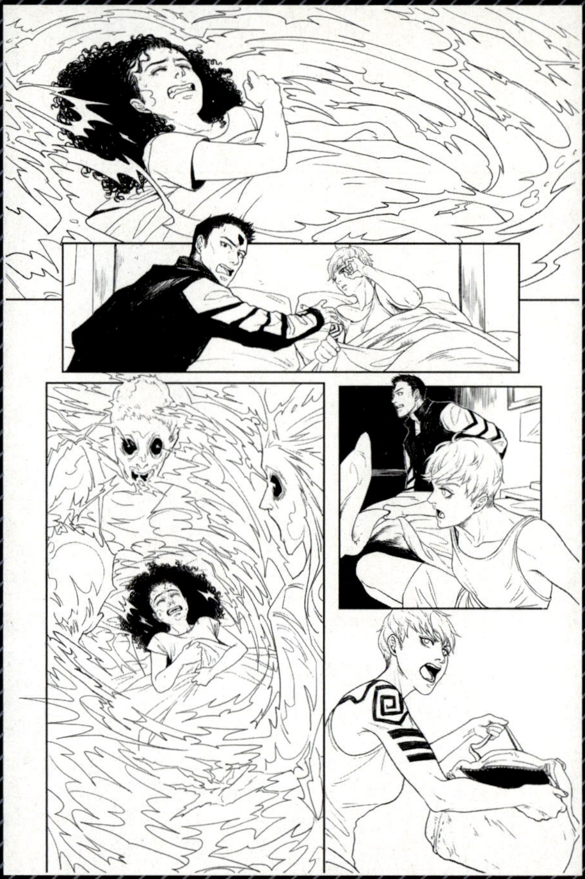

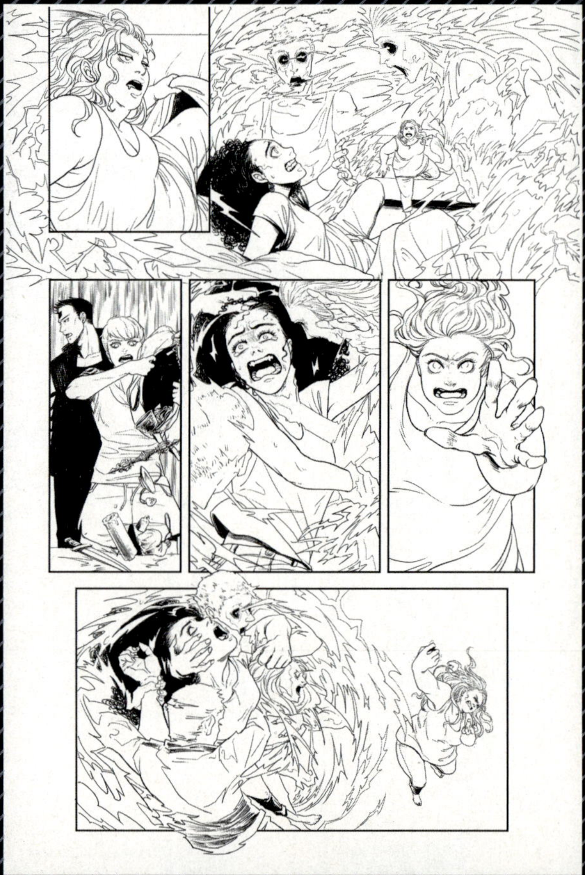

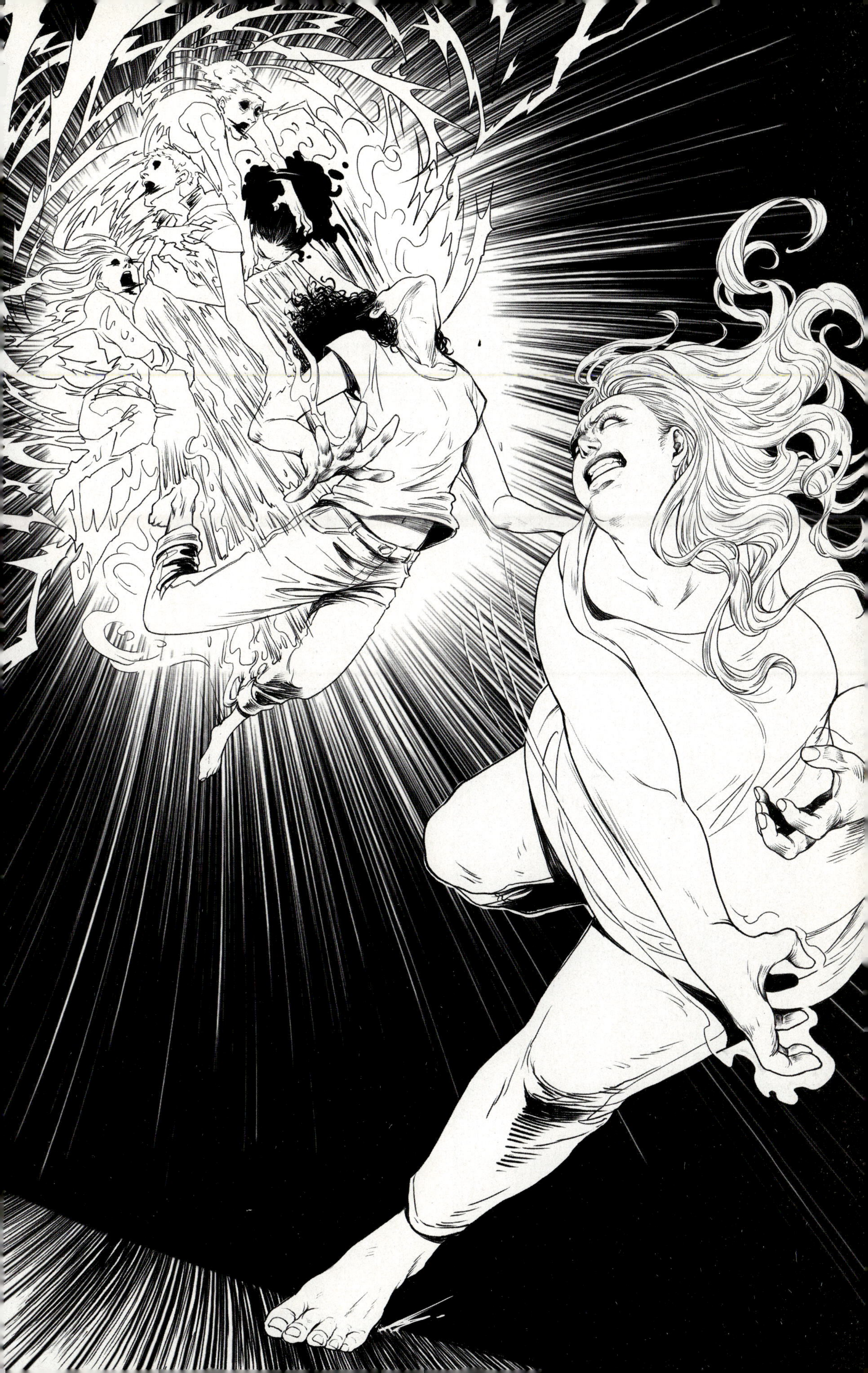

FAITH DREAMSIDE #3, p. 20, 21, and (facing) 22
Art by MJ KIM

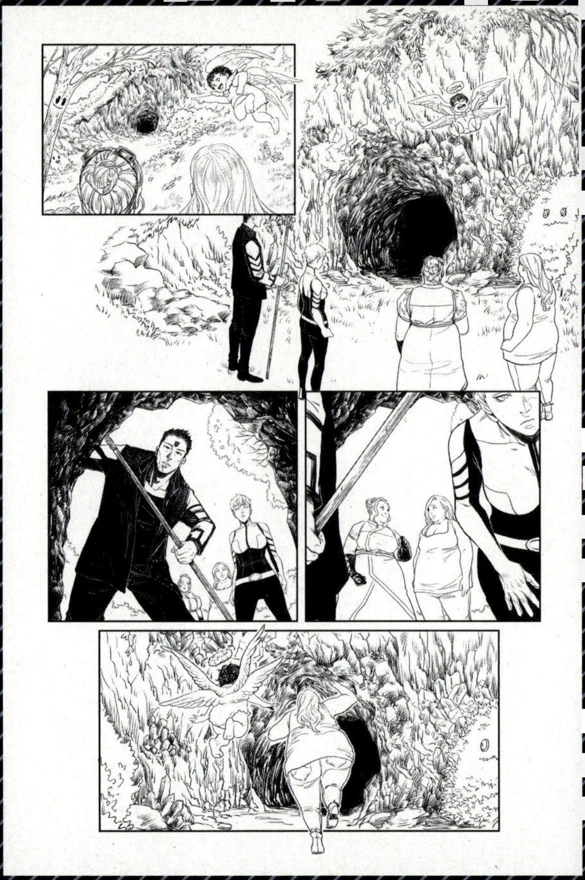

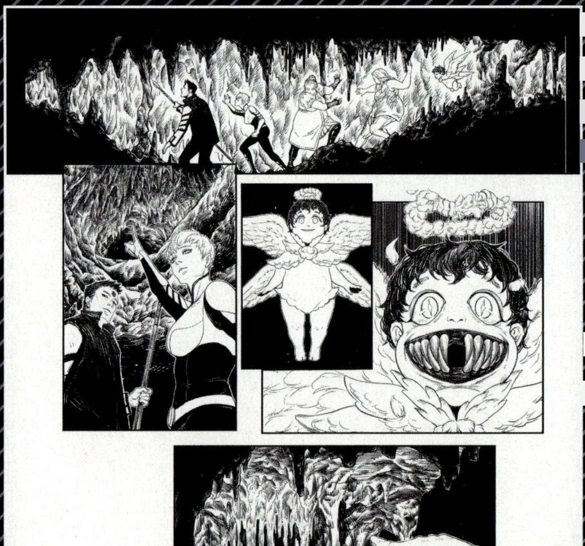

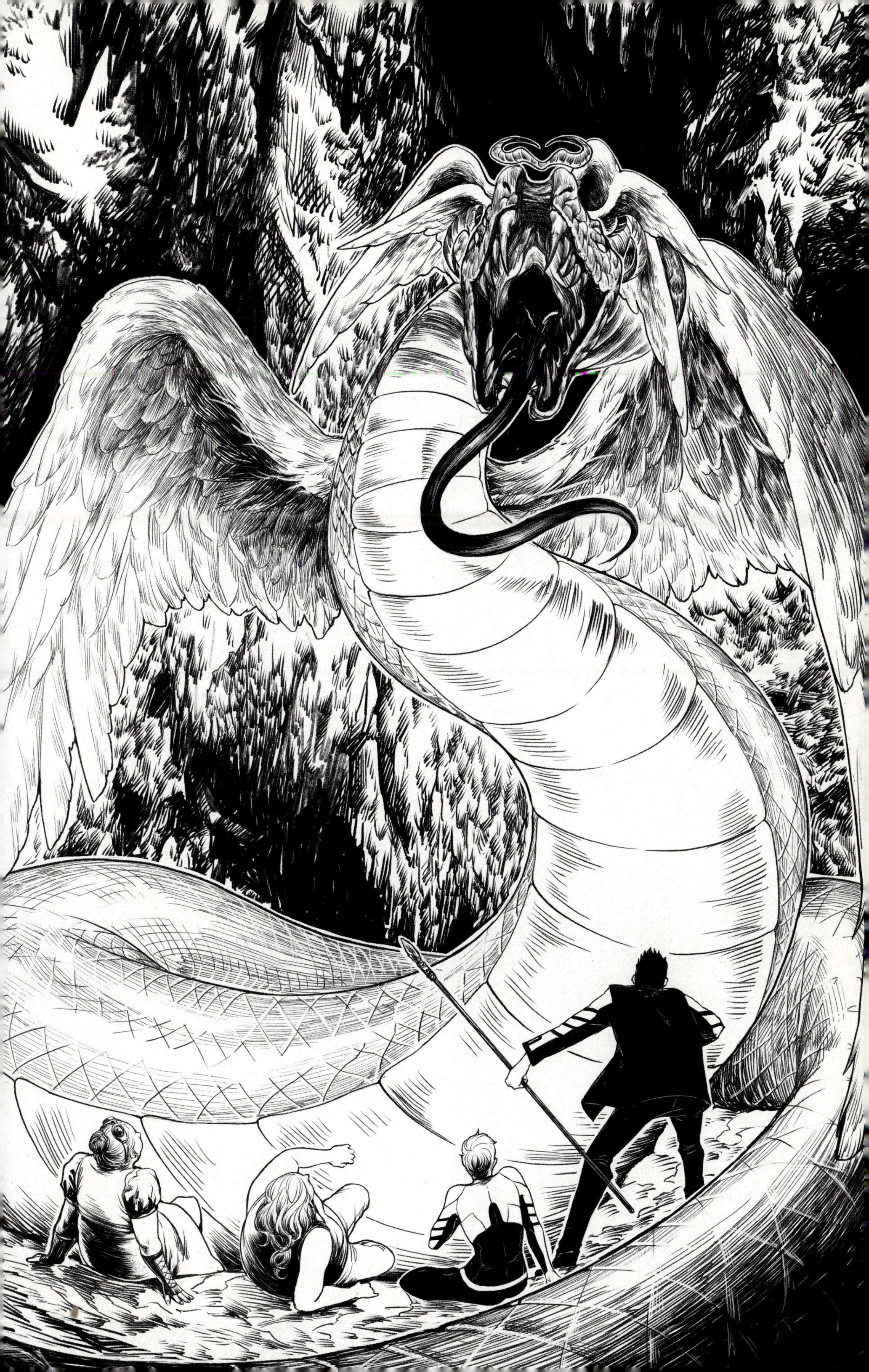

FA [illegible] *AMSIDE #4*, p. 12, 13, and (facing) 14
Art by MJ KIM

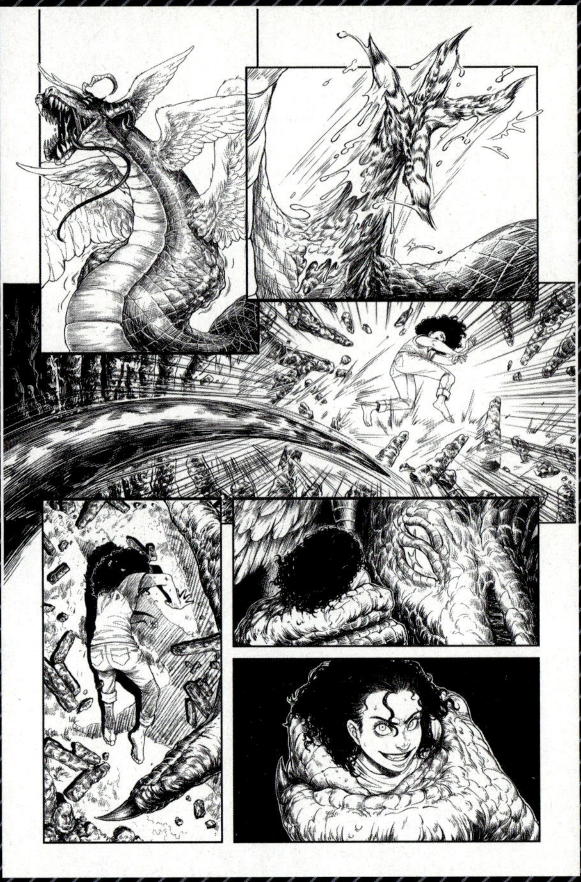

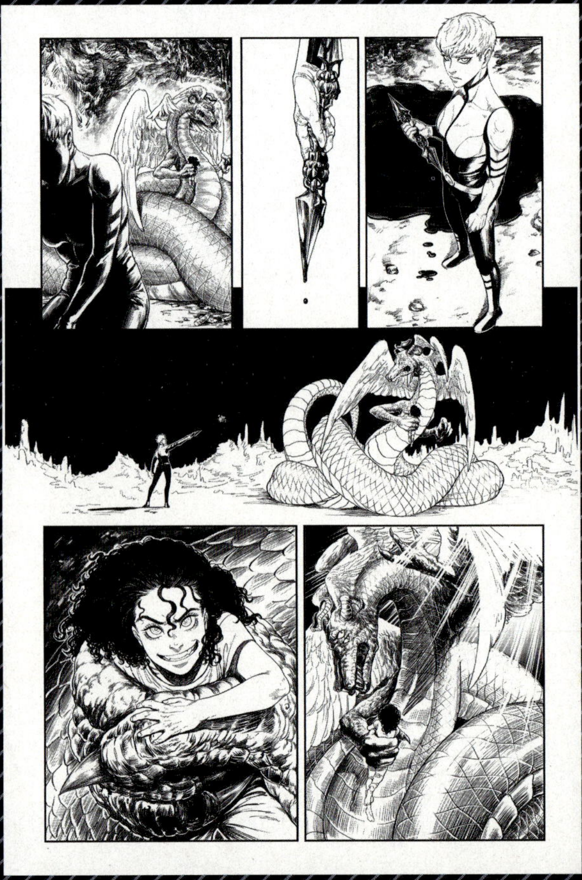

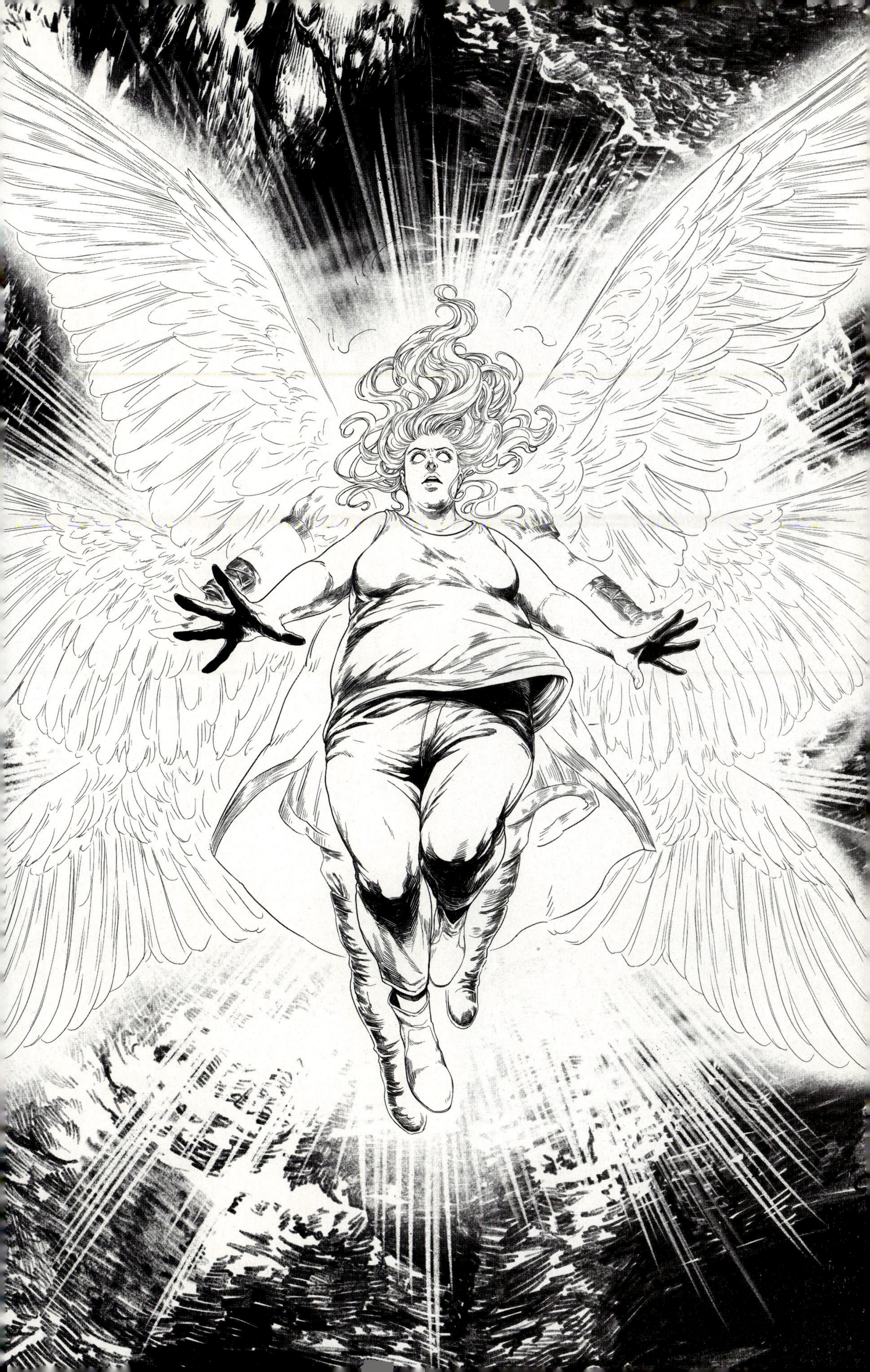

FAITH'S WINTER WONDERLAND SPECIAL #1,
p. 10, 11, and (facing) 12
Art by FRANCIS PORTELA

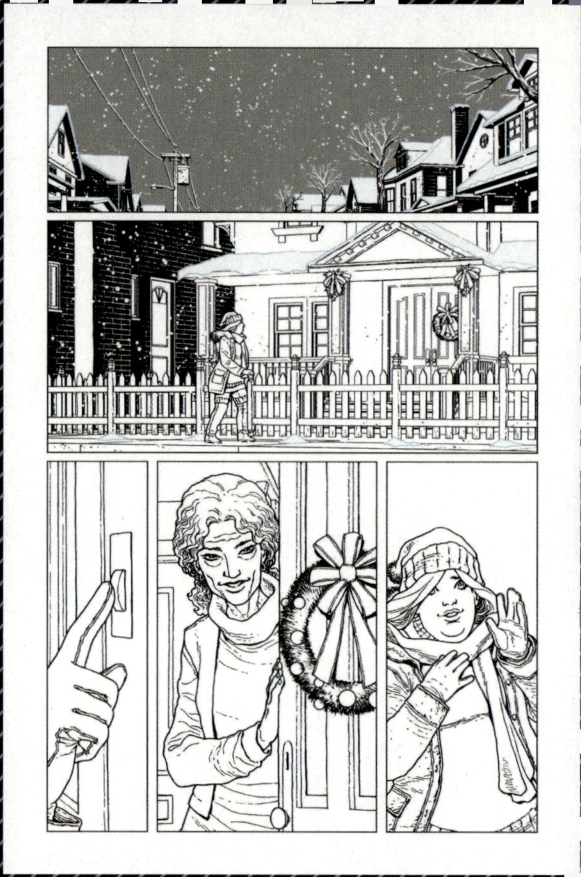

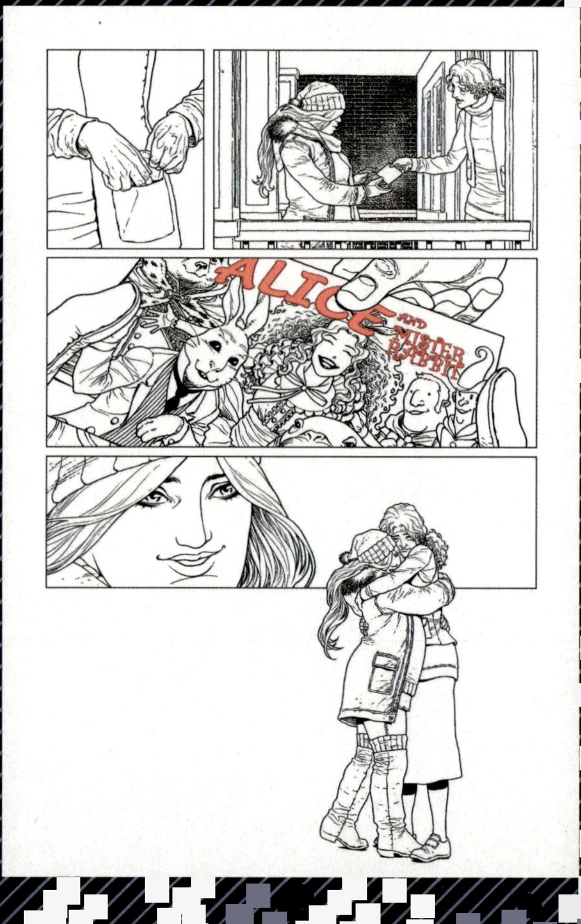
ALICE
AND
MISTER
RABBIT

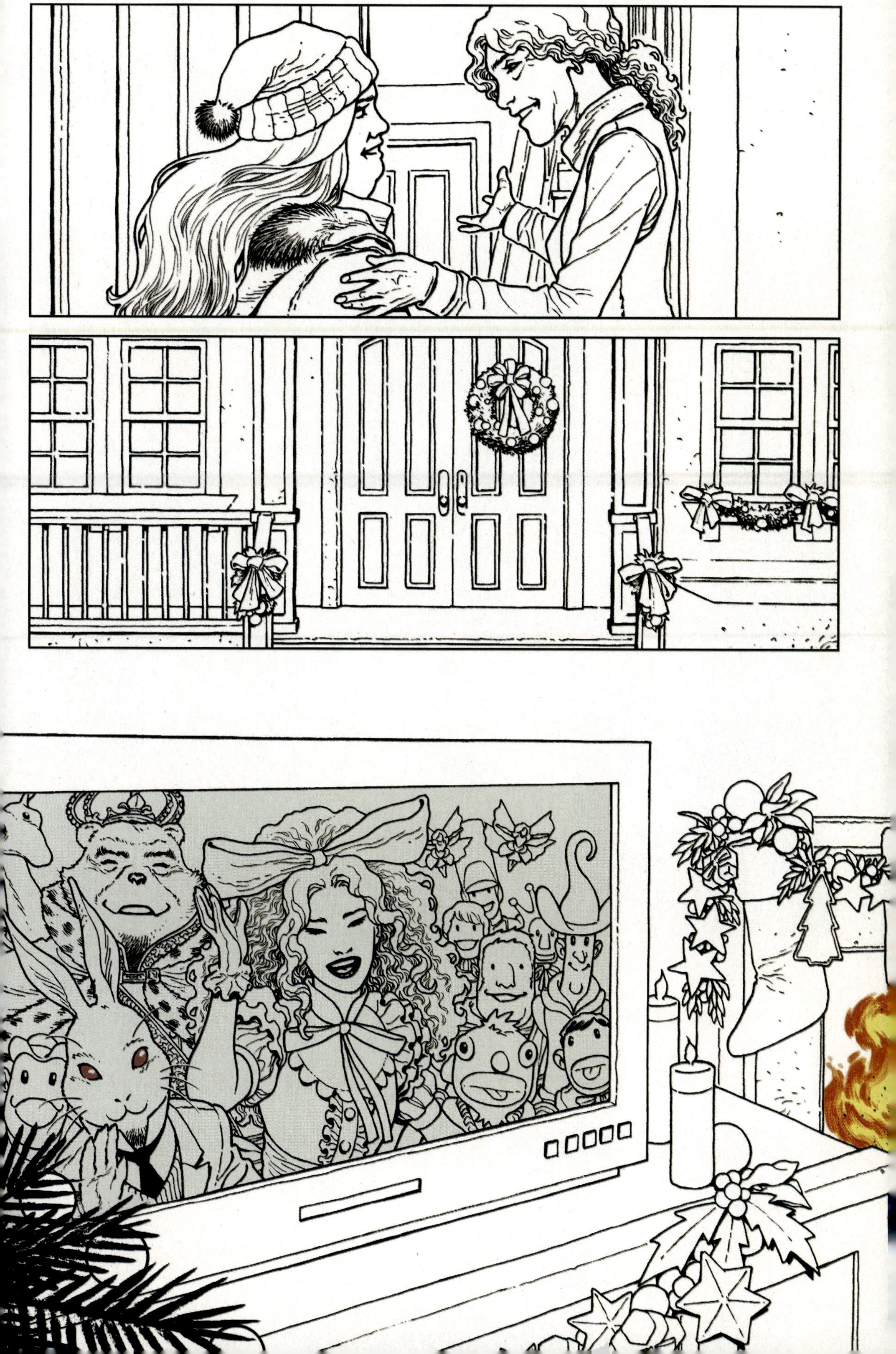

EXPLORE THE VALIANT

UNIVERSE FOR ONLY $9.99

HORROR & MYSTERY

SCIENCE FICTION & FANTASY

TEEN ADVENTURE

BRITANNIA
ISBN: 978-1-68215-185-3

THE DEATH-DEFYING DOCTOR MIRAGE
ISBN: 978-1-939346-49-0

RAPTURE
ISBN: 978-1-68215-225-6

**SHADOWMAN (2018) VOL. 1:
FEAR OF THE DARK**
ISBN: 978-1-68215-239-3

DIVINITY
ISBN: 978-1-939346-76-6

IMPERIUM VOL. 1: COLLECTING MONSTERS
ISBN: 978-1-939346-75-9

IVAR, TIMEWALKER VOL. 1: MAKING HISTORY
ISBN: 978-1-939346-63-6

RAI VOL. 1: WELCOME TO NEW JAPAN
ISBN: 978-1-939346-41-4

WAR MOTHER
ISBN: 978-1-68215-237-9

FAITH VOL. 1: HOLLYWOOD AND VINE
ISBN: 978-1-68215-121-1

**GENERATION ZERO VOL. 1:
WE ARE THE FUTURE**
ISBN: 978-1-68215-175-4

**HARBINGER RENEGADE VOL. 1:
THE JUDGMENT OF SOLOMON**
ISBN: 978-1-68215-169-3

SECRET WEAPONS
ISBN: 978-1-68215-229-4

Discover the entire Valiant Universe of titles at VALIANTENTERTAINMENT.COM/ALL-SERIES/

VALIANT

LIVEWIRE

VOLUME ONE: FUGITIVE

FOR THE FIRST TIME, LIVEWIRE TAKES CENTER STAGE!

Accomplice. Mentor. Savior. And now, Enemy of the State. Seeking to protect other vulnerable super-powered psiots like herself, Livewire plunged the United States into a nationwide blackout with her technopathic abilities, causing untold devastation. After choosing the few over the many, she must now outrun the government she served - and those she once called allies. With the whole world hunting her, what kind of hero will Livewire be...or will she be one at all?

Start reading here with the stunning new ongoing series from rising star Vita Ayala (*Supergirl*, *Submerged*) and fan-favorite artists Raúl Allén (WRATH OF THE ETERNAL WARRIOR) and Patricia Martín (SECRET WEAPONS) as they stand poised to launch the Valiant Universe into a new age of champions!

Collecting LIVEWIRE #1-4.

TRADE PAPERBACK
ISBN: 978-1-68215-301-7

VITA AYALA | RAÚL ALLÉN | PATRICIA MARTÍN
LIVEWIRE
VALIANT
FUGITIVE

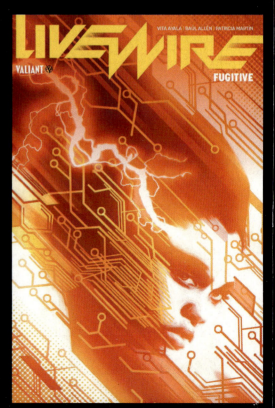